Neighboring on the Air

A Bur Oak Original

NEIGHBORING
ON THE AIR
Cooking with the
KMA Radio Homemakers
By Evelyn Birkby

University of Iowa Press ⵜ Iowa City

University of Iowa Press, Iowa City 52242
Copyright © 1991 by the University of Iowa
All rights reserved
Printed in the United States of America
First edition, 1991

Printed on acid-free paper

Library of Congress Cataloging-in-Publication Data
Birkby, Evelyn.
    Neighboring on the air: cooking with the KMA
Radio homemakers / by Evelyn Birkby.—1st ed.
        p.   cm.—(A Bur oak original)
    Includes index.
    ISBN 0-87745-316-0 (paper).
    1. Cookery.   I. KMA (Radio station:
Shenandoah, Iowa).   II. Title.   III. Series.
TX714.B56   1991   91-6304
641.5—dc20   CIP

To all the
KMA radio homemakers
and their faithful listeners

Lucile Driftmier Verness.

CONTENTS

Evelyn Birkby at Cottonwood Farm.

Preface and Acknowledgments

This is a cookbook. You will find it filled with exciting recipes from sixty-five years of collecting, testing, and broadcasting by the KMA radio homemakers. Except for minor editing, the recipes are given with the same abbreviations and terminology as they were aired and printed by each homemaker.

This is a storybook. It opens a window into the lives of sharing, caring broadcasters from the past and present. It is a biography of an era.

This is a picture book. The photographs will help you visualize people and places as the events actually happened.

This is also a trip back into my own past, for I knew most of the people in this book. I had the pleasure of interviewing the living KMA homemakers and communicating with their friends, associates, relatives, and radio listeners. My thanks to everyone who shared memories, pictures, and favorite recipes from the radio homemakers.

I wish to extend my thanks to KMA for permission to use resource materials from the *KMA Guide*, memos, pamphlets, cookbooks, and photographs that the station has published through the years and for the use of information in the book *KMA Radio: The First Sixty Years* (written by Robert Birkby and published by the May Broadcasting Company), to the *Shenandoah Evening Sentinel* for permission to use materials from my column "Up a Country Lane," and to Juliana Lowey and the Driftmier Company for permission to use items from the *Kitchen-Klatter Magazine* and the *Kitchen-Klatter Cookbook*.

I am especially grateful to my family—sons Bob, Jeff, and Craig and husband Robert—who ate many meals based on the recipes in this book and who encouraged me when the hours grew long and the end of this project seemed never in sight. I am indebted to the exceedingly kind and imaginative staff at the University of Iowa Press, who discovered new values in the story of the radio homemakers and always sensed when my spirits needed a boost.

I wish to express special thanks to those at KMA who showed interest in continuing the story of the KMA homemakers and Andy Andersen, who expressed a sense of urgency to conserve this information when he said, "The creators of this book will never come this way again."

The ways in which women are moving into new work areas and life-styles will make a difference in radio homemaking in the future, but differences can have value. . . . The kitchen is still the heart of the home, and the homemaker is still an important ingredient in that home. As long as there are people, we will have a need for radio homemakers.

—Billie Oakley

Earl and Gertrude May with Edward and Frances.

The Adventure Begins

At the end of World War I, the farmlands and small towns of the Midwest were poised for the beginning of great changes. Within the next decade, electrical lines would spread warmth and illumination over the countryside. Roads that had always been either dust or mud were slowly being graveled and in some cases paved. Still, travel was not easy, and people tended to center their lives around their homes. The kitchen served as a gathering place, social center, workroom, and storage bin.

The kitchen of the 1920s was almost always dominated by a coal- or wood-burning range used for cooking and canning and for heating water for washing dishes and bathing. An ice chest in the corner cooled the perishable foods for people fortunate enough to live along an iceman's route or near ponds, from which blocks of ice could be cut in winter and stored for summer use under piles of icehouse sawdust. Those without iceboxes often cooled their cream and butter in wells and springs. Meat was smoked—frequently in the farmers' own smokehouses—or canned, usually from livestock raised by the family. Fresh produce came right out of the garden. In the summer and fall, the kitchens were rich with the aroma of vegetables, fruits, and jams the housewives were canning for winter use.

The radio companies of that era were as far removed from the broadcasting stations of today as were the kitchens of the 1920s from our modern plastic and chrome facilities. One of those whose imagination and energy helped mold radio into a force that could serve rural America was Earl May. As president of the Earl May Seed & Nursery Company, founded in 1919, Earl learned much about the nursery business from his father-in-law, E. S. Welch, president of the Mount Arbor Nurseries. A few years later, when the new medium of

1

radio came to the Midwest, Earl realized that a broadcasting station would greatly enhance the success of his nursery business. He also believed that radio could do much to satisfy the information and entertainment demands of the people of the farms and small towns. In 1925, with the help of his father-in-law and the encouragement of his wife, Gertrude, Earl constructed radio station KMA in the seedhouse of the May Seed & Nursery Company in Shenandoah, Iowa, and the great adventure in broadcasting was underway.

GERTRUDE'S BING CHERRY SALAD

1 envelope gelatin
½ cup cold water
1 cup hot cherry juice
1 pinch salt
¼ cup lemon or grapefruit juice
1 cup bing cherries

½ cup celery
½ cup pineapple
¼ cup nuts (almonds or
    black walnuts)
¼ cup sugar

Dissolve gelatin in cold water. Add hot juice and stir to mix. Stir in salt, sugar, and lemon or grapefruit juice. Cool until syrupy. Add remaining ingredients.

GERTRUDE'S HONEY SALAD DRESSING

4 cups sugar (or less)
1 pint vinegar
1 small onion (grated fine)
    (use juice also)
2 tablespoons celery seed

1 tablespoon mustard
1 tablespoon paprika
1 tablespoon salt
1 quart Mazola oil
1 cup honey

Mix dry ingredients with vinegar. With a very fine stream, add oil so that a stable emulsion will form. Add honey last. Use blender for mixing. This is a large amount. It may be cut in half. It keeps well in the refrigerator.

The original recipe calls for 4 cups of sugar, which is too sweet for many present-day tastes. This is an excellent recipe, though, and can be adapted with a lesser amount of sugar, perhaps 2 cups.

Gertrude May enjoyed singing on the radio. Accompanying her during many of her broadcasts was Louise McGlone, a Shenandoah pianist who was a KMA musician from 1925 into the 1930s.

Frances and Edward May remember the radio appearances of their mother, especially her Sunday musical programs. The family would attend church first and then go to the KMA studio, where Gertrude would sing over the air. She had a lovely voice, and among the songs she chose were many old German tunes.

After Gertrude's Sunday program was completed, the May family walked the short distance to the Delmonico Hotel, where they enjoyed dinner in Shenandoah's most elegant dining room.

Gertrude May continued singing over radio KMA until a bout of laryngitis in 1938 caused her to lose her singing voice for several months. She did not sing on the air again.

GERTRUDE'S PEACH PUDDING

3 eggs; 4 tablespoons sugar; 3 tablespoons milk; 3 tablespoons sifted flour; peaches. Fill baking dish with peaches and cover with sugar. Beat yolks and sugar and milk; then add flour and whites of egg beaten stiff. Pour batter over peaches and bake (at 375 degrees about 45 minutes). Serve with cream.

GERTRUDE'S BLUEBERRY PUDDING

½ cup butter	1 egg
1 cup sugar	Pinch of salt
2 cups flour	1 teaspoon vanilla
2½ teaspoons baking powder	1½ cups blueberries
1 cup milk	

Cream butter and sugar together; sift dry ingredients and mix in, alternating with milk and egg beaten together. Stir in vanilla and fold in blueberries. Pour into 8 x 8 greased pan and bake at 350 degrees 20 to 30 minutes or until done. Serve with lemon sauce.

Lemon Sauce

1½ cups hot water	⅛ teaspoon salt
Juice of 1 lemon	⅛ teaspoon nutmeg
¼ cup butter	3 tablespoons cornstarch
Sugar to taste	

Mix ingredients and cook, stirring, until mixture bubbles and thickens to desired consistency.

This chicken started life as Jenny. When "she" grew larger, it became evident that Jenny was really Johnny. Earl May had his picture taken with the changeling chicken for his own enjoyment—and ours.

GERTRUDE'S GROUND BEEF RECIPE

2 pounds ground beef
1 6-ounce can tomato sauce
1 cup cream-style cottage
  cheese
1 8-ounce package cream
  cheese

¼ cup sour cream
⅓ cup finely chopped onion
1 tablespoon chopped green
  pepper
2 tablespoons melted butter
1 8-ounce package noodles

Brown beef, drain off excess fat, and stir in tomato sauce. Remove from heat. In bowl combine remaining ingredients except for noodles. Put them in boiling water and cook according to directions; drain. In a buttered 2-quart casserole, put ½ the cooked noodles. Put cheese mixture in, then rest of noodles, and top with meat. Cover. Bake at 350 degrees for 20 minutes. Remove cover and bake 10 minutes longer to brown on top. (This is a good party dish.)

Because of her busy life helping at the radio station and her church and community service, Gertrude May was assisted in food preparation in her home by Shenandoah cooks Katie Davey and Edna Buntz. Gertrude did more cooking during the summer months when the family was at Echo Lake near Mercer, Wisconsin. In this idyllic location, several members of the family built cottages. The May children recall food prepared with blueberries, which used to grow wild in the woods near their cottage. They also remember big kettles of beans, which were a staple food in the cool north country.

"Mother's bean soup was very simple," Frances recalls. "It had no real recipe—she just soaked the beans in water overnight, put in a ham bone, and let it simmer."

KATIE'S LIMA BEANS

2 pounds lima beans
1 cup catsup
1 cup brown sugar

1 cup heavy cream (sweet or
    sour) or half-and-half

Cook lima beans in salted water until just tender. Drain. Stir remaining ingredients together and pour over beans. Bake at 350 degrees for 1½ to 2 hours.

Buckwheat pancakes were one of Gertrude May's specialties. They are as good today as when Earl, Gertrude, Frances, and Edward used to sit around the kitchen table and enjoy them for breakfast.

MAYS' BUCKWHEAT CAKES

2 cups milk
2 cups boiling water
1 yeast cake (or 1 package dry
    yeast)

4 cups buckwheat flour
½ teaspoon soda, dissolved in
    1 cup hot water
1 tablespoon molasses
1 teaspoon salt

Scald the milk and add the boiling water. Cool to lukewarm temperature and dissolve the yeast cake (or dry yeast) in mixture. Sift enough flour (possibly more than 4 cups) to make a batter thin enough to pour. Let rise overnight in an earthenware crock. In A.M. add dissolved soda, molasses, and salt. Fry on a greased griddle. Makes 3½ dozen cakes.

Keep ½ cup of this batter in a cool place to use in place of yeast for next day's pancakes and proceed as above.

As long as Grandfather and Grandmother Welch were alive, the major holiday dinners were held in their Shenandoah home. As many as forty people would gather for the traditional foods. Grandmother Welch's elegant Washington Pie and Gertrude May's Chocolate Steamed Pudding were two of the most popular dishes at those gatherings.

MRS. WELCH'S WASHINGTON PIE

¼ cup butter	1½ cups flour
1 cup sugar	2 teaspoons baking powder
2 eggs	½ cup milk
¼ teaspoon salt	1 teaspoon vanilla

Cream butter and sugar together. Beat in eggs. Sift dry ingredients together and blend in alternately with milk. Add vanilla. Bake in 2 greased pie tins (or round 8-inch layer cake pans) at 350 degrees for 20 to 25 minutes or until they test done. Split each layer so you have 4 layers and fill.

Filling

½ to 1 cup sugar	2 eggs, beaten
3 tablespoons cornstarch	1½ cups milk
1 tablespoon butter	Vanilla to taste

Mix dry ingredients. Add remaining ingredients. Cook in double boiler over hot water, stirring constantly, for 20 minutes or until mixture thickens. Cool. Fill cake layers. Sprinkle powdered sugar over top. Keep refrigerated.

CHOCOLATE STEAMED PUDDING
(Gertrude's Favorite)

Between 1 and 2 squares of	½ cup milk
melted chocolate	½ cup sugar
2 tablespoons melted butter	1 cup flour
1 egg, beaten	3 teaspoons baking powder

Combine ingredients in the order given. Steam 30 to 45 minutes. Serve with whipped cream. Good warmed up. The pudding pan must have a lid over it as well as the steamer pan or the pudding will be soggy. This is an excellent dessert.

After Earl May's death in 1946, Gertrude continued to be involved in the decision-making areas of the May Seed & Nursery Company and radio station KMA. Edward May became president of the company and shouldered many of the responsibilities, which included broadcasting a daily message from KMA to the families in the four-state listening area.

In 1973 Gertrude May died in a fire in the family's summer home near Echo Lake, Wisconsin. Although her physical presence is gone, her influence and inspiration continue to be felt by the present staff at KMA.

"When I think about the early days at KMA," Edward May says, "I always remember the system I had worked out to get nickels and dimes out of my father for my favorite treat—hamburgers! I'd wait until Dad was in the studio making a broadcast and then walk in and ask him for a nickel or so while he was still on the air. He couldn't stop to say no, so nine times out of ten the scheme would work."

Through the years the children of radio personalities—especially those of the radio homemakers who broadcast from their homes—discovered this same ploy worked equally well for them.

The May family in the early 1960s enjoying one of their frequent outdoor meals. Edward and Ed junior are seated at the left; Karen, E. J., and Annette are on the right.

With his deep interest in horticulture, his love of people, and his desire to serve the listeners of KMA radio, Edward May followed in his father's and mother's footsteps. He graduated from the Shenandoah school system and then attended the University of Nebraska at Lincoln. Following his graduation, he did special work in botany at Iowa State College in Ames and had a summer of study at Tarkio College in Tarkio, Missouri.

Edward was six years old when his father founded KMA, so he grew up in radio. His broadcasting career started when he sat on his father's lap and visited with the radio friends.

In 1941, Edward went with his mother to the University of Mexico in Mexico City for a special summer study session. The following year, he married Eleanor Jean Petty of Red Oak, Iowa. The two went to Lima, Peru, where Ed worked in the office of the agricultural attaché at the United States embassy.

Mrs. Edward May, known as E. J., graduated from Lindenwood College, St. Charles, Missouri, and then attended the University of Nebraska at Lincoln. Edward saw E. J.'s picture in the student directory, liked what he saw, and noted that she was from Red Oak, not far from his hometown of Shenandoah.

"Edward called me up for a 'Coke date,'" E. J. recalls. "That really reflects our age. But it was a good beginning for a long friendship and a good marriage."

The Mays' elder daughter, Annette, is married to John Marra, an electrical engineer. They live in a suburb of Milwaukee, Wisconsin. Daughter Karen is married to Dr. James Sislo, and they live in Wausau, Wisconsin. They have two children, Amy and Bill. Son Ed junior and his wife, Carrie, live in Omaha and are the parents of Benjamin and Jeffrey.

Edward officially retired January 1, 1987. He and E. J. continue to enjoy their winter home in Tucson, Arizona, and their summer cottage on Echo Lake near Mercer, Wisconsin. Whenever possible, they return to Shenandoah for special events or a family gathering.

Edward May is certain that he has had popcorn "every Sunday night all my life!" He now eats it plain without salt or butter. "Once a person trains his or her palate, plain popcorn can be delicious." Through the years, members of the May family have experimented with many recipes and various ways to use popcorn.

PINK PEARL POPCORN BALLS

1 cup light corn syrup
½ cup sugar
1 package red gelatin

1 cup coarsely chopped peanuts
9 cups popped corn

Combine syrup and sugar, bring to boil. Remove from heat, add gelatin stirring until dissolved. Add peanuts and mix well. Pour over popcorn. Form into balls. These may be formed around suckers for the youngsters—provides a handle to keep stickiness at a minimum!

Edward May still laughs when he remembers this incident.

"On my noon program one day, I told how our eighteen-month-old boy had gone to the cupboard and found a sack of popcorn after hearing me suggest that we pop some corn. I meant to finish the conversation by saying I thought that was pretty good for an eighteen-month-old boy. Actually I mistakenly said, 'I thought that was pretty good for an eighteen-year-old boy.'

"The next day the mail was very interesting regarding my statement. For example, one letter said, 'May I extend congratulations to you upon your eighteen-year-old son liking popcorn—mine likes girls.' Another person stated, 'I have a well-balanced boy. He likes both girls and popcorn.'

"We all had a good many laughs from that situation, and I realized that a great many people listen to their radios."

CARAMELED CORN

2 cups brown sugar
½ cup corn syrup
½ cup butter

1 tablespoon vinegar
Pinch of soda
3 quarts popped corn

Combine sugar, butter, and syrup. Cook until it forms a hard ball. Put vinegar in just before removing from heat. Add soda after removing from heat and pour this mixture over the popped corn.

E. J.'S PUMPKIN BREAD

Sift together:
3½ cups sifted flour
2 teaspoons soda
1 teaspoon cinnamon
1 teaspoon nutmeg
½ teaspoon salt
3 cups sugar

Mix and add to dry ingredients:
1 cup salad oil
4 eggs, beaten
1 can pumpkin (2 cups)
⅔ cup water

Bake in greased loaf pans (2 large or 4 7 × 3 pans) at 325 degrees for over one hour.

E. J.'S SNOW PEAS WITH WATER CHESTNUTS

½ pound fresh or 1 8-ounce
   package of frozen pods
   (thawed)
1 tablespoon salad oil
1 teaspoon soy sauce
1 medium clove garlic (minced)
1 5-ounce can bamboo shoots,
   drained

1 5-ounce can water chestnuts,
   drained and sliced
1 chicken bouillon cube
¼ cup boiling water
1 teaspoon cornstarch

If fresh peas are used, wash and remove ends and strings. In a preheated skillet, place oil, soy sauce, and garlic. Cook over low heat till garlic has browned.

Add peas, bamboo shoots, and water chestnuts. Toss and cook over high heat for 1 minute. Dissolve bouillon cube in water and add to the peas. Cover and cook over medium heat for 2 minutes. Combine cornstarch and 1 teaspoon cold water. Stir into peas.

Cook, uncovered, over high heat until sauce thickens—about 1 minute. 4 servings.

E. J.'S CHOW MEIN

¼ cup shortening
2 pounds lean pork, cut in
   strips
1 cup onions, chopped
1 teaspoon salt
1/16 teaspoon pepper
2 cups celery (cut in 1-inch
   pieces and then strips
   lengthwise)

1½ cups hot water
1 can mixed Chinese vegetables,
   drained
For flavoring and thickening:
   2 tablespoons cold water
   2 tablespoons cornstarch
   2 teaspoons soy sauce
   (I prefer shoyu sauce)

Sear meat in shortening quickly without browning or burning. Add onions and fry 5 minutes. Add celery, salt, pepper, and hot water. Cover and cook for 5 minutes. Add drained mixed vegetables. Mix thoroughly and heat to boiling point. Combine and add flavoring and thickening. Stir lightly and cook 1 minute. Serve over Chinese noodles or cooked rice. Add soy or shoyu sauce to taste.

PEAS—FRENCH STYLE

Cut a slice of bacon with shears in shreds crosswise. Cook bacon in 2 tablespoons butter for 10 minutes. Add 2 cups peas, ½ dozen small white onions, 1 small sprig of mint, and ¼ cup boiling water. Cook until tender. Drain. Beat 1 egg yolk slightly, and add ⅓ cup cream. Add to peas. Reheat and serve.

BETTY JANE'S WILD RICE WITH MUSHROOMS

1 cup wild rice	1 cup hot water
1 cup grated American cheese	½ cup salad oil
1 cup chopped mushrooms	1 cup canned tomatoes
1 cup chopped ripe olives	Salt and pepper to taste
½ cup chopped onions	

Soak wild rice overnight; drain and add above ingredients. Cover and bake at 350 degrees for 1 hour. Serves 10 to 12 people.

ANNETTE'S ZUCCHINI CASSEROLE

½ large or 1 medium zucchini, chopped or cubed (unpeeled)	Dash garlic powder
2 cups whole-wheat bread cubes	1½ teaspoons dill weed
1 stick butter or margarine	1 cup cubed cheddar cheese
1 large onion, chopped	1 cup cubed mozzarella or Colby cheese
2 tablespoons parsley	Salt and pepper

Brown bread cubes and onion in butter until bread is toasted. Mix all ingredients together. Put in casserole and top with grated cheddar cheese. Bake at 350 degrees for 30 to 40 minutes or until all cheese melts.

Frances May attended National Park Seminary at Forest Glenn, Maryland, and Northwestern University, Evanston, Illinois. She has been active through the years in a number of positions of responsibility with the May Broadcasting Company and the Earl May Seed & Nursery Company.

Frances married J. D. Rankin, Jr., who for many years served as vice-president of May Broadcasting and as executive vice-president of the May Seed & Nursery Company. Mr. Rankin died in September 1983.

Frances is now exclusively involved in the Earl May Seed & Nursery Company. She continues to make her home in Shenandoah and maintains a summer cottage near Mercer, Wisconsin. She has a winter home in Tucson, Arizona. Her daughters, Diane Kidd and Betty Jane Shaw, and their families live in Shenandoah.

FRANCES'S HOT CHICKEN SALAD

1 cup diced chicken (or more)
1 cup diced celery
1 can cream of chicken soup
2 teaspoons chopped onion
1 cup cooked instant rice
½ teaspoon salt

¾ cup Hellmann's mayonnaise
½ cup toasted slivered almonds
3 teaspoons lemon juice
1 jar diced pimiento
3 hard-boiled eggs, chopped

Mix, put in greased pan, and cover with crushed cornflakes. Bake at 350 degrees about 30 minutes. Serves 6 to 8.

FRANCES'S FRIED ZUCCHINI

Zucchini
Wesson or Mazola oil
2 egg yolks
1 egg white

Flour
Sugar
Lemon juice

Wash zucchini with soap and water. Rinse. Do not peel. Slice lengthwise in very thin slices. Heat Wesson or Mazola oil in skillet, about

A photograph of the Rankin family taken in 1965. Left to right: Diane,
Frances, Betty Jane, J. D., and Betty Jane's son, Gordon Sherman.

½-inch deep. Dip slices first in flour, then in egg mixture (2 egg yolks
and 1 egg white that have been beaten together), and then in flour.
Fry until brown. Drain. Sprinkle with sugar and lemon juice. The
eggs keep disappearing, so just beat together more.

Edward May, Jr., was two years old when he first sat on his father's
lap and visited with radio friends. He grew up in the environment of
the seed company and radio station KMA. As he grew, so did the
company. A chain of retail stores was developed across the Midwest.
The communication department expanded with the addition of television stations KMTV in Omaha, Nebraska, and KGUN in Tucson,
Arizona. Radio stations WKTY and WSPL-FM in LaCrosse, Wisconsin, were acquired, as well as a sizable interest in KFAB and KGOR-
FM in Omaha.

Ed junior graduated from high school in Shenandoah and then attended the alma mater of his father and grandfather, the University of
Nebraska in Lincoln, where he majored in communications.

"I began broadcasting 'for real' about 1970," Ed junior says.
"Whenever it was possible I broadcast with my father on the noon

The Ed May junior family in 1990. From left: Jeffrey, Carrie, Ed, and Benjamin.

weather and gardening programs. Then, after graduating from the university in 1976, I began learning about the family business in earnest."

ED JUNIOR'S LAZY ITALIAN LASAGNE

1½ pounds hamburger
1 28-ounce can tomatoes
1 8-ounce can tomato sauce
2 12-ounce cans V-8 juice
2 envelopes dry spaghetti sauce
  mix

1 pound lasagne noodles
1 12-ounce carton cottage
  cheese
½ cup Parmesan cheese
1 8-ounce package shredded
  mozzarella cheese

Brown meat and drain. Stir in tomatoes, tomato sauce, V-8, and spaghetti sauce. Bring to a boil, lower heat, and simmer for 10 minutes. Cover bottom of an oiled 9 × 13-inch baking dish with a thin layer of meat sauce; then add a layer of uncooked noodles followed by a layer made of the cheeses. Repeat layers, ending with some sauce and topped with some of the cheeses. Cover pan tightly with foil; set on jelly roll pan in a 350-degree oven and bake 1 hour. Serves 12.

In 1986, Edward May, Sr., retired. At that time it was the desire of the May and Rankin families to separate the two entities of the company, with each family focusing on its primary area of interest. The television stations KMTV and KGUN were sold along with the interests in the KFAB and KGOR radio stations. The Rankin family retained the Earl May Seed & Nursery Company. The May family continued with the broadcasting interests, which include KMA in Shenandoah and WKTY and WSPL-FM in LaCrosse, Wisconsin.

The Mays purchased KQIS-FM in Clarinda and went on the air under the call letters KMA-FM in September of 1989. Ed May, Jr., is actively involved with these stations. In 1990 he also purchased KFOR and KFRX in Lincoln, Nebraska, to expand his own business interests, just as his father and grandfather had done before him.

KAREN'S BANANA-CHIP BREAD

1 stick butter
1 cup sugar
1 beaten egg
1 teaspoon soda
3 tablespoons milk (more, if necessary, for medium-thin batter)

2 large bananas, mashed
1 cup flour
½ cup chopped nuts
½ teaspoon baking powder
½ cup chocolate chips
Maraschino cherries, sliced

Cream butter and sugar; add egg, soda, and milk; add bananas. Blend in flour, baking powder, and nuts. Fold in cherries and chocolate chips. Spoon into greased loaf pan. Bake at 350 degrees for 1 hour or until done.

Jessie Young, the Reverend Edythe Stirlen, Gertrude May, Margaret Perry (who assisted for a time in the May home), and Doris Murphy are shown viewing flowers in Earl May's garden.

The KMA Homemakers

From its beginning in 1925, KMA has relied on talented and creative women. Gertrude May served on the first board of directors, and she also broadcast programs of vocal music, gardening suggestions, and inspirational messages. Lina Ferguson developed a one-hour daily program on the growing and arranging of flowers. Ormah Carmean served as program director, announcer, and sometime musician. The Reverend Edythe Stirlen's religious broadcasting was to span many decades. Eva Hopkins had a beauty program and sold the cosmetics she made at home. Ella Murphy gave book reviews. And many women worked behind the broadcasting scene in the continuity, business, secretarial, and mailing departments.

Among those who have served on the KMA staff, a few specialized in giving daily programs that included suggestions for beautifying the home, growing gardens, storing produce, developing menus, cleaning the furniture, raising a family, collecting recipes, and making the home a more pleasant, worthwhile place in which to live. These women came to be called *radio homemakers*. For over sixty-five years their willingness to share their lives and the lives of their families has enriched the lives of their listeners.

The women's programs on KMA had such titles as the "Home Hour," "Domestic Science Talks," and just simply, "Visit." In the early days they were usually conducted by people who had other duties at the station. Among the best remembered were Gertrude May, Mamie Miller, LeOna Teget, June Case, and Bernice Currier. Their programs were followed in later years by regularly scheduled homemaker programs, each featuring a broadcaster who became closely identified with KMA. Jessie Young, Doris Murphy, Leanna Driftmier and her daughters, Edith Hansen, Sue Conrad, Adella Shoemaker,

Evelyn Birkby, Florence Falk, Martha Bohlsen, Mary Williams, Billie Oakley, Joni Baillon, Jo Freed, Brenda Kay McConahay, Colleen Ketcham, Sue Jones, Marilyn Lee, and Verlene Looker—all developed and maintained a tradition of women broadcasters unknown anywhere else in the world of radio.

KMA's women came to the microphone for many reasons. Some got their first taste of broadcasting as radio musicians. A few moved from other jobs at the station into the studio; several were pressed into service by relatives already on the air. At least one was blown in by a tornado. Just as their origins differ, each of the radio homemakers has approached the duties of broadcasting in her own way and brought to the listeners her own philosophy of life. Some of KMA's women broadcasters have been trained as home economists, and they structured their programs around teaching the techniques of homemaking. Others relied for inspiration on experience rather than on coursework.

Still, the radio homemakers all share a few indispensable qualities. They can talk. While that may seem simple enough, it has never been just a matter of filling airtime with words. In order to succeed, the homemakers have projected a sincerity, enthusiasm, and optimism that cannot be faked. They have been willing to share their personal lives with listeners in much the same way close neighbors confide in one another. They work to stay current with developments in the techniques of cooking, housekeeping, family care, and interests pertaining to midwesterners. Finally, via letters, phone calls, and visits, they have paid attention to those listeners who wish to share their own joys and sorrows. The audience has come to trust these radio personalities as friends.

The radio homemakers have long filled a need in the lives of those who listen. Men as well as women have enjoyed following the experiences of their favorite homemakers and their families for years, tuning in the programs every day as one might turn on a soap opera. Many lonely listeners have found in the radio homemakers people whose feelings they can share. Still others have sought guidance as they started their homes, raised their families, and coped with everyday life. Since preparing food is a daily occurrence in most households, the radio homemakers have always made menu ideas and recipes a part of each program.

For more than sixty-five years, a trademark of KMA has been its radio homemakers. By sharing of themselves, by encouraging, educating, and especially by listening, they have helped give KMA something few other stations can boast—an audience that is a great and varied extended family.

Gertrude May helped her husband, Earl, in every way she could to encourage the development of radio station KMA. Among her various responsibilities was the sharing of her cooking expertise. LeOna Teget, who sometimes gave flower talks and worked in the recipe department at the station, assisted Gertrude in publishing what seems to be the first book of recipes published by KMA. The frontispiece of the book, *KMA Radio Recipes,* is this photograph of the two ladies working at a 1920s range. The recipes are just as fine to use today as they were when Gertrude and LeOna put together the first of a long line of popular KMA cookbooks. If not specifically identified, the recipes in this chapter are from Gertrude and LeOna.

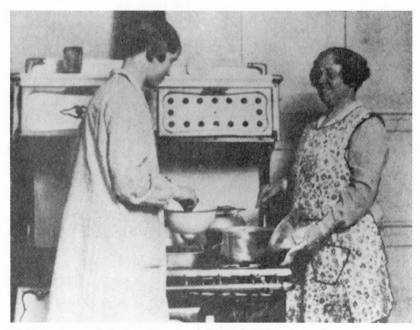

KMA Recipe Lady LeOna Teget and Gertrude May getting dinner in Gertrude's kitchen.

As an ordained minister, the Reverend Edythe Stirlen performed hundreds of weddings, both privately and on the air. The ceremony shown in this photograph was broadcast from the stage of the Mayfair Auditorium. The groom is Cleil Ostrander of Sterling, Nebraska, and the bride is Ilah Funk of Glenwood, Iowa.

An ordained minister with fifty years of active service is not un-usual, but when that person is a woman who has conducted daily radio broadcasts for at least that many years, she symbolizes a personal and spiritual victory.

Edythe Elam Swartz's first radio work was done on station KFEQ in St. Joseph, Missouri. A short time later, she came to Shenandoah to serve as religious director for KFNF, Henry Field's radio station based just a few blocks east of KMA. Initially, Edythe sang hymns and gave religious readings. She was proficient on the guitar, ukulele, and pump organ. She usually played one of those instruments to accompany her singing.

In 1930, Edythe became an ordained minister in the Disciples of Christ Church and brought her religious and social service programs to KMA. In July of that same year, she married Carl Stirlen, who worked in the retail store of the May Company.

Edythe began publishing her monthly magazine, the *S.O.S. Signal*, in 1935. The initials stood for "Send Out Sunshine," a phrase that reflected Edythe's philosophy of life. A microphone was installed in her home, and she began her daily broadcasts with the announcer saying, "It's time for the Little Minister—we now take you to a little white house on 6th Avenue." With the help of her singing canary and

Homemaker Jessie Young and the Little Minister, the Reverend Edythe Stirlen. This 1938 photograph was taken near the driveway of the May home in Shenandoah.

her musical instruments, Edythe shared her music, sermons, Sunday school lessons, inspirational messages, and requests for help for those in need.

The Little Minister gave up active broadcasting on the last Sunday of December 1981, but like most pastors, she continued in local church activities. Edythe celebrated her ninetieth birthday in March 1985 by attending Sunday school and church at the Shenandoah First Christian Church, speaking at both services. That evening her daughters, Rosalee and Josephine, stopped at the little white house on 6th Avenue to visit their mother, but she wasn't home. It did not take them long to find her a block away, seated in a church sanctuary participating in an evening service. She was exactly where she wanted to be.

Edythe passed away on September 17, 1987. Her daughters chose wheat for their mother's casket spray because Edythe was born and raised in Kansas and had attended the university at Lawrence. Wheat not only is associated with the state of Kansas but is, more importantly, the sign of eternal life.

Edythe would have been pleased.

EDYTHE'S TOFFEE BARS

⅔ cup margarine	2½ cups flour
1 1-pound box brown sugar	¼ teaspoon salt
3 eggs, well beaten	1 package chocolate chips
2½ teaspoons baking powder	Nuts, if desired

Melt margarine in saucepan, add sugar, and cool. Add eggs, baking powder sifted with the flour, and salt; stir in chocolate chips and nuts. Spread in well-greased 9 × 15 pan and bake in oven at 350 degrees ½ hour.

May be frosted by using 1 package butterscotch chips melted with powdered sugar.

EDYTHE'S SOUTHERN-STYLE CORN BREAD

1½ cups yellow cornmeal
1 teaspoon salt
1 teaspoon sugar
¾ teaspoon soda

1½ cups buttermilk or sour milk
2 eggs, separated
¼ cup melted shortening

Stir dry ingredients together. Add milk to beaten egg yolks and stir into dry mixture; beat well. Add the shortening. Beat the egg whites until stiff and fold into batter. Pour into greased 8 × 8 pan. Bake at 400 degrees for 8 minutes; then turn heat to 350 degrees and continue baking 25 minutes or until golden brown on top.

PRALINES

4 cups sugar; 1 teaspoon salt; 3 cups pecan nutmeats; 2 cups cream. Make a syrup out of 3 cups of sugar and the cream. Caramelize the other cup of sugar by melting it in an iron pan, stirring constantly with the back of a spoon. Into it pour all the syrup at one time, stirring constantly and rapidly. (Be careful, as this is very hot.) Add the salt. Boil the mixture to the soft ball stage without stirring. Pour into a flat pan and cool. Beat to a cream consistency. Add nuts. Form into flat, round cakes about 3 inches in diameter on a waxed paper. This amount makes about 20 cakes. During the creaming process the nuts must be added before the mixture shows signs of hardening so they will be well mixed. As this candy is to be in the form of round cakes and not in a mass, one must work quickly to keep the candy from hardening before the cakes are placed on the waxed paper.

Lina Ferguson was the Flower Lady on KMA for fourteen years. "I always loved gardens and flowers," Lina remembers. "When I was very young, the first money I ever earned was from selling garden sass." (Sass is an old-fashioned term meaning vegetables, usually those that are cooked and combined with a sauce.)

Lina Coxedge was a teacher who had come from Kansas to teach German and Latin in the Shenandoah high school. She married law-

Lina Ferguson, the Flower Lady.

yer Paul Ferguson in 1916. The two became close friends of Gertrude and Earl May.

Gertrude and Lina shared a mutual interest in flowers. Together they attended many shows and training seminars featuring gardening and flower arranging. Not long after KMA took to the air in 1925, Lina began broadcasting programs listed in the schedules as "Talk" or "Garden Club Hour." Later, when KMA was publishing the *KMA Guide*, Lina wrote columns entitled "Fun with Flowers" and "A Line from Lina."

In 1926 the Shenandoah Kiwanis Club sponsored a trip to the British Isles. A number of KMA people, including Gertrude May, went on this tour. Earl May encouraged Lina to go and arranged for company money to pay for part of her passage. She brought back information on British gardens to present on her programs. Lina also traveled to Yorkshire to see the area from which her ancestors had come. There she discovered her famous Yorkshire Pudding recipe.

When the Fergusons' daughter, Julia, was born, Lina took a leave of absence, during which time Marian Welch presented the flower broadcasts. When Julia started school, Lina returned to the air.

During World War II, when many of the men who worked in radio stations were leaving for the armed forces, Lina took a course in radio engineering. She felt it was a patriotic action, and she found the study fascinating.

"The war ended before my new knowledge was needed, but I was happy I had studied the subject and actually had graduated with an engineer's certificate. It was good to have the war over, and I could continue with my first love—flowers." Lina retired from broadcasting in 1947.

Now past the age of one hundred, Lina lives in a bright, cheerful room in one of Shenandoah's care facilities. Blossoms and plants continue to bring her the same pleasure as they did during the years she was broadcasting as the Flower Lady.

LINA'S DRIED BEEF FILLING

Dried beef, cheese, pimiento, and 2 hard-cooked eggs. Chop all together and mix with dressing.

LINA'S YORKSHIRE PUDDING

⅞ cup flour	2 eggs
½ teaspoon salt	½ cup water
½ cup milk	Beef drippings or melted butter

Sift flour and salt into bowl. Make a well in the center of these dry ingredients. Pour in milk and stir to blend. Beat eggs until fluffy and beat into batter. Add water and beat until large bubbles rise to the surface. Permit this mixture to stand for an hour if you have time, then beat again. Have ready an oven-proof dish (10 × 10 or 9 × 11) containing about ½ inch of hot beef drippings or melted butter. ("I usually add these to the pan and place in oven to heat while I am mixing the batter.") Pour the batter into the hot grease (*carefully!*)

and bake at 400 degrees for about 20 minutes; then reduce heat to 350 degrees and bake 10 to 15 minutes longer. For variety, this can also be baked in muffin tins with a shorter baking time for the smaller puddings. Serve with gravy and roast beef.

MAMIE'S SOUR CREAM CAKE

Mix 2½ cups cake flour (before sifting). Mix with 2 cups sugar and a pinch salt. Combine 3 well-beaten eggs with 2 cups sour cream. Pour into dry ingredients and mix well. In separate bowl put 6 level tablespoons cocoa with 2 level teaspoons soda. Add ¾ cup boiling water. Add to first mixture. Bake in greased loaf pan or 9 × 13 pan at 350 degrees until done.

MAMIE'S BUSY-DAY CAKE

1⅔ cups flour—sift once and measure. 1 cup sugar, ¼ teaspoon salt, 2½ teaspoons baking powder, ⅓ cup shortening (part butter), ⅔ cup milk (room temperature), 1 egg, 1 teaspoon vanilla. Beat all ingredients together with rotary beater 2 minutes. Bake in greased 8-inch square pan or 9-inch round pan for 25 to 35 minutes at 350 degrees.

For spice cake add 1 teaspoon cinnamon, ½ teaspoon nutmeg, and ¼ teaspoon cloves.

For chocolate cake add 2 squares melted chocolate.

BAKED SQUASH

Cut the squash in strips after it is peeled. Slice in a baking dish until full. Add ½ teaspoon salt and a little water. Put on lid and bake till done. Then add ½ cup water, ½ cup brown sugar, and 1 teaspoon butter or more. Bake another 20 minutes.

Mamie Miller.

Those who remember her describe Mamie Miller as a woman of great dignity, kindness, beauty, and talent. She was a graduate of Shenandoah's Western Normal College, a musician who sang beautifully and taught both voice and piano.

Mamie broadcast "Domestic Science" each afternoon on KMA. The sixth edition of the "Behind the Mike" booklet reports that "[Mamie] can make your mouth water for all the good things she tells you about on her program." In those early, informal days of radio, she also used her many talents on various other shows.

A source of information about Mamie surfaced recently with the discovery of a yellowed newspaper clipping—with the date and newspaper name cut away—that tells of Mamie's wedding. The flowery terms of early twentieth-century reporting are evident.

> Dudley B. Miller and Miss Mary Reneau were married Wednesday evening, Dec. 17, at 6:30 o'clock at the home of Col. T. N. and Mrs. Pace on Church St. [in Shenandoah, Iowa] . . . The bride is the popular young lady familiarly known as Mamie Pace. . . .
>
> At the age of seven years, her mother being dead, Mamie was adopted into the Pace home by . . . filial affection, but never in

legal form. The hearts of Mr. and Mrs. Pace were aching for a child, having lost one of their own (a girl about the age of seven) and Mamie was just as glad to find a papa and mamma she could love. . . . She chose to be known as Mamie Pace. . . .

Mr. Miller is a man of fine character and ability, a banker by vocation. His little son David, a bright child of seven, played the part of cupid in this story. . . .

And so it was that Mamie obtained a ready-made family. She and Dudley also had a daughter, Florence. Now Mrs. Ehlers, Florence lives in Blythe, California.

Mamie passed away on June 5, 1951, and is buried in Riverside, California.

HARVARD BEETS

Wash 6 small beets, cook in boiling water until soft. Remove skins and cut beets in thin slices, small cubes, or fancy shapes, using French vegetable cutter. Mix ¾ cup sugar and ½ tablespoon cornstarch. Add ½ cup vinegar and let boil 5 minutes. Pour over beets and let stand on back of range ½ hour. Just before serving add 2 tablespoons butter and reheat.

ASPARAGUS

1 bunch asparagus; 1½ cups rich white sauce; ¼ cup bread crumbs; 4 sliced hard-cooked eggs. Cook the asparagus till tender. Brown the bread crumbs in butter. Place a layer of eggs and crumbs in the bottom of a baking dish, and a layer of asparagus and the white sauce. After all is used, have a layer of crumbs on top and sprinkle over the top with grated cheese and cook in the oven until the cheese is melted and crumbs are brown. Instead of eggs, ¼ cup chopped peanuts are good.

Earl May, founder of KMA radio, in the flower gardens west of the great Mayfair Auditorium.

The Mayfair Auditorium was built in 1927 as a place to hold various meetings, performances, and exhibitions, to show films, and to provide seating space for the crowds of people who wished to watch the KMA radio programs. Many of the special homemaker events originated from its stage.

Besides the one-thousand-seat theater, this Moorish-style building contained the business, engineering, and small broadcast rooms of KMA.

Memories of the early days of radio station KMA conjure up thoughts of the big jubilee days. The forerunner of those unforget-

Serving certain foods at the jubilees, pancake days, and popcorn festivals provided a vehicle for companies to introduce their wares to potential customers. The pancakes, syrups, butter, coffee, etc., served were advertised in various ways. This ad tells about the golden syrup that people ate on their pancakes when they came to Earl May's Seed & Nursery Company and KMA radio celebrations.

table events was held in 1926 on KMA's first anniversary. Then, in 1927 when the great Mayfair Auditorium was dedicated, thousands of people arrived for the event.

For the first time, pancakes were offered to the hungry multitudes.

Fidelity Pancake Flour was sold by the Mays and thus was used as the base for pancakes when the thousands of visitors came to Shenandoah for the various celebrations. This ad includes a recipe for the pancakes—the only such recipe for pancakes that has survived from those early jubilee days.

The company that supplied the May retail store in Shenandoah with its flour came with its product and whipped up huge vats of batter. Helpers fried mountains of pancakes on large griddles. A tradition had begun.

Pancake Days were continued through the years. This is one of the serving areas in the May building on such an occasion.

FORTY-NINE PUNCH BUNS

Dissolve 1 cake Fleischmann's yeast (or 1 package dry yeast) in 2 cups warm water. Add 3 cups warm water; 1 teaspoon salt; 1 teaspoon sugar; flour enough for sponge. Let rise. Add 1 cup shortening (lard); 3 eggs; 1 cup sugar; flour enough for soft dough. Let rise and punch back at intervals all day. Then put in a cool place and occasionally punch back. Can be made 2 or 3 days ahead of time. Allow 2½ hours at least for them to rise after being molded out before baking. Bake at 375 degrees until brown. By starting in the A.M. they can be ready for evening dinner.

HOREHOUND CANDY

1 ounce dry horehound; 1½ cups water; 1¾ pounds brown sugar. Boil water and horehound steadily for about 20 minutes. Strain, add sugar, let boil without stirring until a few drops form a hard ball in cold water. Pour into a well-greased tin, and as soon as cool enough to hold its shape, mark in squares.

CANDLE SALAD

Place a whole slice of canned pineapple on a lettuce leaf. Stick half a banana upright in the center of the pineapple. Top the banana with a red cherry. Garnish the banana with yellow salad dressing to represent tallow running down the sides of a lighted candle.

RADIO PEANUT BRITTLE

2 cups sugar; 1 cup white Karo syrup; 1 cup water. Boil until thick. Add 2 cups (raw or unroasted) peanuts. Stir constantly until the syrup as well as the cracked-open peanuts are light brown in color (about 10 minutes). Remove from stove. Add 2 teaspoons soda, 1 teaspoon vanilla, and lump of butter. Spread thin on well-buttered pans, and just as soon as cool break into small pieces.

INDIAN-MEAL DOUGHNUTS

Pour ¾ cup boiling milk over 1½ cups fine cornmeal, stir, and allow to cool. Add ½ cup soft butter, ¾ cup sugar, a teaspoon cinnamon, ¼ grated nutmeg, 2 beaten eggs, and a cup of flour in which there are 2 teaspoons baking powder. Work the dough smooth, roll on a board three quarters of an inch thick, cut out, and fry in hot lard. Dust with powdered sugar.

BUTTERFLY SALAD

Cut a slice of pineapple in half. Place the curved edges opposite each other with a date between them to represent the body of the butterfly. Use thin strips of lettuce for the antennae. Sliced stuffed olives are placed on the pineapple "wings" with bits of nuts and maraschino cherries. Drops of yellow salad dressing are placed between the olives on the wings.

MINCEMEAT

4 pounds lean boiled meat (chop fine, do not grind). Twice as much chopped apples; 1 pound chopped suet; 4 pounds seedless raisins; 2 pounds currants; 2 pounds brown sugar; 1 pint boiled cider; 1 tablespoon salt; 1 teaspoon allspice; 4 teaspoons cinnamon; 2 grated nutmegs; 1 tablespoon cloves; 2 cups vinegar; 1 quart fruit juice. More sugar if not sweet enough. Add juice from peach pickles. Cook slowly about 1½ hours. Seal in quart jars. Process in hot water bath or pressure canner according to current recommended directions. Enough for about 12 quarts.

PEAR AND APPLE CONSERVE

Nine hard pears; 6 tart apples; 1½ lemons; ⅛ pound Canton ginger; ½ quart water; sugar. Pare, quarter, and core the pears. Pare the apples, core and cut crosswise in ½-inch slices. Grate the rind of the lemons and add the juice to the water. Cut ginger in small pieces. For every pound of fruit allow one pound of sugar. Boil sugar and water to a syrup, add rest of ingredients, and boil ¾ of an hour or until thick and clear. Place in cans or glasses and cover well.

CHICKEN SOUP

Cut up one large chicken. Cook until tender in 5 quarts of water. Each pound of meat requires one quart of water. Keep adding water so you have five quarts when cooking is completed. Salt and boil ½ cup of rice in double boiler (covered with chicken broth). When tender add to rice, 1 pinch of mace, 1 of nutmeg, 1 of saffron. Salt to taste. Add 3 quarts of clear soup. Bring to boil. Add 1 egg, well beaten in ½ cup of cream, and chicken removed from bone as desired.

*This little girl stopped at the Mayway
Hatchery in 1926 to help her father pick up
newly hatched chickens for their farm.*

FEATHERWEIGHT WHITE CAKE

This cake is easy to make and always turns out right. 1 cup of sugar, and if it is a little coarse roll it with a rolling pin; ½ cup fat; ⅔ cup milk; 3 egg whites; 2 cups sifted cake flour; ½ teaspoon salt; 2 teaspoons baking powder; 1 teaspoon vanilla. Cream fat and sugar gradually until mixture is very light. Stir in alternately milk and sifted dry ingredients. Fold in egg whites which have been beaten stiff but not dry. Add vanilla and turn batter into two greased layer pans. Bake in 350-degree oven for about 30 minutes or until cake tests done. Frost with any kind of icing.

Jessie Young

essie Young was the first—the first to broadcast directly from her home and the first of the KMA women broadcasters to share her experiences and her housekeeping, sewing, and cooking expertise with her listeners in depth and detail over many years.

In 1925 KMA went on the air as one of the pioneer radio stations of the Midwest. Before then Earl and Gertrude May and their friends had ridden back and forth to Omaha to put the very first of their programs on the air via station WOAW. The programs included agricultural and garden lectures, religious talks, entertainers and musicians, and solos by Gertrude May. The Mays were intensely loyal to those people who had volunteered to help in the earliest part of their venture into this new medium of communication. Many became regular broadcasters and employees of the May Seed & Nursery Company.

One of these was Jessie Young. She and her husband, Floyd, belonged to the Congregational church choir in Shenandoah, and their choir participated in the very first broadcast on January 17, 1925. As time went on, Floyd and Jessie began singing duets on the fledgling programs.

Both of the Youngs were working in a bank in Shenandoah and thought their future was secure. Unfortunately, the bank closed and its employees were out of work. The circumstances could have been devastating, but Jessie had been through difficult times before; somehow she and her husband would survive.

Earl May never forgot a friend, and he considered the Youngs his friends. When he learned that the two had lost their jobs, he asked them to come and work for him—Floyd in the sales department of the May Seed & Nursery Company and Jessie at KMA.

Jessie began her new occupation by filling in for the vacationing program director. She started writing commercials and soon was giving them on the air. She was the perfect salesperson—relaxed, sincere, and convincing.

By late 1926 Jessie had her own program. "The Stitch and Chat Club" gradually became "A Visit with Jessie Young." She had become an important part of the lives of Midwest listeners.

EGG YOLK COOKIES

9 egg yolks beaten with egg
　beater until very light
1½ cups brown sugar
1 cup soft shortening
1 teaspoon soda
2 teaspoons baking powder

1 cup raisins
½ cup nuts
¼ teaspoon salt
Flour to stiffen
1 teaspoon maple flavoring

Cream sugar and shortening, add beaten egg yolks, sifted dry ingredients, raisins, nuts, and flavoring. Drop by spoonfuls on greased cookie sheet. Bake in moderate oven for 15 minutes.

INDIAN HARVEST BAKE

2 cans tuna in oil
1½ cups chopped onion
1 teaspoon chili powder
1 teaspoon dried leaf oregano
½ teaspoon salt
¼ teaspoon cumin seed

2 medium zucchini, sliced
1 green pepper, cut into strips
2 tomatoes, sliced
1 10-ounce package frozen corn,
　whole kernel
2 cups grated mild cheddar
　cheese

Drain 1 tablespoon oil from tuna into 2-quart casserole. Add onion and cook until golden. Mix together chili powder, oregano, salt, and cumin seed. Layer ⅓ of each vegetable, ⅓ of tuna, and ⅓ cup cheese over onion in casserole, sprinkling each layer with a small amount of seasoning mixture. Repeat layers 2 more times. Cover and bake in 350-degree oven for about 1 hour. Serves 6.

Robert and Jessie Young and Jessie's mother, Rosa Susanka.

As the Depression deepened in the late 1920s and early 1930s, Jessie empathized with and helped those of her radio listeners who were struggling. As a youngster, she too had known hardship, scrimping, and the need to be tenacious.

Jessie's Grandfather Cuhel had come to Nebraska in 1867 as an immigrant from Bohemia. He brought with him his motherless children, the youngest of whom was Rosa. A series of business disasters, many due to his ignorance of the language and the new land, finally led to a situation where the children had to fend for themselves.

Rosa was only seven years old when she began working for her room and board by washing dishes in a saloon. In the years that followed, Rosa did needlework, housekeeping, washing and ironing of clothes, cooking—anything to survive.

Rosa married George Susanka and moved to Essex, Iowa, seven miles north of Shenandoah. The couple had four daughters, the youngest of whom was Jessie. George was not a good provider, and the family was terribly poor; he finally left his wife and children, and they never saw him again.

To keep the family together, Rosa and her daughters did laundry, cleaning, sewing, and cooking. Jessie did many jobs; among them she went from door to door to find customers to buy magazines, books, bluing, and her mother's baked goods. The skills she was learning were one day to make her a super salesperson.

LAZY DAISY CAKE

Put 1 cup milk and 1 tablespoon butter on to heat in a saucepan. Beat 2 eggs till light and add 1 cup sugar, beating vigorously. Sift 1 cup flour, 1 teaspoon baking powder, and ½ teaspoon salt. Stir into the egg mixture and add vanilla. Add milk mixture, stirring carefully as added. Pour into 8 × 8 pan and bake 25 minutes in moderate oven.

Frost with ⅔ cup brown sugar, ⅓ cup melted butter, 2 tablespoons thick cream, and ½ cup coconut. Spread on cake while warm and return to oven to caramelize.

When she was seventeen years old and newly graduated from high school, Jessie moved to Shenandoah, where she obtained work as a secretary at the Henry Field Seed Company. She lived in a nearby boarding house, where she met Floyd Young. The following year they were married. The two were active in the Congregational church and enjoyed singing in the choir.

Not long after she began her regular daily broadcasting, KMA ran a wire from the studio and installed a microphone in Jessie's home so she could do her broadcasts directly from her kitchen. Much to the delight of the listeners, members of the Young family would wander in and out and stop to talk. These included sons Robert, Richard, and

Jessie Young with her daughter, Eileen, and her mother, Rosa.

Ronnie and a daughter, Eileen, whom Floyd and Jessie adopted as an undernourished, neglected child. In their care and with the watchful interest of the radio audience, Eileen blossomed into a strong, healthy girl.

PEAR HONEY

4 pounds pears   1 pint water
3 pounds sugar   1 can crushed pineapple
                                               (undrained)

Grind pared and cored pears in food chopper. Add water and boil until clear. Add sugar and pineapple. Boil rapidly until thick. Fill hot jars. Seal.

RADIO CAKE

1 cup sugar
2 tablespoons butter
2 tablespoons cocoa
¼ cup boiling water
1 cup sour milk or buttermilk

1⅓ cups flour
1 teaspoon soda
½ teaspoon salt
1 teaspoon vanilla

To the creamed butter and sugar, add the cocoa mixed with boiling water. Then sour milk, flour, soda, salt, and vanilla. Beat together and bake in two pans, greased and floured.

Filling

1½ tablespoons cocoa
1½ tablespoons cornstarch
⅔ cup sugar

¾ cup water
½ teaspoon vanilla

Mix dry ingredients, then water, and cook until thick and creamy. Spread between layers and use any desired icing for top.

TOASTED OATMEAL DROP COOKIES

1½ cups oatmeal
⅓ cup sour milk
2 cups brown sugar
¾ cup shortening
2 eggs beaten
1 teaspoon vanilla flavoring
1 cup seeded chopped dates

1 cup chopped nuts
2½ cups flour
1 teaspoon soda
½ teaspoon salt
1 teaspoon baking powder
1 teaspoon cinnamon
1 teaspoon nutmeg

Sprinkle oatmeal in pan and brown lightly in moderate oven. Place in bowl. Add sour milk and let stand 5 minutes. Cream sugar and shortening. Add eggs and vanilla. Mix thoroughly. Add soaked oatmeal. Stir in flour sifted with soda, baking powder, and salt. Also spices. Mix until smooth. Add dates and nuts. Drop from spoon on greased baking sheet and bake at 375 degrees for 15 minutes.

RICHARD YOUNG'S BURNT-SUGAR BIRTHDAY CAKE

½ cup sugar
¼ cup water
1½ cups sugar
½ cup shortening
3 egg yolks
¾ cup milk

4 tablespoons cooled burnt-
 sugar syrup
1 teaspoon vanilla
¼ teaspoon salt
2½ cups flour
2 teaspoons baking powder
3 egg whites, beaten stiff

Put ½ cup sugar into skillet. Cook and stir until light brown. Add ¼ cup boiling water (carefully), stir until mixture is dissolved and syrupy. Set aside to cool. Cream 1½ cups sugar and shortening together until fluffy. Beat in egg yolks, milk, 4 tablespoons burnt-sugar syrup, and vanilla. Sift dry ingredients and beat in. Fold in beaten egg whites. Makes 3 layers. Bake in a 350-degree oven.

Frosting

3 tablespoons butter
Remaining burnt-sugar syrup
1 egg

Pinch of salt
2½ cups powdered sugar
1 teaspoon vanilla

Warm butter and syrup together. Gradually add egg and beat well. Add rest of ingredients. Spread on cake.

Jessie carefully thought through all her own commercials, but she did not work from a script. She would ad-lib twelve to thirteen commercials for her one-hour homemaker visit. Jessie recalled: "I sold cosmetics, roses, fish, prunes, horse collars, harnesses, jackets, boots, jam, tires, blankets, and dress goods. I don't think you can mention anything that I didn't sell. But I never sold anything I didn't believe in. Listeners can tell right away if someone isn't being honest with them."

SEPTEMBER
1967

Jessie's
HOMEMAKER

Radio...Visit

Price
25¢

VARNISHED CHICKEN

Place cut-up chicken in a single layer in a large pan.

Mix: *2 tablespoons brown sugar*
  1 envelope of onion soup mix   *½ cup water*
  ½ cup catsup

Pour this over the chicken and cover with foil. Bake in 300-degree oven for 20 minutes. Uncover and bake 20 minutes more.

MARBLED MACARONI

1 can cream of celery soup   *½ cup shredded American*
1 teaspoon Worcestershire sauce   *cheese*
1 can tomato sauce   *3 ounces elbow macaroni*
1 can luncheon meat cut into   *1 tablespoon flour*
  ¼-inch cubes   *Dash pepper*
¼ cup finely chopped onion   *Dash paprika*
                                 Buttered bread crumbs

Cook macaroni in boiling salted water until tender, about 7 minutes. Drain. Blend in tomato sauce and flour. Cook until thick, stirring constantly. Combine tomato mixture, meat, onion, green pepper,

Worcestershire sauce, and pepper. Stir soup until smooth, mix lightly with macaroni, and spread half the macaroni mixture in a 9-inch square pan, greased. Cover with meat sauce, then remaining macaroni mixture. Sprinkle with cheese, buttered bread crumbs, and paprika. Bake at 350 degrees for 40 minutes. Serves 6.

Leanna Driftmier, Jessie's good friend and colleague, suggested that Jessie start a magazine. It took a number of years for Jessie to save enough money to finance the printing, but in 1946 she began publishing *Jessie's Homemaker Radio . . . Visit.* It was a family production from start to finish—writing, typing, layout, assisting with the printing, and doing the addressing and mailing. Each issue included photographs, letters, recipes, patterns, and helpful suggestions from family members and radio listeners. Publication continued until 1980, when Jessie's eyesight began to fail. Over the years, Jessie also published twenty cookbooks and sewing books.

BANANA PIE

1 egg and 1 yolk of another	2 tablespoons flour
1 cup sugar	Little butter
1 scant cup milk	1 banana, mashed fine

Cook and place in baked pie shell. Cover with meringue. Put back in oven and brown.

ONE-DISH MEAL

2 carrots, sliced lengthwise	1 onion, chopped
2 turnips, sliced	1 pound sausage
4 potatoes, diced	1 cup tomatoes

Brown sausage in heavy pan, breaking meat into pieces with a fork. Place vegetables around sausage and add a little water and tomatoes. Season to taste. Cover. Simmer until done, about 45 minutes.

HOT SLAW

4 slices crisp bacon
1 tablespoon brown sugar
1 tablespoon chopped green
 onions
1 teaspoon salt
¼ cup vinegar

1 medium head cabbage, thinly
 sliced
¼ cup thinly sliced red radishes
1 small stalk celery, thinly
 sliced

In a medium skillet, fry the bacon until crisp. Drain on paper towel but reserve drippings in the skillet. Add the brown sugar, green onions, salt, and vinegar to drippings, stirring until smooth. Add crumbled bacon, cabbage, radishes, and celery. Toss lightly. Heat through. Serve at once. Garnish with parsley, if desired.
    Serves 6.

Jessie found unusual ways to use her sewing skills. When Earl May brought an elephant to town for publicity purposes, he decided it needed a blanket. Jessie agreed to sew the blanket but refused to have anything to do with measuring the animal. Earl had some of the men employees do that task. Jessie bought yards and yards of material and stitched up a blanket for the elephant to wear for its public appearances.

JESSIE'S CROCKPOT PORK CHOPS

6 thick pork chops
½ cup flour
1 tablespoon salt
1½ teaspoons dry mustard

½ teaspoon garlic powder
2 tablespoons oil
1 can chicken and rice soup

Trim fat from chops. Combine all dry ingredients (less salt can be used, if desired). Dip chops in dry mix and brown in oil. Place browned chops in crockpot and pour soup over top. Cover. Cook on high for 3½ hours or on low for 6 to 8 hours.

KATCHY KINKS FOR THE KITCHEN

The use of alliterations, especially those using the letter K, became popular among the radio homemakers. Such words used in titles attracted readers' attention and were imaginatively used in everything from column titles to the names of magazines and programs. In her monthly *Homemaker* magazine, Jessie's column, "Katchy Kinks for the Kitchen," gave her readers thirty-four years of helpful suggestions.

LEMON CHIFFON PIE

1 tablespoon unflavored gelatin
¼ cup cold water
3 egg yolks, beaten
½ cup sugar
½ teaspoon salt

½ cup hot water
¼ cup lemon juice
3 egg whites
½ cup sugar

Dissolve gelatin in cold water. Combine egg yolks, ½ cup sugar, and salt. Gradually beat in hot water and cook, stirring, until thick. Add dissolved gelatin and lemon juice. Cool until it just begins to congeal. Beat egg whites until soft peaks form. Gradually add ½ cup sugar, beating until stiff peaks form. Fold into lemon mixture. Spoon into baked pie shell. Sprinkle top with nutmeg. Chill.

CORNHUSKER SALAD

Break crisp lettuce into small pieces. Add sliced radishes, cucumbers, a quartered tomato, julienne-cut green pepper, celery, carrots, green onions, and 1 cup ham cut in medium-size chunks. Toss with salad dressing of your choice.

UNCOOKED DATE ROLL

2 dozen crushed graham
  crackers
1 pound finely chopped dates
2 dozen marshmallows,
  chopped

1 cup chopped nutmeats
3 tablespoons (or more) cream

Mix and make into a roll and store in refrigerator. Cut in slices and serve with whipped cream.

As late as 1940, people were still writing to Jessie about ways to care for food when they had no refrigeration. A publicity memo mailed out in December of that year stated:

"Problems in refrigeration which have almost disappeared in the city are very real to farm women who have no electricity, and to the many others who have electricity but cannot afford electric refrigerators. Jessie Young helps her listeners solve such problems by giving frequent recipes for canning and smoking meats. Entertainment for farm bureau meetings, suggestions for parties, games for children, exercises and plays for rural school functions—all these are requested by her listeners, and each request is carefully answered."

GARLIC GRITS

1 cup grits
1 quart water
2 to 3 teaspoons salt
3 ounces cheese, grated
1½ cloves garlic

½ stick butter
2 eggs, slightly beaten
1 cup milk
Parmesan cheese, grated

Cook grits in boiling water until tender but pourable. Remove from heat and add cheese, garlic, and butter. Stir until melted. Cool. Then add slightly beaten eggs and milk. Pour into well-greased casserole and bake at 350 degrees for 1 hour. Remove from oven, sprinkle with Parmesan cheese, and bake 10 minutes longer.

JESSIE'S EASY QUICHE

This recipe makes its own crust; you do not have to make a separate crust.

3 eggs
½ cup melted oleo
½ cup Bisquick
1½ cups milk
½ teaspoon salt
Pepper

½ cup shredded *Swiss cheese*
2 tablespoons *minced onion or*
    onion flakes
½ cup *ham or bacon or any*
    meat

Mix in blender (or food processor) all except meat. Add that just before putting into a 9 × 9 buttered Pyrex dish. Bake at 350 degrees for 40 minutes.

Jessie broadcasting from the kitchen of her home in Shenandoah.

SALMON LOAF WITH SAUCE

Mix 1 can salmon with 1 or 2 eggs and sufficient cracker crumbs, bread crumbs, or cornflakes to make into a loaf. Season. Make into loaf; place in greased casserole or baking pan. Have loaf in center of baking pan. Have ready a nice rich cream sauce. Pour over and around. Bake ½ hour. Very good, quick dish.

Jessie is the first Shenandoah woman to be elected president of the Iowa Federation of Business and Professional Women's Organizations. She served the state BPW in this capacity during 1936–1937.

Jessie continued her radio homemaker broadcasts for KMA until 1942 when the Youngs went to Philadelphia, where she did a similar program for a year. Homesick for the Midwest, the family returned to Lincoln, Nebraska, where Jessie became affiliated with radio station KFAB. Later, she and her family moved to Colorado, where she continued to tape her shows and send them back to the station.

Jessie returned to Shenandoah and Essex a number of times. In 1967 she and her son Robert drove from Colorado to attend the fiftieth reunion of the 1917 Essex High School graduating class. The classmates and their relatives had dinner in the same old Butler Hotel building in Essex, where Jessie had helped her mother cater meals so many years ago.

Jessie returned again in 1975 to participate in KMA's fiftieth anniversary celebration. She appeared with the other radio homemakers, past and present, and spoke on the air. She was also interviewed on a broadcast by longtime KMA announcer Warren Nielson.

Although Jessie stopped broadcasting in 1955, she continued publication of her *Homemaker* magazine until 1980.

Jessie's husband, Floyd, died in 1966. In June 1987, Jessie suffered a stroke from which she never recovered. She died that same year on the twelfth of September. Her youngest son, Ronald, still lives in the home on Blue Bell Street in Fort Collins, Colorado, where he lived and cared for his mother after her eyesight failed. Her eldest son, Robert, lives in Vicksburg, Mississippi. Daughter Eileen Nevein resides in Tucson and son Richard is in Denver. Robi, the grandson whom Jessie raised, lives in Seattle.

BRAISED SHORT RIBS

Brown short ribs in hot fat; season with salt and pepper. Add ½ cup hot water; cover tightly and bake in slow oven about 1½ hours.

APPLE GOODIE

3 cups sliced or diced apples
¾ cup white sugar
¼ teaspoon soda
¼ teaspoon baking powder
⅓ cup melted butter

1 rounded tablespoon flour
   (2 level tablespoons)
Salt and cinnamon to taste
¾ cup oatmeal
¾ cup flour
¾ cup brown sugar, firmly
   packed

Combine apples and white sugar and put in buttered 8 × 8 Pyrex pan. Mix soda, baking powder, melted butter, flour, and salt and cinnamon to taste. Spread over top of apples. Combine remaining ingredients and crumble over the top. Bake 30 or 40 minutes at 350 degrees. Cut in squares and serve with hard sauce or whipped cream. I don't use either one; good without.

BEST EVERS

½ cup butter
1 cup sugar
2 egg yolks
2 tablespoons milk
2 cups flour
1 teaspoon salt

1 teaspoon baking powder
1 cup seeded raisins
1 cup dry, shredded coconut
2 egg whites
2 teaspoons vanilla
2 cups flaked, toasted
   breakfast food

Mix the ingredients in the order given. Use one rounded teaspoon of the mixture for each cookie. Drop by spoonfuls on a buttered sheet ½ inch apart. Bake in a moderate oven. Watch closely, for they burn easily. Remove from the pan while hot. This makes about 65 cookies.

Bernice Currier

The idea of being a radio homemaker was far from Bernice Currier's mind when she joined the KMA staff in March 1927. On that date she began what the *KMA Guide* eventually called "a career in radio matched by few people."

Bernice Chambers had attended the University of Nebraska in Lincoln, where she met fellow students Gertrude Welch and Earl May. In fact, it has been said that Bernice is the person who introduced the two, a happy circumstance, as their relationship developed into a romance and resulted in their marriage. Thus began a lifelong friendship between the Mays and Bernice. It eventually became a working relationship as well.

By 1927, when Bernice moved with her children to Shenandoah, KMA had been on the air for twenty months. In March of that year, Earl asked Bernice to join the radio staff. Since she was a highly trained concert violinist, much of her early airtime was spent as a musician. As was true with most of the earliest performers, however, she served wherever she was needed.

Bernice's name is listed on the schedule as early as November 1927 for the "Home Hour." She also was involved in the "Domestic Science" show and one program simply called "Visit." She narrated fashion shows (yes, on the radio), gave commercials, and had a contest for prune recipes. KMA provided the framework through which Bernice could use her many talents.

Some of the radio homemakers developed individual styles for giving recipes. As the years went by, Bernice created the A-B-C method of listing ingredients and describing the mixing. Although she used other styles from time to time, Bernice came to prefer the A-B-C technique as simple, direct, and easy to follow.

BISCUIT TORTONI

A – ¾ cup sugar
½ cup water
B – 6 egg yolks, beaten
C – ½ teaspoon plain gelatin
1 tablespoon cold water

D – 2 cups heavy cream,
whipped
E – 1 tablespoon vanilla
¾ cup chopped blanched
almonds
¾ cup finely crushed
macaroons

Boil A to soft ball stage (238 degrees). Pour slowly over B. Cook in double boiler over simmering water until thick (8 minutes). Stir constantly. Combine C and add. Stir until dissolved. Cool. Fold in D. Add E. Pour into 12 paper cups. Sprinkle with macaroon crumbs. Place in freezing part of refrigerator at coldest setting. Freeze without stirring.

SWEDISH MOVER WAGON COOKIES

A – 3 cups sifted flour
2 teaspoons baking powder
1 teaspoon soda
B – 1 cup shortening

C – 1 cup sugar
2 eggs, beaten
4 tablespoons sweet milk
1 teaspoon lemon extract

Sift A into mixing bowl. Add B and cut in as for pie crust. Combine C, add to first mixture, and mix well. Roll to ⅛ inch thick on floured board. Cut with floured cutter in any desired shape. Bake about 10 to 12 minutes at 375 degrees. (These are often baked over molds in such a manner as to make small, covered wagon–shaped cookies.)

Bernice's father, A. E. Chambers, had come to the Midwest in a covered wagon and settled in Gosper County, Nebraska, where Bernice was born. Soon after her birth, the family moved to Colorado, where they lived for thirteen years before returning to Nebraska. After Bernice graduated from high school, she attended the University of Nebraska in Lincoln, where she majored in music. After receiving her degree, she married Edwin L. Currier, who was also in the music department. They had four children.

The marriage was not a happy one. After a separation and an attempted reconciliation, the two decided on a permanent parting. Bernice accepted responsibility for the children.

By this time Mr. and Mrs. Chambers had moved to Shenandoah, Iowa, and it was to their home that Bernice came with her four children. The year was 1927.

Besides her broadcasting and related work at KMA, Bernice taught music in the schools of Essex on a part-time basis. She directed the Glee Club, taught grade school music, and enjoyed using her violin for accompaniment.

During this same period of time, Bernice was directing the student orchestra in the high school in Shenandoah. She also led a band at KMA and performed with the KMA string trio and the station's Elysian Symphony Orchestra.

Young people who worked with Bernice during the late 1920s and early 1930s remember her with affection and respect. One recently remarked, "Bernice had so much talent and training and enjoyed her craft so much she just spilled that enthusiasm over all of us."

RANGER COOKIES

1 cup butter	½ teaspoon baking powder
1 cup white sugar	½ teaspoon salt
1 cup brown sugar	2 cups quick oatmeal
2 eggs	2 cups Rice Krispies, cornflakes,
1 teaspoon vanilla	or wheat flakes
2 cups flour	1 cup shredded coconut
1 teaspoon soda	

Cream the butter and sugars, add the eggs and vanilla, and mix until smooth. Add flour, which has been sifted with the soda, baking powder, and salt. Mix thoroughly; add the oatmeal, cereal, and coconut, and mix. The dough will be quite crumbly. Mold with the hands into balls the size of a walnut. Place on a greased cookie sheet and press slightly with spatula. Bake 10 to 12 minutes in a 375-degree oven.

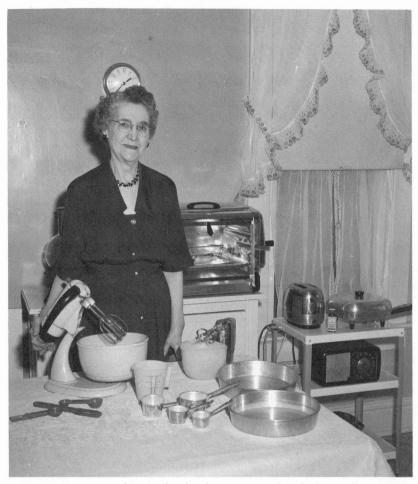

Bernice Currier working in her kitchen, equipped with the modern conveniences of the 1940s.

After her children were grown, Bernice left KMA to work for stations in South Dakota, in Texas, and in Cairo, Illinois. In Cairo she assisted her son Merrill (known as "Red"), who was station manager for WKRO.

Following the death of her mother in 1948, Bernice returned to Shenandoah to make a home for her father. Soon she was back on KMA.

By then the effects of a long siege of crippling arthritis had eroded her ability to play her beloved violin. Mr. May, who tried to solve as many problems for his faithful staff as he could, suggested that a place be made for Bernice in the women's department.

Like a workhorse going home to the barn, Bernice took to radio homemaking with professionalism and enthusiasm. She started her first 1948 program, "A Visit with Bernice," with the words, "I've reared my family and managed a home for forty years. Now I would like to share my experiences with you listeners so you can learn easily what it took me years to find out."

PIONEER BREAD PUDDING

2 cups stale but not dry bread
  cubes
2 cups milk
3 tablespoons butter

¼ cup sugar
2 eggs
Dash salt
¼ teaspoon vanilla

Place bread cubes in a 1-quart buttered baking dish. Scald the milk with the butter and sugar. Beat eggs slightly, add the salt, then stir in the warm milk and vanilla. Pour over the bread cubes. Set the baking dish in a pan containing warm water up to the level of the pudding and bake about 1 hour at 350 degrees, or until a knife comes out clean when inserted in center of pudding. Makes 4 to 6 servings. Serve warm with plain cream, currant jelly, or a lemon pudding sauce.

Lemon Pudding Sauce

½ cup sugar
1 tablespoon cornstarch
1 cup boiling water
2 tablespoons butter

1 tablespoon grated lemon rind
3 tablespoons lemon juice
⅛ teaspoon salt

Combine sugar and cornstarch; add boiling water slowly and stir until dissolved. Cook slowly, stirring constantly, until thickened and clear. Remove from heat and add remaining ingredients. Serve warm.

KIDNEY BEAN RICE SALAD

6 slices crisp bacon, crumbled
1 no. 2 can kidney beans,
   drained (reserve the juice)
1½ cups cooked rice
1 cup diced celery

½ cup diced green onions or
   minced onion
½ cup chopped sweet pickle
½ cup chili sauce
2 teaspoons horseradish
Salt to taste

Drain the beans and save the liquid. Combine all ingredients and mix well. Add just enough of the bean liquid to make desired consistency. Makes 6 servings.

BERNICE'S STRAWBERRY PRESERVES

In a large kettle put 1 cup water, a handful of berries, and 9 cups sugar. Over a slow fire bring to a boil. Stir often. When boiling, add remainder of 2 quarts of berries. Boil 15 minutes without stirring. Shake kettle often. Pour into a long flat pan and let stand all day, shaking often. This puffs up the berries. Put into sterilized glasses cold and cover with paraffin.

RAISED GLAZED POTATO DOUGHNUTS

A– Cook and sieve potatoes to
   make 1 cup
B– ⅓ cup butter, melted
   2 eggs, beaten
   1½ cups scalded, cooled
   milk
   ½ cup sugar

C– 2 packages dry yeast
   1 tablespoon warm water
D– 4½ to 5 cups sifted flour
   1 teaspoon salt

Put A in large bowl; add B and beat well; add C and beat; add 2 cups of D and beat. Then add remaining D gradually to make soft dough. Put out on floured board and knead gently until smooth. Put in greased bowl, cover, let rise to double; punch down and let rise

again. Roll out on board to about ½ inch thick. Cut with floured cutter; cover on board and let rise until light. Put into deep hot fat, carefully inverting doughnuts and putting top side down, then turning to
brown both sides evenly. Drain on brown paper. Glaze while hot.

Glaze

Mix together: 1 tablespoon sweet cream
  1 pound powdered sugar   1 teaspoon vanilla
  1 tablespoon butter   A little water to make it liquid
  1 tablespoon cornstarch

Bring to a boil, remove from fire, dip the fried doughnuts, and drain
on cake racks.

Bernice's favorite food was yeast bread. She made it often and well.
She experimented with new recipes and shared her knowledge with
her listeners.

For snacks, however, Bernice enjoyed plain cake doughnuts. Since she was a rabid baseball fan, she spent many hours in front of the radio and, eventually, the television, nibbling on her doughnuts and cheering for her favorite team. Interruptions during ball games were not welcome.

POTATO REFRIGERATOR ROLLS

A–1½ cups warm water
   1 package dry yeast
B–⅔ cup sugar
   1½ teaspoons salt
   ⅔ cup soft shortening

2 eggs
1 cup lukewarm mashed
potatoes
C–7 to 7½ cups sifted flour

Dissolve A in mixing bowl; stir in B and beat well; mix in C to make dough easy to knead. Put out on floured board and knead until smooth and elastic. Place in greased bowl, and cover with damp cloth (do not use waxed paper); place in refrigerator. Punch down as necessary. When ready to use, let warm to room temperature about an hour. Then make into any rolls desired, put in greased pan, cover, and let rise to double. Then bake about 15 minutes at 375 degrees. Makes about 4 dozen.

SOUR CREAM DRESSING
(For Vegetable Salad)

1 cup sour cream
¼ cup vinegar or lemon juice
1 teaspoon salt

2 tablespoons sugar
Dash cayenne pepper
½ teaspoon grated onion

Combine all ingredients; beat until stiff. Makes about 1¾ cups.

Bernice and announcer Warren Nielson broadcast directly from the scene of a 1951 pancake feed. The Fidelity Pancake Flour chef is answering questions about his products, used during the exciting Jubilee Days.

CANNED SWEET GREEN PEPPERS

Wash peppers and cut in halves. Clean out seeds and membrane. Pack in hot sterilized jars. Make a syrup of 1 cup vinegar (either pure apple cider or distilled white) and ½ cup sugar; bring to boil; then pour over peppers and seal jars. These are delicious for salads, eating as pickles, or in sandwiches.

DEVILED EGGS SPANISH STYLE

A – ⅓ cup butter or margarine
  ⅓ cup chopped onion
  ⅓ cup chopped celery
B – 3 tablespoons flour
C – 3 cups cooked tomatoes
  1 teaspoon sugar
  Salt and pepper to taste
  ¼ teaspoon garlic salt

6 hard-cooked eggs, deviled
½ cup buttered bread crumbs
6 slices toast

Cook A over low heat until tender. Blend in B, add C, and cook, stirring constantly until thickened. Pour into shallow 2-quart baking dish. Arrange deviled eggs in sauce, deviled side up. Top with buttered crumbs. Place in hot oven (425 degrees) until sauce is bubbly (10 to 15 minutes). Serve over toast, rice, spaghetti, or noodles. Makes 6 servings.

OATMEAL SLUGS

1 cup butter
¾ cup margarine
4 cups rolled oats
2 cups raisins
Water (or milk)
4 eggs

2 cups sugar
⅔ cup water from raisins
  (or milk)
2 teaspoons soda
2 teaspoons baking powder
4 cups sifted flour

Melt butter and margarine together. Stir in rolled oats and toast over moderate heat, stirring, for about 10 minutes or until lightly browned. Set aside. Cover raisins with water (or milk) and cook to a good rolling boil. Remove from fire and cool. Drain liquid from raisins and reserve. Combine eggs, sugar, raisin water (or milk), and mix well. Combine dry ingredients and stir into egg mixture. Lastly, add raisins. Drop by teaspoon on greased cookie sheet and bake at 375 degrees for 10 to 12 minutes or until done.

    These are excellent despite the name!

MULBERRY JAM

Measure out 4½ cups mulberries. Clean them, and then run through food mill. Add 1 package raspberry Kool-Aid and the juice of 1 lemon. Bring to a boil; add 1 package commercial powdered pectin. Add 6 cups sugar, stir, bring to a boil, and boil for 1 minute. Put in sterilized glasses and seal with paraffin.

Although Bernice started her musical career as a classical violinist, Earl May suggested that she learn to play the fiddle music that was popular in the first years of radio. She became a regular on programs such as "Country School" and with the Jig and Reel Orchestra. When arthritis finally put a stop to the violin playing, Bernice stated, "I am so thankful the Lord allowed me to keep the use of my hands long enough to put my four kids through college playing that fiddle."

GREEN TOMATO DILL PICKLES

½ bushel green tomatoes
8 large onions
4 cups sugar

1½ quarts cider vinegar
2 packages (1¼ ounces each)
   pickling spices

Slice a layer of tomatoes in a kettle, add a few onion slices, and sprinkle with a very light layer of salt. Continue until tomatoes and onions are all used. Let stand overnight; then drain well. Mix together the sugar, vinegar, and spices and pour over the tomatoes. Cook till tomatoes are tender but still hold their shape. Pour into hot sterilized jars; put 1 head of dill in each jar. Seal immediately.

CHOCOLATE PARTY COOKIES

3 egg whites, beaten stiff
1 cup sifted powdered sugar
½ cup crushed saltines
½ cup chopped pecans

1 teaspoon vanilla
6 ounces semisweet chocolate
   chips, melted

Fold sugar into egg whites; then fold in remaining ingredients. Drop by teaspoon about 1½ inches apart onto greased cookie sheet. Bake 12 minutes at 325 degrees. Remove with spatula. Makes three dozen.

Billie Oakley gave this description of Bernice: "[She was] a gutsy woman, one who was born before her time. She did her own thing without too much concern for public opinion as long as she knew it was right. She resented being paid less than men. She made $50 per week, and out of that she paid for the food which she was expected to serve the radio visitors who stopped at her house.

"In fact, so many listeners came that they wore out her living room rug. When Bernice told Earl May about it, he realized it was the responsibility of KMA to replace the carpet, and he saw that it was done.

"Bernice was a colorful, vibrant person with a keen sense of humor. She helped the other homemakers in every way she could. A perfectionist herself, she wanted others to be equally careful and accurate in whatever they undertook."

Bernice's daughter, Margaret Currier Boylen, lived in New York City and was the author of two novels, *The Marble Orchard* and *The Moveable Feast*. She received the Guggenheim Fellowship award for her writings. She died in 1970.

Bernice's other children include Helen, the widow of Dr. J. T. Armstrong, who lives in Houston, Texas; Edwin L. Currier, retired from the Bechtel Company in San Raphael, California; and Merrill "Red" Currier, the Cairo, Illinois, radio station manager, who died in 1979.

HAND LOTION

½ pint glycerine	1 large tablespoon quince seed
½ pint bay rum	Soak in rosewater 24 hours.
1 pint rosewater or rainwater	Strain and mix all together.
½ ounce tincture of Benzoin	

Use each time after having hands in water.

Bernice and fellow KMA homemakers Adella Shoemaker (left) and
Florence Falk (right) spent a November afternoon in 1953 visiting the
George Teachout family on their turkey farm west of Shenandoah. This
prize 20½-pound bird was chosen for a special portrait with the
homemakers.

FRIED CARROTS

Use cold boiled carrots. Cut off small round ends and cut lengthwise.
Dip in cold milk, roll in flour, and drop in hot lard or Crisco. Fry
until brown. Drain on soft paper. Sprinkle with salt.

VEGETABLE SOUP

To each quart of meat stock, add 2 tablespoons each of carrots, turnips, cabbage, and onion that have been cut in fine pieces. Add ¼ cup
of stewed tomatoes and ¼ cup of diced potatoes. Simmer for an hour
and season before serving.

CORN NUGGET WAFFLES

3 cups buttermilk pancake mix   ⅓ cup melted butter
3 cups milk   1½ cups drained canned whole-
3 eggs   kernel corn

Put pancake mix into large bowl; beat the milk and eggs together and stir into the pancake mix. Stir in the cooled melted butter and the corn. Beat hard until fairly smooth. Ladle into preheated waffle iron and bake. Serve hot with syrup.

POPCORN ON THE GRILL

Cut 12-inch squares of heavy-duty aluminum foil. In center of each square, place 1 teaspoon vegetable oil and 1 tablespoon unpopped popcorn. Twist ends to seal packets loosely. Place packets on hot coals or grill and let corn pop. As soon as popping ceases, remove packet and fold back top. Season with melted butter and salt.

RHUBARB PINEAPPLE ORANGE MARMALADE

7 pounds rhubarb   2 oranges
1 no. 2 can crushed pineapple   1 lemon
   with juice   8 cups sugar

Cut oranges and lemon in quarters after washing carefully; discard seeds and slice very thin; add water to equal 1½ times orange and lemon measure. Bring to boil; then simmer gently for 1 hour. Cook rhubarb in very small amount water just until tender. Combine all ingredients; cook until thick and juice sheets off the spoon. Pour into sterilized glasses to within ¼ inch of top. Seal with paraffin.

In 1952 in her column in the *KMA Guide*, Bernice shared these thoughts about her career: "If I had it to do all over again, I would certainly choose a career as a radio homemaker. There can't be a grander bunch of persons anywhere than my listeners, many of whom seem like close personal friends to me today. Radio homemaking has been not only my work and my hobby but my life."

Then, as she had done for so many years, she closed by saying, "Bless your hearts."

SOUTHERN FRIED CORN

Cut corn from 5 or 6 ears, cutting not too close to the cob. Then scrape each cob thoroughly with back of knife so as to get all the milk left on cob. Fry the corn for 5 minutes in skillet with 2 tablespoons hot bacon drippings. Then add 2 cups rich milk, half-and-half, or cream, and salt and pepper to taste. Stir constantly to avoid sticking; keep fire low until mixture thickens.

Bernice continued her radio visits until January 19, 1963. After her retirement, she stayed in her Shenandoah home south of Priest Park as long as physically possible. In August 1975, Bernice moved to a nearby health care facility, where she died on February 17, 1976.

Driving by her house today brings back memories of Bernice standing on the front steps to greet the many radio friends who stopped by to meet her. If you were one of the lucky ones, she might have invited you inside for tea and cookies or homemade rolls.

CHILI-FRANK FILLING

Combine:
1 can condensed bean with
bacon soup
⅓ cup water

¼ cup ketchup
⅛ teaspoon chili powder
8 frankfurters, thinly sliced

Spread this mixture evenly over toasted bread or bun surfaces, covering edges completely. Broil about 4 inches from heat about 7 minutes. Serve on plate garnished with pickles and olives. Serves 10 to 12.

Doris Murphy

M other must have been at KMA when they laid the cornerstone—if she wasn't, she came soon after," Tom Murphy is quoted as saying as he grew up in the home of radio broadcaster–continuity writer–editor–women's director Doris Murphy. Tom's attitude was shared by many who were aware of the great influence wielded by Doris Murphy during the thirty-five years she served KMA and its listeners.

Doris Ambler graduated from the University of Missouri School of Journalism and worked for a time for the *St. Louis Post Dispatch*. She returned to her hometown of Shenandoah, where she became city editor of the *Shenandoah Evening Sentinel*. In 1921 she married Thomas R. Murphy. The couple lived in Chicago for a time and then returned to Shenandoah. Their son, Tom, was born in 1927. Sadly, just twenty-two months later, Doris's husband died.

So it was actually about four years after the KMA cornerstone was laid that Doris, now a young widow with a son to support, brought her talents to KMA. She first served as a news reporter, gathering her own news—often from the daily newspapers—then writing and presenting it on the air. She wrote her own commercials so successfully that she was soon a continuity writer, preparing ads for the entire station. Eventually Doris was selected as women's director for KMA.

Doris's writing and editing abilities were brought to bear in various ways with the publication of the station's chatty, informational, promotional monthly magazine, the *KMA Guide*. In the very first issue of June 1944, Doris began "Party Line." In 1949 Doris took to the air with the "Party Line" broadcast. It included news, hints, home beautification, and recipes. Along with all her other tasks at KMA, Doris Murphy had become a full-fledged radio homemaker.

IN-A-JIFFY CAKE

1½ cups sifted cake flour   ¾ cup milk
¾ cup sugar   1 teaspoon vanilla
¼ teaspoon salt   ¼ cup melted shortening
2 teaspoons baking powder   1 egg, beaten

Sift dry ingredients together 3 times. Combine remaining ingredients
and add gradually to dry ingredients. Beat mixture 2 minutes. Pour
into greased pan and bake in moderate oven (350 degrees F.) 30
minutes. Makes one 8 × 8 cake.

Doris influenced many of the great homemaker days that were held
in the Mayfair Auditorium. For a time they were monthly events,
each built around a theme. One time the subject was paint, the next
time the way to carpet your home; many were built around food
preparation. In 1953 fourteen hundred people tried to jam into the
auditorium built to seat only a thousand. It was necessary to hold the
program for a second session on the following day to accommodate
everyone. As the KMA Guide reported, "It was the biggest homemaker event, ever."

And what was the program that attracted so many observers? A
style show of the latest spring fashions, audience participation, quiz
games, music by Marge Parker (KMA organist), greetings from all the
KMA homemakers, and door prizes galore.

FRENCH DRESSING

1 can tomato soup   1 cup salad oil (scant)
1 cup sugar   1 teaspoon salt
1 cup vinegar

Mix together in bowl; then put in quart jar and shake. Very delicious.
Keep on hand.

The Mayfair Auditorium, filled for one of KMA's popular programs.

ORANGE RAISIN CAKE

1 cup brown sugar
1 egg
½ cup buttermilk
2 cups flour
1 teaspoon soda

1 teaspoon baking powder
Pinch salt
½ cup nutmeats
½ cup raisins
1 orange

Beat sugar, egg, butter, and buttermilk together. Add flour, soda, baking powder, and salt. Grind together orange rind, raisins, and nuts. Add half of ground mixture to batter. Mix and pour into cake pans and bake 40 minutes at 350 degrees. Pour juice of orange over cake as soon as pan is removed from the oven. Add remaining ground mixture to powdered sugar icing and spread over cake.

NEVER-FAIL CHEESE SOUFFLE

2 tablespoons flour	1 cup cooked rice
2 tablespoons butter	3 well-beaten egg yolks
1 cup milk	3 egg whites
1 cup grated cheese	¼ teaspoon cream of tartar
½ teaspoon salt	

Blend flour and butter together over low heat. Gradually add milk, stirring constantly. Add cheese and salt; cook until thick. Add cooked rice. Cool. Stir in egg yolks. Beat egg whites with cream of tartar until they stand up in stiff peaks. Fold into first mixture. Bake in greased baking dish, uncovered, for 35 minutes at 350 degrees or until golden brown. If using glass baking dish, turn oven to 325 degrees.

The *KMA Guide* was created in June 1944 as a way of filling the many requests from listeners for pictures, recipes, program information, and stories about the personalities who worked at the station. During the war, paper was expensive and difficult to obtain. Putting together a sixteen-page magazine was a more economical and, in some respects, a simpler way to provide materials the listeners wanted sent to them.

It was not an easy project, but the task was lightened by the efforts of Owen Saddler, editor, for he had a newspaper background, had written for magazines, and had published four periodicals before coming to KMA as station manager. Doris Murphy brought her expertise in journalism to the new magazine as feature editor.

On its second anniversary, the KMA Guide held a celebration. Left to right, front row: homemaker Leanna Driftmier, Guide editor Owen Saddler, KMA president and owner Earl May, and homemaker Edith Hansen. Second row: associate editor Mildred Diehl (James), Flower Lady Lina Ferguson, and feature editor Doris Murphy. Third row: Evalyn Saner (who listed the programs in each copy of the Guide) and mail clerks Ina Hahn, Geraldine Berg, and Klea Newman. Back row: Merrill Langfitt, Gayle Maher, Bill Bailey, Ina Burdick, and Bob Hillyer, all with various other Guide responsibilities.

The Ambler family was well known for many years in southwest Iowa. Tappan Nance Ambler and his wife, Nellie Paul Ambler, were living in Thurman, Iowa, some twenty-seven miles west of Shenandoah, when their daughter Doris was born. Not long after that event the family moved to Shenandoah, where Mr. Ambler established a grocery store and later a coal company.

By **DORIS MURPHY**

The three sons and three daughters of the Amblers received recognition in various ways in their professions; several were involved in forms of communication. Frena Ambler was one of KMA's story ladies in the very early days of the station, reading children's stories on the air and assisting around the studio. Walter founded the Ambler Players, a traveling troupe of performers. Doris started as a working journalist on several newspapers and then moved into the medium of radio when she came to KMA.

GRAPEFRUIT MERINGUE PIE

1 cup sugar	½ tablespoon butter
5 tablespoons cornstarch	¾ cup grapefruit juice
½ teaspoon salt	¼ cup lemon juice
Grated rind of one lemon	1 baked 8-inch pie shell
1½ cups boiling water	½ teaspoon baking powder
3 eggs, separated	6 tablespoons sugar

Combine sugar, cornstarch, salt, and grated lemon rind in top of double boiler. Add boiling water gradually and cook over flame, stirring constantly until thick. Place over hot water and cook 10 minutes. Beat egg yolks slightly and add to mixture. Cook one minute. Remove from fire and add butter and fruit juices. Cool and pour into pie crust.

Meringue

Beat egg whites until frothy; add baking powder and beat until stiff. Cut and fold the six tablespoons sugar into whites. Spread over pie and brown under broiler for one minute.

Doris serviced her own accounts and those for many of the other broadcasters. She would go to a sponsor's place of business and look over the items to be advertised. She would talk to the owner about any special product or sales to emphasize on the air at a particular time. Then Doris returned to the station, where she wrote the copy—called *continuity* in radio circles. With so many different kinds of products, the work of servicing accounts and writing continuity was—and still is—a varied and often difficult task.

SEAFOAM SALAD

1 package lime gelatin
1 cup hot pear juice
1 cup cream, whipped

1 large can pears, mashed
1 package cream cheese

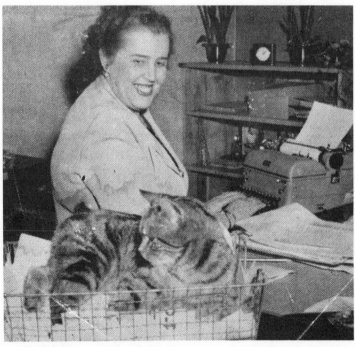

Doris's desk and letter basket were always full, especially with the addition of her pet cat.

Mix cream cheese with pear pulp. Dissolve gelatin in hot pear juice. Let stand till partially jelled; then beat, and add whipped cream and cheese mashed with pulp of pear. Put in individual molds. Serve with whipped cream mixed with salad dressing.

CHEESE LIMA BEAN CASSEROLE

2 cups grated American,
   pimiento, or cheddar cheese
2 cups cooked lima beans
¼ cup chopped green pepper
¼ cup chopped onion
1½ cups canned tomatoes

½ teaspoon salt
⅛ teaspoon pepper
2 tablespoons flour
¼ cup water
1 cup cracker crumbs
2 tablespoons butter

Combine 1 cup cheese with beans, green pepper, and onion and place in 1½-quart casserole. Heat tomatoes with seasonings, stir in flour and water mixed to a paste, and cook until thickened. Pour over lima bean mixture. Combine cracker crumbs with remaining cheese and spread on top. Top with the butter. Bake in 350-degree oven for 30 minutes or until browned. 6 servings.

APPLE CINNAMON SALAD

Add 1 cup boiling water to ¼ cup red-hots (candy) and 2 tablespoons sugar. Put on stove but do not let come to a boil—just cook until dissolved. Add this liquid to 1 box cherry gelatin. Then add 1 cup cold water in regular way. When gelatin begins to congeal add:
   1 cup chopped apples
   1 small can crushed pineapple
   ½ cup nutmeats
   ½ cup celery, diced

Doris opened her home and her heart to those of her family who needed both. She owned a large white house on Church Street in Shenandoah. After her parents retired, they lived with Doris, as did an aunt and Doris's sister Carol.

CHEESE CASSEROLE

1 cup scalded milk	½ teaspoon salt
1 cup soft bread crumbs	⅛ teaspoon pepper
½ cup grated American cheese	3 egg yolks
2 tablespoons melted butter	3 stiffly beaten egg whites

Combine milk, bread crumbs, cheese, butter, and seasoning. Stir in unbeaten egg yolks. Carefully fold in egg whites. Bake in a greased baking dish in pan of hot water in a moderate oven until firm. Takes about 30 minutes.

ORANGE BREAD

Parboil peel of 3 large or 4 small oranges cut in small pieces with 1 cup water and 1 teaspoon soda for 5 minutes. Drain and rinse. Then place 1 cup sugar and ¾ cup water over rind and cook until mushy. Stir often while this is cooking.

While the above is cooking, cream together:	Mix together:
1 cup sugar	3¼ cups flour
2 tablespoons fat	3 teaspoons baking powder
2 eggs	½ teaspoon salt

Add the flour mixture and 1 cup milk alternately to creamed mixture. Use ¼ cup flour to dredge 1 cup nuts. Stir in. Add the hot orange mixture to the batter. Mix well. This makes two loaves. Bake at 350 degrees until toothpick comes clean. Can be made two days in advance. Slice thin for sandwiches.

Doris Murphy was highly respected in her profession. When the radio and television women in the eastern part of the United States were attempting to start a professional organization, they called Doris to come to New York and assist in the project. The result was American Women in Radio and Television, which gradually became known by its initials, AWRT.

Doris Murphy was elected as the first national membership chairperson for AWRT. When she returned to Iowa, she organized the Heart of America chapter of the association and became its first president.

It was Doris who started the tradition of the famous KMA Cookie Tea. "I got the idea when I was back east at an AWRT meeting. One of the women at the meeting told about a gathering where each person attending brought a paper plate holding a dozen of her favorite cookies along with the recipe," Doris remembered. "Various types of programs were given. I came back to Shenandoah and got the KMA homemakers all enthused about our starting one, so we did!

"The first tea was held in 1954 near Christmastime, so we called it the 'KMA Christmas Cookie Tea.' I worked very hard to make the first event beautiful, interesting, and entertaining."

Each of the homemakers made cookies and decorations for display and arranged her own table with some kind of Christmas arrangement. Doris bought pink plastic tablecloths ("pink was IN for Christmas that year") and borrowed Gertrude May's large silver candelabras. Pink and green candles were placed in the silver holders, and evergreens were added to the table centerpieces. Live talent furnished music, and a speaker talked about Christmas decorations.

The first tea was held in the old Elks building located west of the Shenandoah library. More than three hundred women came with their cookies and recipes. Everyone enjoyed the day, and it far surpassed expectations. "Especially," Doris chuckled, "some of the people at the station who didn't think the idea would work."

The Cookie Tea became an annual affair that continued for years under Doris's direction.

DATE PINWHEEL COOKIES

1 pound dates, cut fine	½ cup sugar
1 cup nuts	½ cup water

Cook dates, sugar, and water until thick. Add chopped nuts. Cool before spreading on following dough.

1 cup shortening
2 cups brown sugar
1 teaspoon vanilla
3 beaten eggs

1 teaspoon soda
1 teaspoon baking powder
½ teaspoon salt
About 4 cups flour

Mix well and roll out to about ¼ inch thick. Spread with the date-nut mixture. Roll up as you would cinnamon rolls. Chill four hours or overnight. Slice and bake on floured cookie sheet in 350-degree oven for about 8 minutes.

GINGER LACE COOKIES

Cream together:
  ¾ cup shortening
  ¼ teaspoon salt
  1 cup sugar
  1 egg, beaten
  4 tablespoons sorghum or
  molasses

Sift together:
  2 cups flour
  2 level teaspoons soda
  1 teaspoon cinnamon
  1 teaspoon ginger

Combine mixtures well. Chill dough. Roll in little balls and then roll in sugar. Put apart in pans. Bake in moderate oven (350 degrees) 8 to 10 minutes.

NEW COCONUT PUMPKIN PIE

⅓ cup boiling water
1¼ teaspoons cinnamon
1 teaspoon ginger
⅛ teaspoon cloves
½ teaspoon salt
Dash of nutmeg

2 eggs, beaten
1 cup light brown sugar
¼ cup toasted shredded
  coconut
1½ cups canned pumpkin
1⅔ cups (1 tall can) evaporated
  milk

Blend boiling water with cinnamon, ginger, cloves, salt, and nutmeg. Cool. Combine with eggs. Add sugar, pumpkin, and evaporated milk.

Mix thoroughly. Pour mixture into unbaked 9-inch pie shell. Bake at 425 degrees for 15 minutes. Reduce to 350 degrees and bake 30 minutes longer. Chill.

Top with whipped cream and toasted coconut. (Spread coconut thinly in shallow pan. Place in moderate oven and toast about 10 minutes, or until delicately browned. Stir occasionally to toast evenly.)

COUNTY FAIR CREAM CANDY
(White Fudge)

2 cups sugar	¼ teaspoon almond flavoring
¾ cup sour cream	½ cup broken pecans
½ teaspoon vanilla	10 candied cherries, sliced

In a 2-quart saucepan, combine sugar and cream, stirring well. Place over heat and continue stirring to dissolve sugar. Cover pan and bring to boil for 1 minute, until sugar crystals are melted. Remove cover. Continue cooking without stirring over gentle heat, to soft ball stage (235 degrees) about 12 minutes. Let cool without stirring or moving to lukewarm. Add flavoring and pecans and cherries. Stir-beat until it becomes creamy and loses its gloss. Pour into lightly greased 8-inch square pan. Cut while still warm. Makes about 1 pound.

SIX-LAYER WASHDAY DINNER

(1) 2 cups diced potato, raw	(5) 1 cup diced carrots, raw
(2) ½ cup uncooked rice	(6) 1 pint tomatoes
(3) 1 cup sweet pepper, cut fine	
(4) 2 cups hamburger and 1 small chopped onion, cooked together a few minutes	

Put in casserole in order given, season with salt and pepper, and cover with water. Cook 2 hours in 350-degree oven.

Doris Murphy (right) visits with a friend in the garden of Earl and
Gertrude May.

CHICKEN AND RICE

6 chicken breasts with bone in
  (can split if large)
1½ cups raw rice
1 can chicken broth

1 can cream of mushroom soup
1 can onion soup
¼ pound butter or margarine

Put rice in a 9 × 13 glass baking dish. Melt the butter in the chicken
broth and combine with onion soup. Pour over the rice. Put chicken
breasts meat side up on top of rice mixture. Salt. Spread mushroom
soup over the chicken. Put in 350-degree oven and bake 1 to 1½
hours or until meat is tender or to the falling-off-the-bone stage.

Doris was among the first from the women's department of KMA to be sent to work in the KMA and May Seed Company booths at the Iowa and Nebraska state fairs. KMA also sent Doris to such diverse places as the National Flower Show in Omaha and the AWRT state, regional, and national conventions during the time she was active in the broadcasting field.

SWEEPSTAKES POTATO SALAD

4 cups diced cold boiled
  potatoes
¾ cup sliced green onions
⅓ cup radish slices
3 hard-cooked eggs, cubed

½ cup mayonnaise
¾ cup commercial sour cream
2½ tablespoons herb vinegar
1½ teaspoons salt
¾ teaspoon celery seed

Combine first 4 ingredients; then add remaining ingredients and mix lightly. Chill. Serve in salad bowl lined with endive or lettuce. Garnish with hard-cooked eggs, pineapples, and radishes (tuck an inch length of green onion tops into hole cut in radish). Makes 6 servings. If desired, add 1 cup shredded carrot to salad. Or add 1 cup diced cucumber. Or omit celery seed and add 1 cup chopped celery or chopped green pepper.

RHUBARB DESSERT WITHOUT SUGAR

1½ cups raw rhubarb
20 marshmallows
Vanilla wafers

1 cup whipped cream
½ cup orange juice

Cook rhubarb in very little water. Then add marshmallows while still hot, and stir till dissolved. Cool a bit and add orange juice. Set in refrigerator. When beginning to set, add whipped cream. Pour into mold lined with vanilla wafers, or place vanilla wafers in a layer at bottom of mold and pour the rhubarb over. Set in refrigerator to chill. Serve with whipped cream.

GOLDEN SLAW

4 hard-cooked eggs, finely
   chopped
4 teaspoons sugar
¾ teaspoon salt
2 teaspoons prepared mustard

2 teaspoons cider or tarragon
   vinegar
¼ cup salad dressing
2 cups shredded cabbage
⅓ cup chopped sweet pickles

Combine all ingredients, tossing lightly. Chill. Serve on beds of lettuce garnished with chopped parsley. Makes 4 generous servings.

Doris frequently expressed gratitude that her work at KMA made it possible for her to raise and educate her son, Tom. After earning degrees at the University of Iowa and the Harvard Business School, Tom became a special assistant at the United States Embassy in Paris. When he returned to the United States, he cofounded Partnership Dankist, a venture capital firm in Stamford, Connecticut. Tom retired in 1985 and lives in La Jolla, California.

After the death of Tom's first wife in 1965, Doris and her sister Carol went east to help take care of Tom's home and his two children. His daughter, Ellen Murphy Courtney, is a lawyer in San Francisco with a son, Benjamin. Tom's son, Tam, is in telemarketing in Troy, New York; he and his wife, Lisa, have a son, Thomas.

Tom remarried, and he and his wife have a daughter, Vickie.

Doris died as the result of a stroke on March 13, 1986, after living eighty-nine productive years.

Doris was considered the strongest supporter of women in radio that KMA ever had. She encouraged women to join the staff, she kept many on the air through difficult and challenging times, and she disseminated information on the value of their work. It took a strong person to overcome the prejudice and indifference facing women in the broadcasting profession, but Doris was equal to the task.

Leanna Driftmier in the broadcast studio of her home.

Leanna Driftmier and the Kitchen-Klatter Family

eanna Field Driftmier was no stranger to radio work when in 1939 she began airing "Kitchen-Klatter" over KMA. Her brother Henry Field had founded Shenandoah radio station KFNF in 1924 and had encouraged his five sisters to help with the broadcasts. Leanna made her first appearance before a microphone that same year, singing a song while her daughter Lucile accompanied her on the piano. Not long afterward, she briefly aired a weekly worship service, during which her young son Donald read the Scripture and her daughter Dorothy sang.

By 1926 Leanna's sister Helen Field Fischer had a regular KFNF program called "The Mother's Hour." Leanna occasionally came to the studio to sit with Helen and, in the casual manner of those early days of radio, to talk a little about her family and the daily events in the Driftmier household.

Henry suggested that Leanna do a half-hour program of her own, but she insisted that she couldn't possibly think of enough to say. Henry and Helen joshed her, pointing out that anyone with seven children ought to have plenty to talk about. Helen, whose true calling was horticulture, began a series of flower talks and turned "The Mother's Hour" over to Leanna.

Not surprisingly, Leanna discovered she could fill not only the first thirty minutes but also many years of half-hour programs. "Kitchen-Klatter" became the longest-running homemaker program in the history of radio.

LEANNA'S ANGEL FOOD CAKE

1 cup sifted cake flour　　　　¼ teaspoon salt
1½ cups sugar　　　　　　　　1¼ teaspoons cream of tartar
1¼ cups egg whites　　　　　　1 teaspoon vanilla

Sift flour; measure and add ½ cup of sugar and sift 4 times. Beat egg whites and salt together. When foamy, add cream of tartar. Continue beating till eggs are stiff enough to hold a peak but not dry. Add remaining sugar, 2 tablespoons at a time, beating after each addition till sugar is blended in. Fold in the flavoring. Sift ¼ cup of flour over mixture. Fold in very lightly and repeat till flour is all used. Turn into ungreased 10-inch tube pan. Cut gently through the batter with a knife to remove the bubbles. Bake in a slow oven (325 degrees) for 1 hour.

LEANNA'S DATE BARS

5 eggs　　　　　　　　　　　1 teaspoon baking powder
1 cup sugar　　　　　　　　　1 pound dates
1 cup flour　　　　　　　　　1½ cups walnut meats

Mix together. Pour batter into pan to about 1-inch thickness. Set oven at 350 degrees and bake until just done—about 30 minutes. Cut in bars and roll in powdered sugar.

Leanna Field was born in 1886 at Sunnyside Farm southeast of Shenandoah in the home built by her pioneer parents, Solomon and Celestia Field. In addition to her brothers Henry and Sol junior, Leanna had four sisters: Helen Fischer, Martha Eaton, Jessie Shambaugh, and Susan Conrad.

Solomon and Celestia were both schoolteachers, and they loved the rich land of Iowa. Theirs was a loving, intellectually stimulating home, and their children all learned the principles of hard work and sharing. Many a passing traveler found a place to stay and a friendly meal at Sunnyside Farm.

Upon completing high school, Leanna taught for a few semesters at a rural grade school near Essex, Iowa. Moving west, she graduated from Los Angeles Normal College, and continued her teaching career in California. Then, in 1913, she married Martin Driftmier, of Shenandoah, a widower with two small children, Howard and Lucile. Five more children were born into the family: Dorothy, Frederick, Wayne, Donald, and Margery.

For more than a decade, Leanna busied herself with the chores of keeping her family fed and clothed and the pleasure of imparting to them the simple pioneer strengths her parents had instilled in her. Little did she know that with the development of radio in the Midwest, her name would became familiar in almost every home.

"The Mother's Hour" was a name devised by Leanna's sister Helen, and as Leanna felt more at home before the microphone, she wanted a program name of her own. She ran a contest, and a Nebraska listener sent in the winning suggestion, "Kitchen-Klatter."

LEANNA'S WHITE BREAD

1 cake (or 1 package) yeast	4 teaspoons salt
1 teaspoon sugar	4 tablespoons melted lard
½ cup lukewarm water	12 cups sifted flour
3½ cups (more) water	
¼ cup sugar (or ½ cup	
corn syrup)	

Dissolve yeast and sugar in lukewarm water. Add rest of water, sugar, salt, and lard. Stir in flour gradually to make a soft dough. Turn out on floured breadboard and knead until light and elastic. Let rise in greased bowl, covered, until double in bulk. Punch down. Knead. Divide into 4 loaves; put into greased bread pans. Let rise until double. Bake at 375 to 400 degrees for about 1 hour or until loaves make a hollow sound when thumped. Turn out on rack to cool. Grease crust if desired.

Leanna wrote out this recipe for Dorothy, and her total directions were, "You know the process."

Many of Leanna's children had their chances to perform before the microphone. "I first appeared on the radio in 1926 when I played a solo on my cornet," Frederick Driftmier remembered. "I think I played 'Nearer My God to Thee.' That and 'Tahitian Love Song' were the only pieces I ever did learn to play, but in spite of my cornet solos, people continued to buy radios."

LEANNA'S YULETIDE BREAD

1 cake or package of yeast
4 tablespoons warm water
1 teaspoon sugar
1 cup thick, warm potato water
½ cup melted butter or
   margarine

½ cup sugar or honey
2 eggs, well beaten
1 cup maraschino cherries,
   diced
2 cups chopped pecans
4½ cups flour (about)

Dissolve yeast in warm water with sugar added. When bubbly, stir in potato water, butter, sugar or honey, and eggs. Add cherries and nuts. Beat flour in gradually until a soft dough is formed. Knead lightly. Let rise until double. Punch down; knead and divide into three parts. Make into long rolls and braid; place on greased cookie sheet and push ends together to make a wreath shape. Let rise until double. Bake at 400 degrees about 30 minutes or until nicely browned on top. Frost with powdered sugar–maraschino cherry juice frosting and sprinkle with pecans.

Leanna gave this recipe on the air on December 23, 1946. It was the day of Earl May's funeral.

LEANNA'S DIVINITY

2 cups granulated sugar
½ cup light corn syrup
½ cup water
2 egg whites, stiffly beaten

Few grains of salt
1 tablespoon Kitchen-Klatter
   vanilla flavoring
½ cup chopped nuts

Mix sugar, corn syrup, and water, stirring over heat until dissolved. Let boil, without stirring, to crack stage (280 degrees on candy thermometer). Pour this syrup a little at a time over the stiffly beaten egg whites, stirring constantly. Take care not to scrape the bottom of the syrup pan. Add the salt and flavoring; continue beating until creamy; add nuts and continue beating until candy will hold its shape. Drop quickly from tip of spoon onto waxed paper, or pour into slightly greased pan and cut in squares when cold.

Flavorings are no longer marketed under the Kitchen-Klatter name.

One of Dorothy's fond memories is of a surprise gift shower given Leanna by her radio listeners at the suggestion of another KFNF broadcaster. Fans mailed her hundreds of tea towels, dishcloths, table runners, and household items. So many gifts arrived that Leanna portioned out a generous boxful for each of her children.

LUCILE'S TOMATO SCALLOP

4 tablespoons butter or
    margarine
1 cup dry bread crumbs
2 tablespoons butter or
    margarine
2 tablespoons minced onion
3 cups canned tomatoes
5 tablespoons minute tapioca

1 tablespoon sugar
Salt and pepper to taste
½ teaspoon paprika
1 cup grated medium cheddar
    cheese
¾ cup sliced stuffed olives

Melt 4 tablespoons butter or margarine in heavy skillet and stir in dry bread crumbs until they are lightly browned and toasted. Put aside.

Melt 2 tablespoons butter or margarine in heavy pan and stir into it the minced onion. Then add tomatoes, tapioca, sugar, and seasonings. Cook for 5 minutes, stirring constantly. (It will bubble up violently and splash unless you keep the fire very low and stir energetically.)

Butter a casserole (not a flat baking type) and sprinkle in a layer of the toasted crumbs. Then cover with a layer of tomato, grated cheese, and green olives; repeat. Top with quite a thick sprinkling of the buttered crumbs and bake for 40 minutes in a 350-degree oven.

Even in an era when large families were more common than they are now, the Driftmier clan could be quite a spectacle. One day, as Leanna loaded her seven children into the car, a man passing by on the sidewalk watched quizzically. "Excuse me, ma'am," he inquired, "but is this a Sunday school class? It looks as if you're taking them on a picnic."

"Oh no," Leanna smiled. "These are all my children." She wedged the last one in, got behind the wheel, and drove away, leaving the man scratching his head in either doubt or awe.

Leanna's skills as a parent became well known. She was named Iowa Mother of the Year in 1954.

In the autumn of 1930, Leanna suffered a broken back in an automobile accident. After months in a hospital strapped into a special traction bed, she returned home just in time for Christmas. Henry Field installed a microphone in her bedroom so that she could conduct a holiday broadcast. Later, when she was able to be up and around, she moved the microphone into the kitchen and continued her programs from there. Eventually, she had a bedroom renovated to serve as a small, soundproof studio in her home.

LUCILE'S FLY-OFF-THE-PLATE ROLLS

2 packages dry yeast
½ cup warm water
2 cups hot water
½ cup sugar

3 tablespoons butter (don't substitute)
3 teaspoons salt
6 to 6½ cups flour (approximately—use as little as possible)

Dissolve yeast in warm water. Heat 2 cups water and pour over the sugar and butter. Add 2 cups flour, beating as hard as possible after each addition. When mixture is warm, not hot, add to the dissolved yeast. Add balance of flour to which you have added the salt. Knead well. Place in greased bowl and let rise until double in bulk. Shape into rolls or buns, let rise again until double, and bake at 375 degrees for about 18 to 20 minutes.

With the microphone on the kitchen table, Leanna enjoyed including a weekly cooking session on "Kitchen-Klatter." Leanna would read and discuss a recipe while one of her daughters prepared the dish. Listeners could hear the sounds of measuring and mixing, and the bang of the oven door as a casserole or cake went in to bake.

Live radio was always full of surprises, even in Leanna's kitchen. One morning, as Leanna sat at the microphone explaining how to bake a special cake, Dorothy stood nearby stirring together the ingredients. "And now Dorothy will break the eggs into the creamed sugar and butter," Leanna explained. Dorothy cracked open two eggs, and as the yolks dropped into the batter, the foul, sulfur smell of rotten eggs drifted out of the bowl.

"I pantomimed to Mother that something was wrong," Dorothy recalls. "In fact, I held my nose. She kept giving the recipe, but motioned for me to take the bowl out on the back porch. Then for the rest of the program I just pretended to mix the cake. I clattered a spoon against a bowl, banged the oven door, and made all the right noises, but didn't use a single ingredient."

Although she had improvised well enough to fool her audience, Leanna felt uneasy about the incident, since it was her habit always to be honest with her listeners. Eventually, she confessed what had really happened, and the story of the rotten eggs became one of her favorites.

And then there was Tippy Toes, the Driftmier mouse. "This was in the days of the live broadcasts from the kitchen," Lucile commented. "Occasionally a mouse would run into the kitchen while we were on the air. It defied all our efforts to catch it, and finally it grew almost tame. We named it Tippy Toes and eventually introduced it to our listeners."

Kitchen-Klatter
(Reg. U. S. Pat. Off.)
MAGAZINE

SHENANDOAH, IOWA
Price 10 cents

Vol. 9   MARCH, 1944   Number 3

Leanna
MY
FAVORITE
IMITATION
VANILLA
FLAVOR
A
Kitchen-Klatter
REG. U.S. PAT. OFF.
QUALITY PRODUCT

Contains water, vanillin, coumarin,
pure vanilla, CP glycerine,
caramel color, propylene glycol

3 Fluid Oz.

Manufactured for
THE DRIFTMIER CO.
Shenandoah, Iowa

Kitchen-Klatter
(Reg. U. S. Pat. Off.)
P I E
COOK BOOK
25c

PUBLISHED BY

THE DRIFTMIER CO.   Shenandoah, Iowa

The Driftmier Company also published many cookbooks and guide-
books for everything from church activities to family parties. Of special interest was *The Story of an American Family*. Written by Lucile
Verness, the book chronicled the history of the Field and Driftmier
families and traced the development of the "Kitchen-Klatter" radio
program.

LUCILE'S BAVARIAN MINT PIE

Crust

1⅓ cups crushed vanilla wafer crumbs

¼ cup sugar
¼ cup butter or margarine, melted

Combine finely crushed crumbs with sugar and melted butter or margarine. Press into 9-inch pie tin. Bake in a 375-degree oven for 5 or 6 minutes.

Bavarian Mint Filling

2 ounces unsweetened chocolate
1 4-ounce bar German sweet chocolate
½ cup butter or margarine
¾ cup sugar
3 eggs

1 teaspoon Kitchen-Klatter mint flavoring
1 cup whipping cream, whipped
2 tablespoons powdered sugar
¼ teaspoon Kitchen-Klatter mint flavoring

Put unsweetened chocolate and German sweet chocolate in top of double boiler to melt. Cream butter or margarine and sugar together until as smooth as whipped cream. Add the eggs that have been beaten until extremely light and frothy. Add the melted chocolate and stir until very smooth. Lastly add the 1 teaspoon mint flavoring and stir well. Turn into the cooled crumb crust. When firm, cover with whipped cream to which you have added the powdered sugar and ¼ teaspoon mint flavoring.

Decorate this pie by reserving a small amount of the crumb crust mixture and sprinkling it very lightly on top of the whipped cream. Or, drain green cherries and cut tiny slivers, arrange to make little flowers with five petals over the top of the whipped cream. Refrigerate.

Lucile liked the taste of Bavarian mint candy so well she tried to duplicate it with this pie. She came very close with this original creation.

DOROTHY'S CURRIED PORK ROAST

4-pound pork shoulder roast
1 teaspoon salt
½ teaspoon curry powder
2 tablespoons oil
½ cup water
1 1-pound can chop suey
　vegetables, drained

1 10½-ounce can cream of
　mushroom soup
¾ cup water
½ cup long grain rice
½ teaspoon curry powder
½ teaspoon salt
⅛ teaspoon pepper

Rub the pork roast with the 1 teaspoon salt and ½ teaspoon curry powder. Heat the oil in a Dutch oven and brown the roast on all sides. Add the ½ cup of water, cover, and roast in a 325-degree oven for 2 hours. Drain off all the liquid and fat. Combine the remaining ingredients and pour around the meat. Cover and roast another 1½ hours.

MARGERY'S CHICKEN 'N NIFFLES

4- to 5-pound stewing hen, cut
　in serving pieces
3 or 4 slices carrot
3 or 4 slices onion
Few sprigs parsley (or a good
　sprinkle of dry parsley flakes)

Few sprigs celery tops (or 1
　teaspoon celery seed)
1 bay leaf
2 large peppercorns
½ teaspoon salt
Butter or margarine

Wipe chicken with damp cloth and place in large kettle. Cover with boiling water. Add carrots, onion, parsley, celery tops, bay leaf, and peppercorns. Cover and simmer for 2 to 3 hours or until meat begins to loosen from the bone. Add salt during the last hour of cooking. When tender, remove chicken from broth, place on platter, brush with butter or margarine, and keep hot in oven at 300 degrees.

Niffles

1 cup biscuit mix
½ teaspoon salt

2 eggs
¼ cup cold water

Combine biscuit mix and salt in bowl. Make a well in center and add whole eggs. Pour in water and work with fork to make a soft batter, adding more water if necessary. Drop pieces of batter, about a teaspoon at a time, into the simmering chicken broth. Cook for 5 minutes. Take niffles from broth with a slotted spoon and place in a serving dish. You can't make them all at once, but probably half of the batter can be cooked at one time. Thicken the broth with a little flour and serve from a gravy boat.

With four sons in the service and three daughters on the West Coast in related efforts, Leanna was deeply involved with World War II. She shared the concerns, frustrations, fears, and sorrows of parents all across the country. She encouraged homemakers to grow victory gardens, preserve food, and develop a sense that in so doing they were helping win the war. Leanna mailed more than three thousand personal messages to fathers and mothers who lost sons in the war.

In 1939 Leanna moved the "Kitchen-Klatter" program from KFNF to the more powerful KMA. For nine years loyal listeners tuned their dials to 960. Then, in 1948, Leanna left KMA and began syndicating her program for replay over a number of stations throughout the Midwest. In 1972 the Driftmier Company again arranged to air "Kitchen-Klatter" over KMA.

In the first years of "Kitchen-Klatter," Leanna received so many letters that she could not personally answer every request for recipes, advice, and encouragement. After describing an angel food cake, for instance, she asked listeners to send in a card describing the cakes they made from her recipe. More than seventeen hundred replies piled up in the mailroom.

To help manage such voluminous correspondence, Leanna began publishing a leaflet called "Mother's Hour Letter" with the subtitle, "Sent Out Every Once In Awhile." Each copy was tucked into a stamped, self-addressed envelope sent in by a listener who had also included a dime to cover printing costs.

"Mother's Hour Letter" gradually grew in size and evolved into the *Kitchen-Klatter Magazine*, a publication that at its peak had a subscription list of nearly ninety thousand.

LUCILE'S REMARKABLE FUDGE

4 cups sugar
1 13-ounce can evaporated milk
¼ pound butter or margarine

2 12-ounce packages chocolate
  chips
1 pint marshmallow creme
1 teaspoon Kitchen-Klatter
  vanilla flavoring

Boil sugar, milk, and butter or margarine together until it reaches the soft ball stage (235 degrees on a candy thermometer). This scorches easily, so stir almost constantly. It will take approximately 45 minutes to reach the right stage. Remove from heat and add the chocolate chips, marshmallow creme, and flavoring. Stir until all is dissolved and then pour into a large, buttered pan. The 9- by 13-inch size is just right. Add nutmeats if desired. But if you don't care for the nuts, yet want the flavor of black walnut meats, add about ½ teaspoon Kitchen-Klatter black walnut flavoring.

When this recipe first came in the radio mail Lucile said, "That is a remarkable fudge." She decided to give it that name. Anytime you see this fudge with that title you know the name was Lucile's original idea.

Leanna frequently told "Kitchen-Klatter" listeners that they were welcome in her home whenever they visited Shenandoah. Hundreds took advantage of the opportunity to wander through the house, enjoy refreshments, and visit with Leanna, but such behavior could be a shock to the uninitiated.

"Soon after my marriage in Washington, D.C., I took my bride, Betty, to Shenandoah to meet the family," Frederick said. "While we were eating breakfast that first morning, an entire busload of radio friends walked through the house! Betty still speaks of that bit of culture shock, but she very quickly learned what it meant to be part of a radio family."

For many years, listeners tuning in the "Kitchen-Klatter" program could expect to hear Leanna and one or another of her daughters sharing the microphone. Each of the younger women mastered the art of visiting easily over the air.

Many visitors came by bus to Shenandoah to tour the radio station and to stop at the homes of the radio homemakers. This group of ladies from Galt, Missouri, visited Leanna Driftmier (at left, seated in her wheelchair).

LUCILE'S WONDERFUL MUSTARD SAUCE

½ cup butter or margarine
½ cup sugar
3 egg yolks

½ cup tomato soup, undiluted
½ cup prepared mustard
⅓ cup cider vinegar

In the top part of a double boiler, cream together the butter or margarine and sugar. When fluffy, add the 3 egg yolks that have been well beaten. Then add the tomato soup, prepared mustard, and vinegar.

Cook over hot water, stirring frequently, until it is smooth and fairly thick. When cool, turn into a pint jar.

Lucile considered this sauce a sensational success with ham but equally delicious with any cold meat. Stored in the refrigerator it keeps indefinitely.

The house on East Summit Avenue is no longer owned by the Driftmier family, but the ramp is still in place at the side of the porch where Leanna maneuvered her wheelchair in and out. Those who remember Leanna often drive by and have the sense that she is still sitting on the porch, waving to her many friends.

Gradually the second generation of Driftmiers accepted the responsibilities of running the company. In 1959 Leanna and Martin retired and sold the firm to Lucile and Russell Verness.

At that time, a studio was constructed in the Verness home, and the remaining "Kitchen-Klatter" programs originated from there until the concluding broadcast.

Martin Driftmier passed away in 1968. As long as her health permitted, Leanna continued to broadcast on birthdays, anniversaries, and other special occasions. In May 1976 Leanna celebrated her ninetieth birthday and the fiftieth anniversary of the Kitchen-Klatter radio broadcasts. In the months that followed, her health gradually deteriorated. She died quietly in her sleep on September 30, 1976, at the age of ninety.

Through the years, third- and fourth-generation members of the Kitchen-Klatter family appeared on the broadcasts: Mary Lea Palo, daughter of Frederick; Kristin Brase, Dorothy's daughter; and Lucile's daughter, Juliana, and her family participated long-distance from their home in New Mexico.

Friends and coworkers took turns in front of the microphone too. Evelyn Birkby broadcast during the twenty-eight years she worked with the Driftmier Company. Hallie Blackman, who held various positions in the business and became executive vice-president and

Lucile Driftmier Verness with her daughter, Juliana, and Margery Driftmier Strom with her son, Martin, early in 1948.

general manager, did considerable broadcasting, as did Verlene Looker, who was with the company for twenty years. Many of these women made frequent public appearances, which became a prerequisite of each radio homemaker's professional life.

DOROTHY'S SCALLOPED TURNIPS

Peel and dice enough turnips to fill a 2-quart casserole. Place turnips in a kettle to which you have added enough cold water to cover and ¼ teaspoon soda. Bring to boiling and cook for a few minutes to parboil. Drain and rinse. Combine about ⅓ cup flour, ⅓ cup sugar, and 1 cup cream and beat until smooth. Place turnips in casserole and pour the cream mixture over them until just covered. (More cream or milk can be stirred in if amount is not sufficient to cover.) Bake at 350 degrees for about 1 hour. Stir every 15 minutes or so while baking.

JULIANA'S SPLIT PEA SOUP

4 ounces salt pork, chopped
½ pound ham, chopped
1 medium onion, chopped
1 cup carrots, chopped
2 garlic cloves, minced
2 cups celery and leaves,
    chopped
2 tablespoons butter (if salt pork
    is lean)
1 teaspoon coarsely ground
    seasoned pepper

3 sprigs parsley
1 bay leaf
1 tablespoon mixed herbs
2 14½-ounce cans chicken broth
2 soup cans water
2 cups green split peas
Parmesan cheese or cooked,
    crumbled bacon (optional)

Lightly fry the salt pork and ham. Add the onion, carrots, garlic, celery, and butter (if necessary). Cook until onion is lightly browned. Add the pepper, parsley, bay leaf, mixed herbs, chicken broth, water, and peas. Cook for 2½ to 3 hours. Put through blender and return to heat until heated through. Serve hot with Parmesan cheese or crumbled bacon sprinkled over top if desired.

Dorothy and Margery look over some of the day's mail as they prepare a Kitchen-Klatter broadcast.

In 1924 Lucile developed bone cancer that resulted in the loss of a leg. She learned to walk again with a prosthesis and managed a normal and extremely active life. After two falls and osteoporosis compounded her problems, Lucile became resigned to living the last years of her life in a wheelchair in the same manner as Leanna had.

After the death of her husband in 1963, Lucile continued to manage the Driftmier Company and helped direct the Triple K Manufacturing Company, which developed, produced, and distributed Kitchen-Klatter flavorings and household cleaning products. When Lucile's health began to fail, her daughter, Juliana, assumed leadership of the firm.

As the third generation of the family to be heard on the "Kitchen-Klatter" radio program, Juliana brought her own interests to the listening audience. A resident of New Mexico, she spoke often of the foods, archeology, and lifestyle of the Southwest—subjects that might have startled a loyal midwesterner like Leanna. But Juliana also visited about her husband, Jed, her children, her home, and everyday events. Leanna would not have found that surprising at all.

On December 31, 1985, the family, which had shared its life for so long with the listening and reading public, announced over the air that it was their last radio visit. The January 1986 issue of the Kitchen-Klatter Magazine was put into the mail sacks and taken to the post office, the final copies to go out to their loyal subscribers. The doors of the Kitchen-Klatter plant were closed and locked. The exciting story of an American family, which had lasted for more than sixty years on radio and in print, was over.

Howard Driftmier, the eldest of the Driftmier children, died in the summer of 1989. The following winter, Lucile Verness suffered a massive stroke from which she never recovered. She passed away on June 17, 1990, at the age of eighty. Frederick Driftmier, a retired United Church of Christ minister, lives in Pawcatuck, Connecticut, with his wife, Betty. Dorothy Johnson's husband, Frank, died in December of 1990. Dorothy lives on their farm near Lucas, Iowa. Stephen Wayne Driftmier is a nurseryman in Denver, Colorado, where he lives with his wife, Abigail. Donald Paul Driftmier and his wife, Mary Beth, live in Delafield, Wisconsin, where he works as a consulting engineer. Margery Strom is retired and lives with her husband, Oliver, in Shenandoah. Leanna had twelve grandchildren and a number of great-grandchildren.

JULIANA'S BARBECUE

1 bottle hot catsup	2 cloves garlic, minced
1 small can taco sauce	¼ teaspoon oregano
1 heaping tablespoon brown sugar	¼ teaspoon dry mustard
1 tablespoon vinegar	¼ teaspoon black pepper
1 onion, chopped	2 tablespoons Worcestershire sauce

Mix all ingredients and pour over 3 to 4 pounds of meat cut in chunks (venison is excellent). Bake at 300 degrees at least 6 hours or until meat shreds.

This recipe came originally from Iowa but is now famous in New Mexico with Juliana's friends. Deer hunters especially like it.

MARGERY'S ZUCCHINI TOMATO DISH

3 tablespoons fat
¼ cup onion, minced
2 8-ounce cans stewed tomatoes
3 cups unpared zucchini, cut
   into ¼-inch slices

¼ teaspoon salt
⅛ teaspoon pepper
⅛ teaspoon garlic powder

In hot fat in a saucepan, sauté the onion until tender. Add stewed tomatoes and heat to boiling. Add salt, garlic powder, pepper, and zucchini. Simmer over low heat, uncovered, until zucchini is tender, about 20 minutes. Serves 4 to 6.

LEANNA'S GRAHAM CRACKER ROLL

12 graham crackers, marshmallows, nutmeats, dates, and enough cream or milk to hold it together. Form in a loaf and chill.

LEANNA'S PLAIN GOOD MEAT LOAF

½ pound ground pork
1 pound ground beef
½ cup soft bread crumbs or
   oatmeal
1 egg, beaten
1 cup milk or tomato sauce

2 tablespoons green pepper,
   chopped (optional)
½ cup onion, chopped
1 teaspoon salt
Dash of pepper

Combine all ingredients and mix very thoroughly. Form into a loaf, place in a shallow pan, and bake about 45 minutes at 350 degrees.

    Leanna felt this quick and easy meat loaf not only tastes downright good but also has the virtues of holding its shape and slicing neatly.

Edith Hansen

Two world wars, a home in Shenandoah, a family, and a career as one of KMA's major radio homemakers were inexorably inter-twined in the life of Edith Hansen.

Edith began her broadcasting experience on Norfolk, Nebraska, station WJAG on December 31, 1940. In the spring of 1942 she and her husband and two sons moved to Shenandoah. On June 1st of that year she began "The Edith Hansen Kitchen Club" on KMA, replacing Jessie Young, who had left the station to move to Philadelphia.

Life was difficult during those lean war years, and Edith worked diligently to find and share the best ways to cope with the many problems that surfaced in her own life and in the lives of her listeners. She searched out recipes that conserved sugar, fats, meats, and other items rationed and hard to obtain. She tested and aired recipes that made life easier for the new and struggling cooks in her audience. "Edith draws on her own experiences in meeting the typical home-maker's problems on the farms and towns of the Midwest," a KMA news release explained.

Little did Edith realize when she started her public career how much sorrow she would share with her listeners. Eldest son Donald joined the marines at age eighteen. He was in the Iwo Jima campaign, where he was wounded and reported missing in action. When he was located and eventually returned to the United States, Don was a paraplegic. His injuries eventually caused his death. Edith's hus-band, Aage, carried the effects of World War I all his life, and he died in 1948 in the Veterans Hospital in Lincoln, Nebraska.

Circumstances mostly related to the war and its effects on her fam-ily took Edith out of Shenandoah several times, but each time she returned. She was never off the KMA airwaves for long.

Eventually, along with fellow broadcaster Martha Bohlsen, Edith became part of the Tidy House syndicated radio network and was heard over ninety stations across the country. She always, however, when she was in Shenandoah, broadcast a live morning program for KMA. It was Edith's personal visit from her kitchen to her loyal friends in the Midwest.

Born of pioneer stock, Edith began her life in Taylor County, Iowa. "My new granddaughter is a sickly baby with a big voice," her grandfather reported to friends. As an adult, Edith often commented that she outgrew her puny beginning but she never lost her big voice.

Eventually the family moved to Silver Creek, Nebraska. When part of the Rosebud Indian Reservation lands in South Dakota were opened in 1912 for settlement by homesteaders, her parents moved the family to an area where they could prove up the land. Here Edith, her two sisters, and her brother started school in a sod schoolhouse.

Edith enjoyed a childhood filled with the beauty of the plains of South Dakota, interesting neighbors, a loving family, and important lessons in self-reliance and resiliency. "Along with other homestead families, we had the thrill of Dakota prairie fires, the hardship of droughts, the grasshopper scourges, and the long blizzards that would snow us in for several weeks at a time," Edith wrote about those early days.

SEATTLE LUNCH

1 pound ground beef	1 package spaghetti, cooked
½ pound grated cheese	1 tablespoon Worcestershire
1 green pepper, diced	sauce
1 can whole-kernel corn	1 large onion, chopped fine
1 can mushrooms and liquid	½ cup cooking oil
1 can tomato soup	Salt and pepper to taste

Brown meat and onion in oil (use less oil if desired). Combine with remaining ingredients; put in casserole and top with buttered bread crumbs. Bake 1 hour at 350–375 degrees.

MOLLY McGEE'S FAVORITE BUTTERSCOTCH PIE

½ cup brown sugar
1 tablespoon butter
2 cups hot water
½ cup white sugar
3 tablespoons cornstarch stirred
   to a paste with 2 tablespoons
   cold water

2 egg yolks
1 pinch salt
1 teaspoon vanilla

Cook brown sugar and butter in frying pan until darker brown. Add hot water and boil 5 minutes until lumps dissolve. Put in double boiler with white sugar and cornstarch paste and cook until thick. Add egg yolks. Cook 5 minutes. Remove and add salt and vanilla. Cool and put in shell. Top with meringue. Bake in moderate (375-degree) oven 15 minutes or until golden brown on top.

NEVER-FAIL NOODLES

2 egg yolks, beaten
1 teaspoon lard
2 tablespoons cream

¼ to ⅓ teaspoon salt
⅛ teaspoon baking powder

Add enough flour (about 2 cups) to make dough stiff enough to roll out. Roll out on floured breadboard and slice into strips any width desired. Drop into salted boiling water or meat broth and simmer until tender. Not sticky; may be used immediately without drying.

MOCK HAMBURGERS

1 large onion, diced fine and browned in 2 tablespoons butter and 1 teaspoon sage or poultry seasoning. Beat 3 eggs; add 1 cup quick-cooking oatmeal, salt, and pepper to taste; then add the onion, sage, and butter. Drop mixture by spoonfuls on greased griddle, brown on each side; then pour 1½ cups tomato juice over them and simmer a few minutes. Serve hot.

YAKIMA MEATLESS

2 cups cooked kidney beans 8 soda crackers
1 cup cottage cheese   1 tablespoon butter
1 medium onion   Salt and pepper to taste

Grind beans, onion, and crackers through food chopper or food processor. Mix thoroughly. Bake 1 hour in 350-degree oven in greased casserole or loaf pan. Serve with tomato sauce.

FRESH PEAS

In the top of your double boiler, put 2 tablespoons butter and 2 tablespoons finely minced fresh green onions. Cook the onions in the butter until slightly transparent; then add 3 cups of shelled peas and put them over the boiling water and cook until done—about 15 to 20 minutes. Cover while cooking. One teaspoon sugar may be added, also.

EDITH'S DOUGHNUTS

1 teaspoon soda   ½ cup sour cream
½ cup buttermilk or sour milk 2½ cups sifted flour
1 egg   1 teaspoon salt
1 cup sugar   ¼ teaspoon nutmeg

Put soda in the sour milk or buttermilk.

 Beat egg, add sugar, and beat well; then add the cream, and buttermilk or sour milk mixture and beat well. Sift the flour, salt, and nutmeg and add. Use a little more flour if necessary to make dough easy to roll. Chill for 1½ hours; then divide it in half and roll it out half at a time to ¼ inch thick. Cut with floured doughnut cutter and fry in hot deep fat that will brown a bread cube in 1 minute. Turn and brown both sides evenly and drain on brown paper or paper toweling. Shake lightly in sack with granulated sugar.

 Bernice Currier called these the best doughnuts she'd ever eaten.

E.E.E. MISSOURI DESSERT

Beat 3 egg whites until light. Gradually fold in 1 cup sugar with a pinch of salt and ½ teaspoon cream of tartar. Add 8 crushed soda crackers, ½ pound nutmeats, and 1 teaspoon vanilla. Bake for 30 minutes in 350-degree oven. Serve with whipped cream. The meaning of the name of this recipe is lost.

Edith taught in rural schools in South Dakota for a time. When she went to Norfolk, Nebraska, to attend the wedding of a friend, she met Aage Hansen, a native of Copenhagen, Denmark.

Aage emigrated to the United States and, by the age of twenty, was working on an uncle's farm near Hampton, Nebraska. He served in World War I, and upon his return he moved to Norfolk to work for a lumber company. He and Edith were married in 1923 and had two sons, Donald and Harold.

CHOCOLATE MALTED-MILK CAKE

1 egg
1 cup sour cream
1 teaspoon vanilla
½ teaspoon salt

1 teaspoon soda
1 cup sifted flour
1½ cups sweetened chocolate malted-milk powder (plain may be used)

Mix well. Beat well after adding the flour. Bake in layers or loaf pan for 25 minutes at 350 degrees.

Frosting

¼ cup butter
¼ cup peanut butter (cream or chunk style)
1 cup chocolate malted-milk powder

Pinch salt
½ teaspoon vanilla
Hot water and sweet cream

Blend together the butter and peanut butter until creamy. Add malted-milk powder and blend well. Set over low heat for about 5 minutes, or until the ingredients are creamy. Remove from heat, and very slowly add enough hot water and sweet cream to make it of spreading consistency. Add salt and vanilla. Beat until cool and spread on cake. It won't run but stays soft and isn't sticky.

This cake and frosting are two of Edith's sugar-saving recipes.

During World War II, Aage, Edith, and Harold moved to Richmond, California, so Aage could help with the war effort by working in the Kaiser Shipyards. Edith read this poem to listeners on what she thought would be her final program for KMA:

> I'd like to be the sort of friend that
> You have always been to me.
> I'd like to be the help that you've been
> Always glad to be.
> I'd like to mean as much to you each
> Minute of the day
> As you have meant, old friends of mine,
> To me along the way.

Little did she know that in a few short months she would return to Shenandoah and the airwaves.

Aage's health deteriorated rapidly to the point that he could no longer work, so the family packed their belongings and started back to Iowa. It was Christmas Eve day of 1944 when they boarded the bus. All through the holidays they rode. Finally, after sixty-eight long, tiring hours, their bus pulled into the Shenandoah bus station. It was good to be home.

Edith's son Donald was wounded on February 27, 1945. It was September before he was settled in the U.S. Naval Hospital, Oceanside, California, and his parents were allowed to visit him.

Every afternoon during their stay, Edith and Aage took treats to Don and the thirty-two boys who were in the ward reserved for young men with injuries resulting in paralysis. The boys would tell them what they wanted, and they brought such things as fresh fruit,

Don Hansen.

pop, cream puffs, and hamburgers. Edith had also taken with her many of Don's home-canned favorites—strawberry jam, pickles, and peaches.

SERVICEMAN'S SPECIAL CANDY

2 cups sugar   1 teaspoon vanilla
1 cup cream   1 pound marshmallows
1 tablespoon butter   1 cup nuts
1½ squares bitter chocolate   3 cups graham cracker crumbs

Combine sugar, cream (can use half-and-half), butter, chocolate, and vanilla. Cook to soft ball stage. Remove from fire and stir in remaining ingredients. Spoon into buttered pan. Press firm. Cut into squares. Excellent for mailing. Can leave uncut for easier packaging.

By June 1952, Edith had been on the air for KMA for ten years. A special Homemaker's Day was held in her honor, and more than twelve hundred radio friends were present for the program at the

Kay Wilkins, Edith Hansen, and Jane Robinson.

Mayfair Auditorium. Other KMA homemakers Bernice Currier, Adella Shoemaker, and women's director Doris Murphy helped greet the guests.

By this time Edith's career was tied to that of Martha Bohlsen. Moreover, the work load had expanded so much that two professional assistants—Kay Wilkins and Jane Robinson—had been brought in to help, and the two were introduced to the audience at Mayfair. Edward May presented Edith with an engraved tray in appreciation of her years with KMA and her excellence in broadcasting.

Edith and her two assistants were also on the staff of Tidy House, a Shenandoah-based firm that manufactured and marketed household cleaning items. The company had been founded by two men who had ties with KMA. J. C. (Cy) Rapp was former general manager of KMA, and A. W. Ramsey had formerly been sales manager.

Kay Wilkins worked closely with Edith. She tested recipes, answered mail, prepared program material, and frequently helped with the broadcasts. Kay had been a broadcaster on five Midwest stations before coming to Shenandoah. Her mother and son Terry lived with her, so she had the experience of a three-generation home to share with the listeners.

Jane Robinson started her communications career as editor of a country newspaper and advertising manager of a large department store. Starting in 1942, she was on radio stations in Virginia and Minnesota. The Robinsons, along with an eight-year-old daughter, arrived in Shenandoah in 1952 when Jane became part of the Tidy House broadcasting team.

CHIPPED DRIED BEEF DELUXE

1-pound package noodles (or
   homemade cooked noodles)
8-ounce can mushrooms
1 pound chipped dried beef
⅓ cup butter

½ cup flour
⅔ pound Old English cheese
⅓ cup chopped pimiento
   (optional)
1 quart milk

Cook mushrooms in butter 5 minutes. Add dried beef and flour. Then add milk all at once. Blend and cook. Add cheese; stir and cook over low heat until cheese is melted. Add pimiento. Combine noodles and other ingredients in layers in large buttered baking dish. Sprinkle with ⅔ cup fine buttered crumbs. Bake in 350-degree oven until browned. Serves 10 or 12.

KAY'S PERFECT CUSTARD

Into a quart container break 4 eggs. Add 4 tablespoons sugar. Beat the eggs slightly and stir in sugar, being sure it is well stirred in. Add a dash of salt. Fill container with milk; stir together. Pour into top half of double boiler, sprinkle generously with nutmeg, set over boiling water; cover and steam exactly 22 minutes. Remove from fire. Serve hot or cold.

QUICK-METHOD BEAN SOUP

Heat canned pork and beans, adding four times the amount of water as you have beans, with diced onion and diced potatoes. Add salt and pepper to taste. Ready to serve as soon as onion and potatoes are tender.

BRAZIL NUT CHERRY JAM

4 cups fresh or canned sour pie
    cherries
¼ cup water or juice from can

7 cups sugar
1 cup sliced Brazil nuts
1 bottle fruit pectin

Pit cherries, if fresh. Place in large kettle and add water or juice. Stir until mixture boils. Cover and simmer 15 minutes. Add sugar and mix well. Stir over high flame until mixture boils rapidly. Add Brazil nuts and boil hard for 3 minutes, stirring constantly. Remove from fire. Stir in fruit pectin. Let cool for 3 minutes. Skim, stir well, put into hot jelly glasses, and cover with paraffin.

PEANUT BRITTLE CRUNCH PIE

¼ cup cold water
2 tablespoons butter
1 cup milk, scalded
2 tablespoons sugar
¼ teaspoon salt
½ teaspoon vanilla

2 beaten egg yolks
¾ cup brown sugar
1 envelope unflavored gelatin
2 stiffly beaten egg whites
1 cup crushed peanut brittle
1 9-inch graham cracker crust

Soften gelatin in cold water. Combine egg yolks, brown sugar, and salt. Gradually add scalded milk. Cook until thick, stirring constantly. Add butter and gelatin, stirring until dissolved. Add vanilla. Cool. Chill until partially set. Gradually add the granulated sugar to the egg whites. Beat until glossy and sugar is dissolved. Fold into chilled mixture. Fold in whipped cream and peanut brittle. Pour into graham cracker crust.

On January 21, 1950, Edith received more than thirty thousand greetings for her forty-ninth birthday.

FRIED APPLES

8 large cooking apples
1 tablespoon butter
1 tablespoon bacon drippings
2 tablespoons brown sugar

2 tablespoons white sugar
½ teaspoon cinnamon
¼ teaspoon salt

Wash and slice apples in ¼-inch rounds; fry them in the skillet with the butter and bacon drippings; cover and let cook until they are almost done. Then add the sugar, salt, and cinnamon and finish cooking. Serves 4.

YELLOW TOMATO PRESERVES

10 cups yellow tomatoes
7 cups white sugar

2 cups crushed pineapple

Drop tomatoes in hot water and remove skins. Dice. Measure 10 cups tomatoes. Boil sugar in 2 cups water until syrup spins a thread. Add tomatoes and pineapple, and cook until done. If desired, red tomatoes may be used instead of yellow tomatoes.

WAR FRENCH FRIES

Peel and slice large potatoes into lengths about ½ inch thick. Dip the slices in melted lard and place on a lightly greased cookie sheet in a 400-degree oven. Turn once as soon as browned on one side—about 15 minutes—and continue baking until both sides are brown. Salt and serve immediately. The result is a mealy slice of potato, deliciously crisp on the outside.

Aage Hansen, Edith's husband of twenty-five years, died in 1948 in the Veterans Hospital in Lincoln, Nebraska. The day after his death, Edith told of her experiences on her radio program. She talked of driving to Lincoln with Aage, knowing he was in critical condition. They arrived at the hospital, but while they were still in the waiting room, Aage died. Edith described on her program the shock she felt when she realized that he was gone and that she had to turn around and come back to Shenandoah alone, knowing that Aage would never return.

I was cleaning the upstairs bedroom of my farm home when I heard Edith's broadcast. Tears ran down my face as I sat in the middle of the bedroom floor, listening. Then I realized that I was not the only one who was sorrowing; other listeners who knew and loved her were crying as well.

HOMEMADE HOMINY

Select ears of corn with nice rounded grains. To each quart of shelled corn, use 1 slightly rounded teaspoon of lye and water to cover. Cook until when a little is taken out into a pan, and with a little water on it, the hull is loosened and comes off easily. Wash well in plenty of water, using a potato masher to stir with. Put back on stove; cover with cold water; heat and cook. Continue to wash, cover with water, and cook several times until all lye is out and corn is tender. Will keep several days when weather is cold, if kept in cool place; or can be canned by processing in pressure cooker 60 minutes at 10 pounds. (Or can be frozen.)

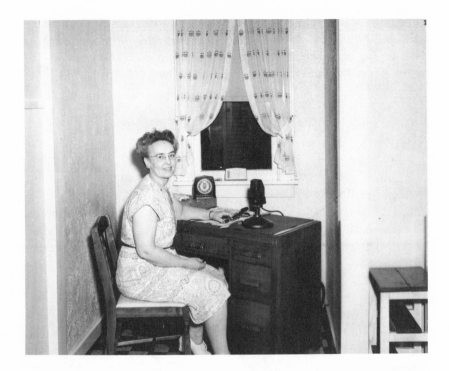

Edith did her broadcasting from a pleasant house at 101 S. Center St. At the back of the house just off the kitchen was a little breakfast nook, and from this corner of the kitchen Edith did her morning radio visits. Her microphone was on a desk directly in front of a window. As part of her daily visit, she would look out the window and tell her listeners exactly what the weather was like in Shenandoah at that precise moment.

One of Edith's radio-connected projects was the printing of a "growing cookbook," Kitchen Club Recipes. The recipes were printed on 8½ by 11 paper and punched in a manner so the pages would fit into a three-ring notebook. In the introduction to the cookbook, Edith explained: "As rapidly as possible, we will have other sets of recipes available. Get each set as soon as they are ready; place them in a three-ring binder and keep them."

Leafing through the pages of this 1950s book gives one a glimpse into cooking patterns of that decade. One recipe begins with "take one fat chicken." Another has glycerine as an ingredient needed for cake icing. Oil of wintergreen, cinnamon, peppermint, and anise are prevalent in the flavorings of candies and cookies. Compressed yeast was used for bread. Lard was the normal shortening for cooking. Far more eggs were used than in present-day dishes.

DELICIOUS DRIED CORN

8 pints sweet corn cut from cob   ½ cup sweet cream
½ cup sugar   ⅛ cup salt

Mix well and cook in large preserving kettle for about 20 minutes. Stir constantly as this burns easily. Spread thinly on trays and place in sunny, airy place to dry thoroughly. Store in glass jars and seal.

SHENANDOAH WHITE CAKE

Cream together: ⅔ cup vegetable shortening or butter, 1 cup sugar, 1 teaspoon each vanilla and almond flavoring. Sift together: 3 cups cake flour, ¼ teaspoon salt, 3 teaspoons baking powder. Add sifted ingredients alternately with 1 cup milk. Beat ¾ cup egg whites, add 1 cup sugar, beat till stiff, and fold into the above. Bake in wax paper–lined pan (no grease) for 30 minutes in 350-degree oven.

SWISS STEAK

2 pounds beef (1-inch thick)   2 tablespoons fat
⅓ cup flour   ½ cup water
1 teaspoon salt   1 cup tomato juice (or 1 can
⅛ teaspoon pepper and paprika   tomato soup)
3 slices onion

Pound flour and seasonings into steak. Brown steak in hot fat. Remove to roaster or casserole and add water, tomato juice, and onion that was browned in the fat after the steak was removed. Put in 350- to 375-degree oven 1 hour.

In 1963 Edith went to visit her son Don in Arizona. As she was driving home through New Mexico on her return trip to Iowa, she was involved in a car accident. Edith spent a considerable amount of time in the hospital in New Mexico before returning to Iowa.

Not long after her return to the Midwest, Edith suffered a stroke. She died in an Omaha hospital on October 28, 1964.

Don lived in Phoenix for a time and then returned to Long Beach, California, where he had a specially constructed home near the Veterans Hospital. He died on January 31, 1971.

Edith's younger son Harold lives in Shenandoah. He retired in 1984 from the Northwestern Bell telephone company. He and his wife are the parents of two daughters and two sons. His younger son, named Donald after his uncle, is now program director for radio station KMA, following in the broadcasting footsteps of his illustrious grandmother.

BAKED CANNED HAM

Take 1 canned ham. Make openings at the top of the can at each end. Put can in 375-degree oven just long enough to liquefy the juices. Remove from oven, pour liquid out through one of the holes into a bowl. Measure. Add 1 part of brown sugar to 3 parts of any fruit juice (pineapple is very good) until these measure a little less than the ham liquid. Add ⅛ teaspoon cloves and 2 tablespoons prepared mustard. Mix with ham liquid. Pour back through the can openings so this mixture surrounds the ham. (If it will not hold all the liquid, the balance can be added as the ham bakes and some of the liquid evaporates.) Put can into a shallow pan and bake 45 minutes to 1 hour in a 375-degree oven. Drain off liquid and reserve to serve with ham. Open can, remove ham, slice, and enjoy.

Martha Bohlsen

Martha was a loving person whose family included her mother, aunt, and brother plus a large extended family made up of her radio friends.

Soon after she graduated from the University of Chicago with a degree in nutrition, Martha returned to her hometown of Omaha, Nebraska, and began working for the Nebraska Electric Power Company as a home economist. Soon she was writing a food column for the *Omaha Bee-News* under the pen name "Prudence Penny."

In 1938 Martha originated her first radio program, "Martha's Kitchen," on radio WOW. Her homemaker program became so popular that she came to the attention of the Shenandoah-based Tidy House Company, which arranged to syndicate her program.

Martha was joined in 1948 by Edith Hansen, the well-known KMA radio homemaker. Their program, "The Tidy House Kitchen Club Show," was eventually heard over ninety stations, including KMA.

In 1949 Martha added television to her credits when she became the first woman to appear on WOW-TV. Later her cooking program was carried over KETV.

Martha's father was a Lutheran minister who was serving a parish in Wasaw, Nebraska, at the time of her birth. The family moved to Wisner, Nebraska, where they spent three years and then went to Omaha, where Martha attended a Lutheran parochial school.

Martha Bohlsen and Edith Hansen did a great deal of advertising and published many memos, fliers, leaflets, cookbooks, and recipe sheets. *More Time-saving Household Hints and Recipes From the Famous Radio "Kitchen Club" (heard every week-day featuring Edith Hansen and Martha Bohlsen)* was the long-winded title of just one of the leaflets the two homemakers published together.

BANANA CRUNCHIES COOKIES

Preheat oven to 400 degrees.

Cream ½ cup sugar and ½ cup shortening. Add 1 egg and ½ teaspoon almond flavoring. Beat well. Sift together ¾ cup flour and ½ teaspoon soda. Add 1½ cups Gerber's oatmeal-with-banana cereal. Stir into creamed mixture until well blended. Shape into small balls. Place on ungreased cookie sheet; flatten with fork. Bake 5 to 7 minutes until *lightly* browned. Makes about 40 2-inch cookies.

APPLE CHUNK CAKE

2 cups flour	½ cup butter or salad oil
2 level teaspoons soda	1 cup raisins, softened in warm
2 teaspoons cinnamon	water
½ teaspoon salt	2 beaten eggs
1 can Wilderness apple pie mix	2 teaspoons vanilla
1 cup sugar	½ cup chopped walnuts

Sift dry ingredients together. Add remaining ingredients ALL AT ONCE. Mix well and turn into 9 × 13 × 2 pan and bake at 350 degrees for 50 minutes (325 degrees for glass baking pan). If you like unfrosted cakes, sprinkle top of batter before baking with a mixture of cinnamon and sugar. This is delicious with a topping of whipped cream. This cake is noted for being quick to toss together when time is short. It stays moist.

SWISS STEAK FOR THE WORKING WOMAN

1 3- to 4-pound 7-bone roast	1 can diced carrots
1 can cream of mushroom soup	1 medium onion, diced
1 can tomato soup	Salt and pepper to taste

Place meat in heavy roaster or Dutch oven; pour all remaining ingredients over the meat (including juice from carrots). Season. Cook covered at 300 degrees for 5 to 6 hours.

Martha participated in many of the KMA Homemaker Days. From left: Gertrude May, Bernice Currier, Martha, and Florence Falk with two visitors to the event.

CREAMY OVEN-BAKED RICE

8 tablespoons rice	1 quart milk
8 tablespoons sugar	1 teaspoon vanilla

Combine and bake at 275 degrees for 3 hours. Cover during first half of baking; uncover for last half.

FARMER'S DELIGHT

1 pound ground beef	1 can chicken soup
½ package noodles	¼ pound American cheese,
1 can cream-style corn	grated
1 can cream of mushroom soup	¼ teaspoon salt

Brown the beef and partially cook the noodles. When beef has started to brown, add the noodles and simmer for a few minutes. Add remaining ingredients and bake at 350 degrees for 40 minutes.

Martha was introduced to frozen foods while she was in Chicago. Freezers were just being developed as well as other work-saving kitchen appliances. World War II brought a halt to the manufacturing of many such items. During the war, food was preserved by canning and dehydration rather than by the newfangled freezing process. Martha broadcast many suggestions on conserving garden foods and emphasized sugarless and fat-free recipes.

After the war ended and consumer goods were being made again, freezers became available. The Birdseye Company even started marketing a line of frozen foods. Martha pulled out all her unused material on preparing and cooking frozen foods and shared her knowledge with her listeners.

MARTHA'S POPOVERS

3 eggs   1 cup milk
½ teaspoon salt   1 cup flour

Heat 8 custard cups. Oil them and put into oven when you start your batter. Mix batter in a 1-quart measure. Beat eggs and salt thoroughly. Add milk. Stir in flour with a fork; then beat with mixer 2 minutes. Pour cups ½ full of batter. Bake in 425-degree oven for 30 minutes. Remove from oven, puncture center of each popover so steam will escape, and return to oven for 2 more minutes. Serve.

SCALLOPED SPINACH

1 egg, beaten   ⅛ teaspoon salt
¼ cup mayonnaise   1 no. 303 can spinach, well
1 tablespoon vinegar   drained and chopped
1 tablespoon sugar

Combine egg, mayonnaise, vinegar, salt, and sugar; blend well. Fold in spinach (1½ cups fresh cooked and chopped spinach may be substituted for canned). Turn mixture into a lightly greased 1½-quart casserole and bake, uncovered, at 350 degrees for about 30 minutes. Serves 4.

As director of women's activities for the Tidy House Company, Martha made many appearances in Shenandoah. In 1953 she attended a homemaker show that was part of a two-day livestock feeders' institute sponsored by KMA. Martha's feature presentation was entitled "Household Magic."

Among her credits were three *McCall's Magazine* awards and a listing in *Who's Who of American Women*. Martha was president of the American Women in Radio and Television Heart of America chapter, which covers a six-state region in the Midwest. She served as president of the women's division of the Omaha Chamber of Commerce.

In 1987 Martha was posthumously elected into the Nebraska Broadcasters Hall of Fame for her more than thirty years in the field of home economics on Midwest radio and television.

COCOA MIX

12 cups dry milk solids
4½ cups sugar
1 6-ounce jar nondairy creamer

2½ cups cocoa
1 teaspoon salt
1 tablespoon cinnamon
  (optional)

Combine all ingredients in a large bowl, using a pastry blender for thorough mixing. Store in airtight container. To make cocoa, use 3 tablespoons of the mix for each cup of hot water. Stir until blended.

DIET BLUE CHEESE DRESSING

¼ cup cold water
⅓ cup instant nonfat dry milk
1½ cups low-cal cottage cheese
⅓ cup crumbled blue cheese

3 tablespoons lemon juice
¾ teaspoon onion salt
¼ teaspoon garlic salt

Combine all ingredients in blender; whip in a stop-and-go fashion until blended and just barely smooth. Cover and chill in refrigerator.

Martha Bohlsen thoroughly enjoyed her role as television homemaker for station WOW-TV. Friends who knew her well as a voice on the radio could see and recognize her as well.

When Martha worked at WOW television, she became acquainted with Johnny Carson. In later years when Johnny would visit Omaha, he would always try to see his good friend Martha.

One memorable day Martha was in the middle of her televised cooking show when Johnny barged onto the set. A live chicken Martha was using for part of her demonstration caught Johnny's attention. He proceeded to tell the viewers all kinds of things that could be done with that fowl. The program concluded with the crew and Martha dissolving in laughter as Johnny pushed the chicken into the cupboard under the sink, shut the door, and said his farewells.

When Martha came to the studio the following morning to organize the equipment for her program, she reached under the sink to pull out a pan. Out squawked one very indignant chicken.

"I used to think that two months after a broadcaster goes off the air the public will have forgotten her," Martha said, "but after I retired I discovered this simply was not true. I go into a store to buy groceries and my fellow shoppers stop to visit. When I walk down the street or go to church, people come up to me to ask how I am and seek my advice on some problem or find out my opinion on the latest home-making trends. It's lovely."

Martha's mother and an aunt lived with her at different times in her pleasant home in Omaha. Her brother Paul was living with her in 1984 when Martha died unexpectedly. She died just as she would have wished, still active, still able to keep a home for herself and her brother.

Martha has not been forgotten.

CHERRY LOAF CAKE
(A Bachelor's Delight)

2 eggs   1 can cherry pie filling
1 package white cake mix

Beat eggs only until blended, then add the package of cake mix (dry) and about ⅓ of the can of cherry pie filling. Mix on low speed until ingredients are moistened; then beat on medium to high for 1 minute or until batter appears smooth (will require from 1 to 1½ minutes of beating). Remove beaters and stir in remaining cherry pie filling. Fold over and over until evenly mixed. Turn into a greased 9 × 13 baking pan and bake at 350 degrees for about 35 minutes or until cake tests done. Frost, when cooled, with any desired frosting. We like the simple thin glaze made by blending 2 tablespoons hot water with 1 cup powdered sugar. A little almond flavoring may be added. Apply this glaze while the cake is still slightly warm. Delicious!

Martha had wise advice for modern young women: "Go into some kind of profession that you can develop for the remainder of your life. When radio first began, women's programs were termed 'domes-tic science' but look at the subject matter now—it is as broad as the whole world.

"Enjoy life but don't just spend it having fun. Be of service. Find a way to help people. There are many lonely people, many elderly,

many needy. You can help whether such activity is part of your vocation or your avocation. And don't criticize your church," Martha continued; "if you don't think your church is doing what it should, get
busy and start to do what needs to be done."

In her life Martha took her own advice. Her good friend Mildred
Gustason said, "Martha was the best person I ever knew. Always
kind, always thoughtful, and always thinking of others. She was basi-
cally very shy, but she responded to others. I would call her a Christian woman in the very best meaning of that term."

QUICK FONDANT EASTER EGGS

⅔ cup sweetened condensed
  milk
1 teaspoon vanilla
4 cups sifted confectioners'
  sugar
Finely chopped nuts

Flaked coconut
Grated chocolate
Colored sugar
Melted semisweet chocolate

Blend condensed milk and vanilla together; gradually add the confectioners' sugar while mixing until smooth and creamy. Flavor and
color as desired and form into Easter eggs. Roll in nuts, coconut,
chocolate, or colored sugar to make a colorful assortment. Or, dip
into melted semisweet chocolate, drain, and write child's name on
egg, using small tip of pastry tube.

HERBED BREAD COATING

2 cups fine dry bread crumbs
¼ cup flour
3 tablespoons paprika
4 teaspoons salt
2 teaspoons sugar

2 teaspoons onion powder
2 teaspoons ground oregano
½ teaspoon garlic salt
¼ cup vegetable shortening

Martha in 1982.

Mix dry ingredients together thoroughly; cut in shortening until mixture is crumbly. Store in tightly covered container. To use: Dip products (chicken, fish, chops, and such) into milk, then in the coating. Arrange in a single layer in an ungreased shallow pan. Bake at 400 degrees for 50 to 60 minutes until brown.

Adella Shoemaker

appy day to you" was the cheerful sign-off signature of Adella Shoemaker during her days as a radio homemaker. Her ability to convey a bright, happy approach to life was apparent in every one of her programs. It was always a pleasure to listen when she was on the air.

"Cookbook Time" was one title for Adella's broadcast, but she also used the term "Kitchen Klinik" when using Ks instead of Cs seemed to be one way to attract attention. Her informal chatter included homemaking tips, recipes, menus, child care hints, stories about sons Donald and George, projects with her husband, Don, and excerpts from the many letters she received from listeners.

For the first two weeks of her broadcasting life, Adella worked without pay on Shenandoah station KFNF to prove that she could relate to the housewives of the area. She was hired by KFNF and spent seven years with that station. When Leanna Driftmier left KMA to syndicate her "Kitchen-Klatter" program, she suggested Adella as her replacement. So it was that Adella came to KMA in August 1948 to become one of their full-time homemakers.

The comfortable home of Don and Adella Shoemaker on West Summit Avenue had a pleasant alcove located just off the dining room. Adella put a desk and bookcases in this space, and it was here that the microphone was positioned for her daily radio visits. Adella appreciated the convenience of being able to leave whatever she was doing and, without changing her clothes or combing her hair, to sit at the desk and begin her visit.

In 1952 Adella became director of women's activities for the Georgie Porgie breakfast cereal company, and her program was syndicated. Fortunately for her listeners, it was still heard on KMA.

STRAWBERRY DUMPLINGS

⅓ cup sugar	½ teaspoon salt
⅔ cup water	¼ cup margarine
½ teaspoon vanilla	½ cup milk
1 cup flour	1 pint strawberries, washed and
2 tablespoons sugar	hulled
1½ teaspoons baking powder	1 tablespoon sugar

Combine ⅓ cup sugar and water in small pan. Bring mixture to boiling. Reduce heat and simmer, uncovered, 5 minutes. Stir in vanilla. Stir together flour, 2 tablespoons sugar, baking powder, and salt. Cut in margarine till mixture is crumbly. Add milk and stir just till well combined. Place strawberries in bottom of 1½-quart casserole. Pour hot sugar-water mixture over berries. Drop dumpling mixture by spoonfuls, about 8 to 10, over berries. Sprinkle with remaining sugar. Bake at 450 degrees for 25 minutes. Serve warm.

WILD GOOSEBERRY PIE

2 cups gooseberries, stemmed	¾ cup flour
1 cup sugar	¼ cup cream

Wash and stem gooseberries. Mix with other ingredients—just use enough cream to make it all stick together. Put into unbaked pie shell and top with crust. Bake at 350 degrees for 40 to 45 minutes. Do not overbake. (¼ cup of cream may be too much; use just enough to make the mixture stick together.)

HONEY NUT CUPCAKES

1 egg	½ teaspoon baking powder
½ cup strained honey	¼ teaspoon soda
Grated rind of 1 lemon	Dash of salt
1 cup cake flour	½ cup sour cream

Beat egg until foamy. Add honey and grated rind. Sift dry ingredients and add to mixture alternately with ½ cup sour cream. Grease muffin pans generously on bottom, lightly on sides. Put 1 tablespoon coarsely chopped nuts in each one. Fill ⅔ full of batter. Bake in moderate oven 20 minutes.

ADELLA'S BRUNCH CHICKEN

Slice chicken (or turkey) in thick slices, using 1 dark and 1 white slice for each serving. Wrap the chicken slices in foil and put in oven to heat. Meanwhile, combine 2 10½-ounce cans chicken gravy with 1 6-ounce can applesauce and 1 3-ounce can mushrooms (drained). Heat this mixture. Arrange chicken slices on platter, top with some of the gravy mixture, and surround with hot biscuits. Serve any remaining gravy in a bowl.

TOMATO SOUP
(To Can)

1 peck (8 quarts) tomatoes	¼ cup salt
6 onions	A little pepper
1 bunch celery	1 cup butter
1 cup sugar	1 cup flour

Wash tomatoes and cut out all the greenish, whitish core. Do not peel! Cook and run through a sieve or food press. Cook onions and celery and also put them through the sieve. Mix vegetables and return to stove. Add sugar, salt, and pepper. When boiling, add butter and flour that have been rubbed together thoroughly. Continue cooking a few minutes longer until soup is slightly thickened. Stir often so it doesn't stick or burn. Pour into sterilized jars and seal. Process 10 minutes at 10 pounds.

When opened, bring to a boil; add a pinch of soda and milk. Add about as much milk as the soup needs, or according to your taste.

Nettie and George Washington Mitchell were living four miles southwest of Shenandoah when their daughter Adella was born. The area where the Mitchells farmed was known as Manti, a community that predated Shenandoah as a pioneer settlement.

Adella was the youngest of six children. She attended the Manti one-room school until she was twelve. The family moved to Shenandoah, where she graduated from high school. She attended Simpson College in Indianola, Iowa, and Tarkio College in Missouri and eventually received her master's degree in English from the University of Northern Colorado in Greeley.

A list of Adella's favorite recipes would invariably include Soda Cracker Pie, Crystal Pickles, and French Chocolate Silk Pie.

A funny story was told recently about the Soda Cracker Pie. A radio listener gave a 1984 bride a copy of the recipe. The young woman read the ingredients and the title, laughingly declared it was a great joke to suggest she put soda crackers into a dessert, and threw the recipe away! The friend who had given the recipe to the newlywed made up the light, delicious pie and presented it as a gift to the bride with a duplicate copy of the recipe.

SODA CRACKER PIE

3 egg whites	¼ teaspoon baking powder
1 cup sugar	½ cup pecans
14 soda crackers	1 teaspoon vanilla

Beat egg whites stiff; gradually beat in sugar. Add soda crackers (rolled very fine), baking powder, and broken pecans. Flavor with vanilla. Fill a buttered pie plate with this mixture. Bake for 30 minutes in a 325-degree oven. Cool. Top with a layer of thinly sliced peaches, either fresh or well drained. Blanket with a layer of sweetened whipped cream (it will take 1 cup) and store in refrigerator overnight. Be sure the cream is stiffly whipped. The pie is much improved by storing, so don't be afraid to follow these directions.

During the Korean conflict, Adella lifted the morale of servicemen by
making and sending them hundreds of her delicious cookies and candies.
She wrapped each piece in self-seal paraffin paper, a forerunner of modern
plastic wrap.

CRYSTAL PICKLES

Wash 25 dill-size cucumbers and put in brine made with 1 quart
coarse salt and 1 gallon water. Use stone jar or enamel kettle. Cover
with a plate and weight down (I use a 2-quart jar half-filled with
water). All cukes must be kept below the brine. Cover with clean
cloth. Skim daily if necessary. Leave for two weeks. Drain and wash.
Cut in slices about ½ inch thick. Cover with cold water and 2 tablespoons powdered alum. Soak 24 hours. Drain and wash. Make a
syrup of 1 quart vinegar, 2 quarts sugar, 2 sticks cinnamon, 1 teaspoon ground mace, and 1 teaspoon whole cloves. Put the spices in a

bag. Bring to a boil and pour over the pickles. Repeat for four days. This means drain pickling syrup, reheat to boiling, and again pour over pickles. This syrup covers about a gallon of chunks.

Good-size cucumbers may be used, but be sure large seeds are not formed. The cucumbers must not be older than 24 hours or they will not make crisp pickles. You may add fresh cucumbers to the brine from time to time, but allow two weeks for the last added. These may be allowed to remain in the brine for a long time but need more soaking to remove the salt.

Put the pickles in jars when process is completed. Can cold. Seal.

FRENCH CHOCOLATE SILK PIE

Cream together ¼ pound butter, ¾ cup sugar, and 1 teaspoon vanilla. Add 2 squares melted chocolate. Then add 2 whole eggs, one at a time, beating 5 minutes after adding each egg. Put in a baked pie shell. Chill in the refrigerator overnight or several hours. Serve with whipped cream. Makes 8 servings.

"JOHN MASETTI"
(Adella's Favorite One-Dish Meal)

1 pound sausage	1 teaspoon salt
1 onion, chopped	1 cup diced cheese
1 cup tomato juice	1 8-ounce package finely cut noodles

Fry onion until light brown. Add sausage and fry until it crumbles. Stir it constantly. Cook noodles 10 minutes in salted water. Drain. Mix together with sausage, cheese, and tomato juice. Bake in greased casserole in slow oven (325 degrees) 40 minutes.

ORANGE HONEY

Combine in a saucepan: ½ cup orange juice concentrate
 1 cup honey   6 whole cloves

Place over medium heat and simmer 5 minutes. Remove cloves before serving. Excellent on waffles, pancakes, or French toast.

COOKED SALAD DRESSING

Put into a bowl, but do not beat   4 tablespoons sugar
 or stir: 3 teaspoons salt
 2 eggs   ¾ cup salad oil
 2 teaspoons dry mustard   ½ cup vinegar

In a pan, mix together 2 cups water and ½ cup cornstarch. Cook over slow heat, stirring constantly, until it is clear. Add this hot mixture to the ingredients in the bowl and beat well with rotary beater or electric mixer until smooth.

ADELLA'S GRAPE JUICE

Wash and remove spoiled grapes from stems of 20 pounds of grapes. You do not need to remove the good grapes from the stems unless you wish. Place in a kettle and smash down with a potato masher. Pour 3 quarts of water into the kettle. Boil complete mixture, timing for 3 to 5 minutes after it comes to a boil. Strain. Return juice to kettle and add 6 cups of sugar (or sugar to taste). Stir until sugar is dissolved. Bring to a good rolling boil, ladle quickly into sterile jars, and cap immediately. Process 5 minutes in hot water bath. This is to be diluted with about half as much water when served.

KMA sponsored a Farm Day on June 1st in 1949. In addition to hearing talks on farm problems, visitors were entertained by an aerial circus, the KMA musical staff, and the opportunity to visit with homemakers Adella Shoemaker and Bernice Currier. Since time was short and hundreds of their listeners wanted to see them, the two had to eat their hot dog lunch under the watchful eyes of their fans.

CHINESE CHEWS

1 cup sugar	2 eggs
¾ cup flour	1 cup nutmeats, chopped
1 teaspoon baking powder	1 cup chopped dates
¼ teaspoon salt	

Mix dry ingredients. Add beaten eggs, then nuts and dates. Spread on cookie sheet and bake in a 375-degree oven. Cut in small squares and form into balls while warm. Roll balls in powdered sugar.

JELLIED CRANBERRIES

2 cups cold water   2 cups sugar
4 cups berries

Combine berries and water in saucepan and cook until the berries
pop. Put through food mill or food processor. Combine pulp and
sugar. Boil exactly 5 minutes. Pour into jars. Refrigerate for a short
time, or freeze if you wish to store for longer period.

MOTHER SHOEMAKER'S BAKED BEANS

3 cups navy beans, soaked   1 cup sugar
   overnight in water to cover   1 tablespoon salt
1 teaspoon soda   2 slices bacon

Cook beans and soda together a few minutes. Pour off water, wash
well, and let cook in clear water for ½ hour. Drain off water as desired, leaving enough to moisten beans. Add more during baking if
needed. Add the other ingredients (putting bacon on top). Bake for
three hours in a moderate (350-degree) oven.

PORK CHOP CORN BAKE

4 pork chops   Milk
1 tablespoon shortening   ¾ cup coarse cracker crumbs
¾ teaspoon salt   1 tablespoon prepared mustard
⅛ teaspoon pepper   1 egg, slightly beaten
1 16-ounce can whole-kernel   2 tablespoons sugar
   corn, drained   1 tablespoon instant minced
                                     onion

Brown pork chops in melted shortening in heavy skillet over low
heat. Sprinkle with salt and pepper. Drain liquid from corn, measure,
and add enough milk to make 1 cup. Stir corn and liquid together

with the remaining ingredients. Spoon into greased 1½- to 2-quart casserole and place browned pork chops on top of corn mixture. Bake at 350 degrees for 50 to 60 minutes.

UNIVERSITY CLUB FAMOUS PECAN ROLLS

Bring to a boil and then cool to
lukewarm:
½ cup sugar
1 teaspoon salt
2 cups water
1¾ cups lard (or other
shortening)

Mix till dissolved:
¼ cup warm water
1 teaspoon sugar
2 yeast cakes (or use 2
packages dry yeast)

Put two mixtures together. Add 2 well-beaten eggs. Then sift in 4 cups flour and beat well. Stir in 2 more cups flour, adding a little more if necessary to make a soft dough. Put in greased bowl. Grease top of dough; cover with wax paper. Keep in refrigerator for 12 hours before using. Roll dough to ½ inch thickness. Spread with mixture of 1 cup butter, 1 cup shortening, and 4 cups brown sugar (mixed thoroughly together in beater). Sprinkle with pecans. Roll up, slice off in 1-inch sections, and place in greased muffin tins in which about 1 tablespoon sugar mixture has been put. Let rise. Bake about 20 minutes in a 375-degree oven. (I use a greased oblong pan, dot the sugar mixture and pecans, and place the rolls close together to rise high, as if they were in the muffin pans. The sugar mixture will provide enough "goo" for several batches of rolls.)

Adella's working hours stretched far into the night. She sent out mimeographed sheets of recipes, helped edit KMA cookbooks, arranged contests, judged baking competitions, and assisted Doris Murphy with the famous cookie teas. She baked cookies for the KMA tours and participated in the homemaker celebrations at the Mayfair Auditorium.

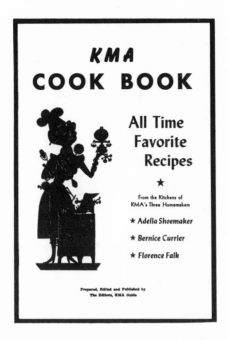

KMA COOK BOOK

All Time
Favorite
Recipes

★

From the Kitchens of
KMA's Three Homemakers

★ Adella Shoemaker

★ Bernice Currier

★ Florence Falk

Prepared, Edited and Published by
The Editors, KMA Guide

After the sudden death of her husband in 1953, Adella kept busy by operating a tearoom in her home. She enjoyed preparing and serving delicious meals to club groups and private parties. She continued broadcasting for a time and then decided to go into teaching. She taught English at the Eagle Grove, Logan, and Shenandoah high schools and at Iowa Central Community College in Fort Dodge. Upon her retirement, she returned to her beloved Shenandoah.

It was a sorrow to all who knew her that Adella was destined to spend the last years of her life suffering from Alzheimer's disease.

SWEEPSTAKE CHOCOLATE CAKE

½ cup cocoa
¾ cup hot water
½ cup butter
2 cups sugar
1 teaspoon vanilla

2 unbeaten eggs
3 cups sifted flour
1 teaspoon soda
⅛ teaspoon salt
1 cup sour cream

Cook cocoa and hot water together over low heat, stirring, until mixture is thick and smooth. Set aside. Cream butter, sugar, and vanilla together. Add eggs and beat well. Sift dry ingredients together and add to creamed mixture alternately with sour cream. Stir in cocoa mixture last. Bake in 9 × 13 greased pan for 45 minutes (or until it tests done) at 350 degrees.

RHUBARB PIE WITH STREUSEL TOPPING

3 cups rhubarb	1¼ cups sugar
2 tablespoons flour	¼ teaspoon cinnamon

Wash rhubarb and cut in ½-inch lengths. Do not peel. Mix with flour, sugar, and cinnamon. Fill unbaked 10-inch pie shell.

Topping

½ cup butter	1 cup flour
½ cup brown sugar	

Cream together the butter and sugar. With a fork, blend in the flour to make a crumbly mixture, or streusel. Sprinkle streusel over rhubarb. Bake in a preheated oven for 15 minutes at 450 degrees. Reduce temperature to 350 degrees and bake for 30 minutes longer.

APPLETS

Soak 2 tablespoons unflavored gelatin in ½ cup unsweetened applesauce for 10 minutes. Put ¾ cup applesauce and 2 cups sugar into a saucepan and bring to a boil. Add the soaked applesauce and gelatin, and cook hard for 15 minutes; stir frequently. Then add 1 cup finely chopped nutmeats and 2 teaspoons vanilla. Pour into buttered shallow pan. Let stand to dry several hours. Cut into squares; roll in powdered sugar.

LEMON DESSERT

2 tablespoons flour
¾ cup sugar
1 tablespoon butter
2 beaten egg yolks

¼ cup lemon juice
1 cup milk
Lemon rind
2 beaten egg whites

Blend flour with sugar and butter. Add egg yolks, lemon juice, milk, and rind. Fold in stiffly beaten egg whites. Pour into unbuttered 8-inch square pan. Set pan in a pan of water. Bake in a 375-degree oven for 30 minutes or until a knife inserted comes out clean (just as you test for custards).

By the time I came on the radio homemaker scene, Adella was well into her popular program. Adella gave me moral support, suggestions for programming, recipes from her extensive files, and cookies baked in her busy kitchen. We became close friends.

Adella's husband, Don, passed away from a heart attack just one week after my daughter Dulcie Jean died, and I was among the first to come to Adella to offer her sympathy. The shared experiences drew us even closer together. Later, when I was expecting my third child, Adella hosted a shower for the new baby.

CHURCH CHEESE SPREAD

2 sticks mild Cracker Barrel
     cheddar cheese

1 pint Kraft sandwich spread
2 ounces pimiento, drained and
     diced

Grind or grate cheese. Combine with sandwich spread. Stir in pimiento. (If more moisture is needed, and it usually is not, add a little mayonnaise or salad dressing.) Excellent on whole wheat, rye, or white bread. Nice for open-face sandwiches.

The brands are suggestions only. These are the ones the church members who developed this particular sandwich filling found to their taste.

Plan Now to Attend Our Big

KMA 40th
Anniversary Celebration
(To be held in conjunction with Shenandoah Farm-Industry Day)

Saturday, September 18

GUEST OF HONOR — Secretary of Agriculture Orville Freeman

-- IT'S ALL FREE --

BAR-B-CUE—3,000 LBS. BEEF AND PORK

TRACTOR PULL—HUNDREDS OF $ IN PRIZES

ENTERTAINMENT—BIG OUTDOOR STAGE
★ BILLY WALKER — GRAND OLE OPRY STAR
With his country/western entertainers featuring
Linda Manning—recording vocalist.

MILE LONG PARADE—BANDS, BEAUTIFUL FLOATS

COIN SHOW AT LIBERTY MEMORIAL BUILDING

Vote for Miss KMA—QUEEN OF FARM-INDUSTRY DAY

You'll vote from four finalists from Missouri, Iowa, Nebraska, Kansas

BRING THE WHOLE FAMILY
COME EARLY AND STAY LATE

— Complete details in next issue of your Guide —

KMA's fortieth anniversary in 1965 was a gala affair with thousands of visitors coming to Shenandoah for the special event. A platform had been erected in the street to the east of Mayfair Auditorium for Grand Ole Opry star Billy Walker, the Strategic Air Command Band from Offut airbase near Omaha, and the KMA musicians.

Billie McNeilly (Oakley), the KMA homemaker at that time, had the pleasure of giving recognition to the past radio homemakers. Accolades were also given to other KMA personalities, past and present. The celebration reminded many of the jubilee days of long ago.

HOT GERMAN APPLE ROLLS

1 can (1 pound, 5 ounce) apple
   pie filling
2 tablespoons brown sugar
½ teaspoon cinnamon
12 brown-and-serve pull-apart
   dinner rolls

Streusel topping:
   2 tablespoons flour
   2 tablespoons brown sugar
   ¼ teaspoon cinnamon
   1 tablespoon butter

Combine pie filling, brown sugar, and cinnamon. Cut slits ½ inch deep in indentations of each roll. Place a small amount of apple mixture in each. Combine ingredients for topping and sprinkle a little over each roll. Bake at 400 degrees for 10 to 15 minutes or until golden brown. 12 servings.

PEPPERS STUFFED WITH ASPARAGUS

Cut slices from the stem end of 6 medium-size green peppers. Remove seeds and white portion. Parboil in boiling salted water 10 minutes. Drain and fill with creamed asparagus cut in small pieces. Cover with buttered bread crumbs and bake 10 minutes in moderate oven. These could be served as a garnish on a platter of sliced tongue.

Adella loved holidays. She was born on December 24, 1908, was married on December 25, 1928, and, characteristically, died just one day after New Year's, January 2, 1985. She lived and worked only four miles from the place where she was born, but she traveled far on the airwaves and farther in the years she studied and taught school. Her son Don now lives in Rolfe, Iowa, where he is a banker, and son George is with the Farm Bureau Insurance Company and lives in Sterling, Colorado. They made Adella a grandmother seven times, and their children made her a great-grandmother eight times. The holiday celebrations continue.

Warren Nielson has long been known for his culinary prowess, especially with wild game. This 1949 photograph shows Warren doing the cleanup tasks following a meal.

Men in the Kitchen

To most people the term *radio homemaker* means women talking to women, but that is not the entire story. Men listen. Men who are specialists in such fields as cooking, decorating, and child care appear as guests. Male broadcasters of the KMA staff have been substitute hosts on the women's programs.

Men have also been radio homemakers. A homemaker program known as "The Man in the Kitchen" aired on KMA with congenial, fun-loving Merl Douglas as host. Announcer Clair Gross headed the program for a time and brought his own special, pleasant personality to the microphone. Larry Parker took over the duties in August 1953.

Through the years, the men of KMA have presented their favorite recipes on a number of different shows—the call-in program, the male homemaker programs, the women's programs, and their own broadcasts. This chapter contains a sampling.

LARRY PARKER'S DINNER IN A DISH

2 tablespoons lard
1 medium onion, chopped
2 green peppers, sliced
1 pound hamburger
4 medium tomatoes
½ to 1 teaspoon salt
¼ teaspoon pepper
2 eggs
2 cups freshly cut corn or 1 can
    whole-kernel corn
½ cup dry bread crumbs

Put lard in skillet and lightly fry pepper and onions for 3 minutes. Add meat and blend thoroughly. Add seasonings. Remove from fire. Drain off excess grease. Cool. Stir in eggs and mix well. Put 1 cup

Larry Parker came to Shenandoah as an announcer in 1947. He arrived via Norfolk, Nebraska (where he was born), Iowa State College, and radio jobs in Nebraska, Missouri, and California. Larry had "The Man in the Kitchen" program for the longest time.

corn in baking dish, then half the meat mixture, then a layer of sliced tomatoes. Then another layer of corn, meat, and tomatoes. Cover with crumbs and dot generously with bits of pure lard (butter or margarine). Bake in moderate oven (375 degrees) for 35 minutes.

LARRY'S FOIL-BAKED POTATOES AND ONIONS

Peel 4 baking potatoes; cut into 1-inch-thick slices. Place potatoes back into original shape, placing a thick slice of onion between each potato piece. Brush generously with melted butter and sprinkle with seasoned salt. Wrap each potato in square of heavy duty aluminum foil. Place on grill and roast over hot coals 40 to 50 minutes, turning occasionally, or until potatoes are done. Makes 4 to 6 servings.

MERRILL LANGFITT'S STUFFED BAKED TOMATOES

Six tomatoes. Remove seeds and sprinkle inside with salt; invert on a platter and let drain. Sauté ⅓ cup finely chopped green pepper, 2 tablespoons butter, 1 cup bread crumbs, ½ cup chopped tomato,

1 teaspoon grated onion, ¼ teaspoon salt, and ¼ teaspoon pepper. Fill tomatoes with mixture. Set in muffin tins to hold upright. Bake at 350 degrees for 15 to 20 minutes, or until heated through.

MERRILL'S SPANISH HAMBURGER

¾ package macaroni
2 cans tomatoes
½ can tomato juice
½ cup minced onion
1½ pounds ground beef

Small bay leaf
3 slices green pepper, minced
3 tablespoons butter
Salt and pepper to taste

Cook ground beef and onion in butter. Add tomatoes and bay leaf. Cook for 20 minutes. Remove bay leaf. To mixture add cooked macaroni, tomato juice, green peppers, salt, and pepper. Simmer for 1½ hours. Serve.

"The outdoor culinary expert of KMA" is the way Merrill Langfitt was described in 1959 when this photograph first appeared in the KMA Guide.

Merl Douglas is filling his plate at one of the famous food days at KMA. To the left in the picture are Mary Williams (promotion) and Lynn Padilla (continuity).

Merl Douglas was an announcer-entertainer and, for a brief time, a radio homemaker. He was crippled with infantile paralysis—polio— when he was fifteen months old and wore a brace on one leg. Twenty-seven of his thirty-four years in broadcasting were spent at KMA. Merl is now retired and lives in Springfield, Missouri.

MERL DOUGLAS'S BEEF LOAF

Grind 3 large sweet green peppers and 1 large onion. Combine with 1 cup cracker crumbs. Drain the liquid from a large can of tomatoes (3½ cups) and reserve for basting. Combine vegetables and add 1 pound ground beef, 1 pound ground pork, ½ teaspoon salt, and ⅛ teaspoon paprika. Shape these ingredients into a loaf. Dredge with flour. Cover with 5 or 6 slices of bacon. Bake for 1 hour in moderate oven (350 degrees). Baste frequently with tomato juice. Remove from pan. Serves 8 to 10.

MERL'S JIFFY CHILI CON QUESO

1 can cheddar cheese soup   ¾ tablespoon cornstarch
1 can tomatoes with chilies   ¾ tablespoon water

Mix soup and tomatoes in a saucepan. Heat. Thicken with cornstarch mixed with water. Serve hot in chafing dish. Use corn chips for dippers. Serves 8 to 10.

A bull pen is a place where prisoners are held, a spot on a baseball field for relief pitchers to warm up, and the center space at radio studios with a work area for the sports, women's, promotion, and other departments as needed. In earlier days, it became the location where the station staff held many of their so-called food days. After the work space was remodeled into neat, modern cubicles, the staff began to hold the food days in the "Memorabilia" conference room near the entrance to the building. Except for those actually on the air and those working on the engineering board, work comes to a screeching halt on food days as the KMA people (and a few others who wander in) enjoy the fellowship and the feasting.

Ike Everly and his wife, Margaret, came to Shenandoah, Iowa, with their two small sons, Phil and Don, because they wanted a small, neighborly town in which to raise their family. By 1947 Ike was part of the musical staff at KMA, and soon Margaret was singing with him. When the boys were ten and twelve years old, they joined their parents on the air. According to the book *KMA Radio: The First Sixty Years*, they were busy, active boys: "At school, Phil sang in the glee club. In addition to working at KMA, the boys had paper routes and lemonade stands, and joined hundreds of other youngsters detasseling corn in the fields owned by Earl May."

The family continued to perform on the KMA airwaves until the middle 1950s. In 1954 the parents moved to their native state of Kentucky, and the Everly brothers grew up and became world famous. In 1986 Don and Phil returned to Shenandoah for a "Homecoming Reunion."

One of Ike's favorite recipes was for fried oysters. He shared this recipe in the *Favorite Recipes* book published by KMA in 1948. Margaret passed along these favorite recipes of her sons. This is the way Ike likes his oysters prepared.

IKE EVERLY'S FRIED OYSTERS

Drain 12 large oysters. Pour 1 cup of cold water over them. Dry them between towels. Beat 1 egg with 2 tablespoons water. Inserting a fork in the tough muscle of the oyster, dip the oysters in the egg then in seasoned bread crumbs. In the egg again and again in the crumbs. Permit the oysters to stand for ½ hour. Fry them in deep fat for 4 minutes or sauté them in butter.

PHIL EVERLY'S BANANA CUSTARD RECIPE

1¼ cups sugar
¼ cup flour
2 tablespoons cornstarch
3½ cups milk (or evaporated milk)
2 egg yolks, lightly beaten
2 tablespoons butter or margarine, softened

1 teaspoon vanilla flavoring
1 package graham crackers
4 or 5 medium bananas, sliced
2 egg whites
4 tablespoons sugar
¼ teaspoon cream of tartar

Combine sugar, flour, and cornstarch in a mixing bowl; mix well and set aside. Pour milk into a heavy saucepan and cook over medium heat until it is scalded, about 160 degrees. (Margaret likes the evaporated milk and usually dilutes it with a little water.) Gradually stir a little of the hot milk into the egg yolks and stir into reserved dry ingredients. Add to remaining hot milk. Cook, stirring, until mixture coats the spoon. Remove from heat and add butter and vanilla. Let cool.

Line bottom of 9 × 13 pan with a layer of graham crackers. Arrange half of banana slices over the top. Top with half the cooled custard.

The Everly Brothers performed with their father and mother and with other musical groups over the KMA airwaves. From left: Don Everly, clarinetist Eddie Comer, Phil Everly, Ike Everly on guitar, and accordion player Jerry Fronek.

Repeat layers. Crumble some graham cracker crumbs over the top custard layer. Cool. Whip the egg whites until soft peaks form. Continue beating and gradually add sugar and cream of tartar. When stiff peaks form, spoon over top of pudding. Bake at 375 to 400 degrees until light brown on top. Excellent eaten warm. Keep any uneaten portions refrigerated.

This is also delicious made with vanilla wafers.

DON EVERLY'S COUNTRY FRIED CHICKEN

½ cup flour   Salt if desired
½ teaspoon paprika   1 (3 to 3½ pounds) fryer, cut up
¼ teaspoon pepper   Safflower oil or Crisco for frying

Combine first four ingredients in plastic or paper bag; shake to mix.
Place 2 or 3 pieces of chicken in bag at a time and shake well to coat.
Repeat until all pieces are coated with flour mixture. In a large skillet, heat shortening to 350 degrees or until a cube of bread sizzles
when dropped into the hot fat. Add chicken and brown on all sides.
Reduce heat to medium and cover. Cook for about 30 minutes, or until chicken is tender. Remove cover and cook another 10 minutes to
crisp, turning occasionally. Drain on paper towel.

News broadcaster Ralph Childs had a deep, resonant voice, a nose
for news, a penchant for playing Santa Claus during the holidays,
and a way with chili that would make a strong man cry. In fact, his
chili was so filled with spices and garlic that his fellow KMA staff
members say they could always tell when Ralph had eaten his
own concoction. They didn't mind, however, for he often shared it
with them.

Ralph sent out a number of recipe sheets and memos to his listeners. Some included ingredients for products for which he aired
commercials. He included some of his homespun philosophy with
his mailers. "Two can live as cheaply as one," one item stated, "but it
takes both of them to work to do it." Another suggested, "Think of
the money that could be saved by letting a pretty girl draw the names
of the lucky political candidates out of a barrel. It might improve the
quality of the office holders we get as well."

"Chili in the Childs's household is a favorite that is a must once a
week and maybe even oftener," Ralph Childs explained in the KMA
Guide. "This recipe is one that evolved by a process of trial and error
over the years and by reference to other standard recipes.

"I got started in this business of personal cookery when I was a
student at the University of Iowa back in very unprosperous years,"
Ralph continued. "Peanut butter sandwiches as a steady diet didn't

Ralph Childs in 1952.

appeal to me, so I bought an electric hot plate for about a dollar and found a room where I could use it. This was the beginning of my chili cooking, and should explain why I have actually several varieties of chili that I make, and why it is difficult to give exact measurements. But this is my favorite of all."

RALPH CHILDS'S CHILI CON CARNE

I prefer to start with the dried red beans. I use the canned beans only when I am in a hurry. It takes 45 minutes to cook the red beans in a pressure cooker. I usually just boil them first instead of bothering with soaking them with water to cover them and a little more. I use a pound of dried red beans.

In the biggest skillet we own, I start frying 2 pounds of hamburger. (It doesn't make any difference how fat it is because grease makes the chili all the better. If the meat is dry, I use plenty of cooking oil, bacon drippings, or whatever is available.)

Cut up three good-sized onions and add while meat is frying, plus a couple small cloves of garlic and 1 teaspoon chili powder. Then clean and cut up a good-sized green pepper and put in. I add what I think is the right amount of salt and pepper to this, and a heaping teaspoonful more of chili powder. Cook about 10 minutes. Stir often.

When the beans are done, I pour the meat into the cooker with them and add a quart or so of tomato juice and whatever other vegetable juices we may have saved in the refrigerator for this occasion.

(At this time, I make another decision. Since chili is simply a stew in Mexico, where they use whatever they have available, I may add a can of peas. They're really good in it. Sometimes we have a lot of little potatoes that nobody has wanted to peel, so I peel them and throw them in whole, or even cut some big ones in half. These really make a hit with the kids.)

To this I add another clove of garlic, put the cooker top on, and cook for another five to ten minutes, according to the size of the potatoes. When it is done, I add another heaping teaspoon of chili powder, stir, and serve with plenty of crisp crackers and milk.

And by my own plate I always put the can of chili powder, cayenne pepper, and maybe a bottle of Tabasco sauce.

RALPH'S NORWEGIAN FATTIGMAND

2 whole eggs
2 yolks
4 tablespoons powdered sugar
4 tablespoons cream
½ teaspoon salt

About 2 cups Mother's Best Flour (to make a dough that can be rolled out like noodles or pie crust)

Beat eggs; add sugar, cream, and salt. Sift flour. Put 2 cups into a bowl, make a well in the center, pour in the first mixture, and stir until all flour is taken up. Knead, adding enough flour to handle and roll out paper-thin. Cut into diamond shapes. (Diamonds may be 9 inches long and 5 inches across.) Put a 2-inch slit near the end of one of the long points of the diamond and draw the other point through it, making a kind of circle. Drop 2 at a time into fat heated to 375 degrees. Fry until a delicate brown, and dash generously with confectioners' sugar. Serve with coffee.

During World War II, fats were used in large quantities in the making of explosives. Since they are also one of the basic ingredients in soap, a shortage of laundry products developed. Many women began saving grease drippings and made their own soap.

Gertrude May and Frank Field's wife, Jennie, found such a solution to their problem. They also got Frank to help with the project. The *KMA Guide* stated: "With Frank supervising, the ladies took their grease, lye, and other ingredients out in the backyard on some cement blocks and made over 100 bars of nice, white, floating soap."

This is one of the recipes given over KMA during the days of soap scarcity.

FRANK'S HOMEMADE SOAP
(Makes One Bar)

Mix and let cool:
½ cup soft water
½ tablespoon lye

When cool, add:
1 tablespoon borax
1 tablespoon liquid ammonia
(watch eyes when using lye)

Pour the above mixture into 1 cup of warm grease (fryings if you wish). Stir occasionally until like heavy cream. Pour into a coffee can and set aside to ripen and whiten.

Just a few cautions when making lye soap! Clean grease is best—surplus bacon drippings and fat rendered from trimmings of meat. If you wish to clarify the grease, heat and drop in several sliced raw potatoes and let cool. Carefully pour off the grease and don't use the part that settles to the bottom. If you wish a real white soap, stir, stir, and stir.

Our grandmothers used talcum powder to perfume the soap.

Be very careful when using lye, especially of the splashes; protect your arms with cloths and wear cotton flannel gloves if you wish.

From the quantity of tomatoes Frank grew and the number of tomato-based recipes he gave on the air, this must have been one of his favorite garden crops. This photograph of Frank and just a few of his tomatoes was taken in the May Seed Company trial grounds.

Frank Field started broadcasting on his father's station, KFNF, in August 1926. He played guitar, sang with a quartet, and announced. He came to KMA in April 1940 to develop the farm, garden, and weather broadcasts for which he became legendary. Later he had a program on KMTV in Omaha called "Over the Garden Fence."

It was not unusual for Frank to receive hundreds of letters a day. It became a challenge for everyone else at KMA to match or beat his record. Billie Oakley well remembers the day she received more fan mail than Frank: "It was a high point in my career." For a time in 1969, Jo Freed's mail ran ahead of Frank's, and she was elated; it was a great achievement. When Frank celebrated his seventy-eighth birthday in 1972, he received more than 1,300 letters in three days.

FRANK FIELD'S SIMPLE TOMATO CATSUP

1 quart tomato juice and pulp
1 onion, grated
1 cup sugar
1 cup vinegar

1 heaping teaspoon celery salt
1 teaspoon salt
$\frac{1}{3}$ teaspoon red pepper
1 tablespoon mixed pickling
   spices

Put the spices and the ground onion in a loosely tied cloth bag so the flavor can boil out into the catsup. Mix all the ingredients together and throw in the bag of spices, and let boil for half an hour. Then cream a heaping tablespoon of cornstarch in a cup of cold water, and slowly stir it into the boiling catsup. Let it boil for two or three minutes longer until it is thickened. Then pour into sterile catsup bottles, and seal with a bottle capper using crown caps. If you don't have the bottles, can in pint fruit jars just the same as you would hot fruit or vegetables.

FRANK'S TOMATO JUICE

1 peck sound, ripe red tomatoes
1 cup grated onion
1 bunch celery, 1 cup chopped
   (leaves and all)

4 teaspoons salt (more, if
   desired)
4 tablespoons sugar

Wash and quarter the tomatoes into a big kettle without peeling them. Add other ingredients and let simmer for 15 minutes, or until celery is soft. Rub through a sieve or colander to remove seed and skins. Put juice back in kettle, bring to a good boil, and seal in hot, sterilized jars. Process in hot-water bath or pressure canner according to current recommended directions.

FRANK'S CORNMEAL DOUGHNUTS

1 scant cup sweet milk
²⁄₃ cup yellow cornmeal
½ cup butter
½ teaspoon salt
²⁄₃ cup white sugar
1 teaspoon cinnamon

¼ teaspoon ground cloves or
   nutmeg or both
2 eggs
1 cup flour
2 teaspoons baking powder

Bring milk to boil. Gradually beat in cornmeal and cook, stirring constantly, until thick. Add butter, salt, sugar, and spices. Cool. Beat eggs and add to cooled mixture with flour and baking powder. Mix well. Take out ⅓ of batter and put on well-floured breadboard. Knead in enough flour so dough handles well. Cut and place to one side until all doughnuts are cut and ready. Fry in hot lard (or other shortening).

Warren Nielson arrived in Shenandoah in late fall 1945, a young bachelor newly discharged from the army. He always liked performing and talking and had worked his way through college playing clarinet and tenor sax in dance bands. It proved to be an excellent background for radio.

Through the years he was on KMA, Warren hosted an amazing variety of programs, including "Kiddie Korner," "Party Line," and "Sportsman." On the "Party Line," people called in to ask Warren all kinds of questions—how to blow soap bubbles, trace down strange noises in the night, what to do with old hens, how to find the owner of twenty stray hogs, the best way to make snickerdoodles, and how a person can unzip the back zipper in a dress when she is all alone—things like that. On the "Sportsman" program, Warren featured stories of hunting and fishing and then gave the listeners recipes for preparing game.

After leaving KMA in 1970, Warren moved to Omaha, where he established Warren Nielson and Associates Public Relations and Advertising. His radio and television broadcasting continued. He was director of agricultural services for radio KFAB from 1970 until 1990. He continues to serve as farm director of KMTV.

WARREN NIELSON'S COZY RABBIT

Fry 6 or 8 slices of bacon. Reserve cooked bacon, and use fat to brown two rabbits, cut into serving pieces. Place browned meat in baking pan, arrange bacon on top, and pour currant jelly sauce over the meat. Bake at 350 degrees until meat is tender.

If bunny has tough muscles, this is sure to tenderize him.

WARREN'S CURRANT JELLY SAUCE

2 tablespoons butter	Salt and pepper
3 tablespoons flour	⅓ cup currant jelly
1 cup water or stock	2 tablespoons sherry wine

Melt butter; stir in flour and brown together. Add stock gradually, simmer gently, and stir until smooth. Add salt and pepper. Melt currant jelly in the sauce and add sherry wine.

WARREN'S NOTHING COOKIES

Small Batch

1 small-size package cake mix	¼ cup salad (cooking) oil
	1 egg

Mix together and drop by teaspoons on ungreased cookie sheet. Bake in 350-degree oven for 10 to 12 minutes.

Big Batch

1 regular-size package cake mix	½ cup salad (cooking) oil
	2 eggs

Mix together and bake as for small batch.

Don Hansen in 1985.

DON HANSEN'S ITALIAN SPAGHETTI

Meatballs

1 pound hamburger
1 egg
Parsley

1 bud garlic, diced
1 tablespoon cheese

Form into balls and brown before dropping into the sauce.

Sauce

In a 2-quart saucepan, put 2 to 4 tablespoons olive oil or bacon grease, 1 large diced onion, 1 bud garlic; add parsley to taste. Fry until clear. Add 2 cans tomato paste and 6 cans water. Simmer over low heat approximately 4 hours. After 1 hour, add grated Parmesan cheese to taste and the meatballs. You can add more water if it gets too thick.

About 20 minutes before serving, cook the spaghetti as usual, adding salt to help keep it from sticking. Serve with lots of garlic bread!

Don Hansen was born and raised in Shenandoah. He can trace his interest in radio back to his childhood friendship with Ed May, Jr. When Ed junior went to the broadcasting studios, Don would go with him. While he was still in high school, Don became a part-time announcer with KMA. In 1974, after attending the Radio Engineering Institute in Omaha, Don returned to KMA and became a full-time member of the staff as chief announcer and music director. In August 1981 Don was promoted to program director. It is unfortunate that his grandmother, Edith Hansen, did not live long enough to see her grandson working in such an important capacity at the radio station where she was so popular.

CRAIGHTON KNAU'S SWEDISH RYE BREAD

1 package dry yeast
¼ cup lukewarm water
1 teaspoon sugar
¼ cup brown sugar
¼ cup light molasses
1 tablespoon salt

2 tablespoons shortening
1½ cups hot water
2½ cups medium rye flour
3½ tablespoons caraway seed
4 cups (about) white flour

Combine yeast, water, and sugar; set aside to dissolve. Combine brown sugar, molasses, salt, and shortening in a big bowl and add the hot water; stir until dissolved. Let cool to lukewarm. Beat in the rye flour, add the yeast mixture and the caraway seed, and mix well. (Be sure to add the caraway seed; it adds much to the flavor.) Add enough white flour to make a soft dough. Let rest 10 minutes, covered, and then turn out on a floured board and knead until smooth and satiny—about 10 minutes. Put in greased bowl, cover, and let rise until double. Punch down. Put on board and cut in two. Knead each lightly and shape into a round loaf. Put the two loaves on a large greased baking sheet or into 2 greased loaf pans.

Cover and let rise until almost double, about 1½ hours. Bake at 375 degrees for 25 to 30 minutes. Cover the loaves with foil the last 10 minutes so they don't get too brown.

Craighton Knau in 1987.

When he arrived at KMA in 1976, Craighton Knau was already a veteran of twenty-eight years in farm broadcasting and agricultural promotion. As head of the KMA farm department, he traveled to far-away lands, met with people in high places (such as presidents and U.S. secretaries of agriculture), and participated in cook-out contests and livestock shows. He would return to the microphone to tell listeners what he had seen and heard on the world scene and how the information related to the midwestern farm experience.

Craighton's sudden death from a heart attack on December 5, 1987, was a tremendous shock to his friends, colleagues, and the radio listeners who had grown to depend on him for information. Farmers and farming were of vital importance to Craighton.

CRAIGHTON'S GRILLED PORK LOIN

5 to 6 pounds boned pork loins   ¼ cup creamy peanut butter
½ cup orange juice

Tie pork loins together at 2-inch intervals with the fat sides out. Balance roast on spit and secure with holding forks; insert meat thermometer. Season with salt and pepper. Roast until meat thermometer reads 185 degrees or till roast shows no pink inside. Allow about 3½ hours cooking time.

Combine orange juice and peanut butter. Brush the peanut butter sauce on roast and continue cooking and basting for 15 minutes.

After Craighton Knau's death, Mike LePorte moved up from associate farm director to become head of the farm department. Mike started his broadcast career as a high school intern at KMA from 1966 through 1967. Later he worked as a newscaster and news director at WREN in Topeka, Kansas, and as an anchorman at KHAS-TV in Hastings, Nebraska. In 1984 he returned to KMA as associate farm director when Jim Ross Lightfoot left that position to become a member of the U.S. Congress.

Mike became director of the farm department in December 1987. In September 1990, he moved from KMA to radio station KRVN in Lexington, Nebraska, where his work parallels that done in Shenandoah.

Mike LePorte in 1990.

MIKE LePORTE'S HUNGARIAN CHEESE SPREAD

1 8-ounce package cream
   cheese
¼ pound butter
3 tablespoons sour cream
3–4 green onions, chopped
   (including stalks)
1 tablespoon Hungarian
   paprika

1½ teaspoons caraway seeds
¼ pound ricotta cheese
   (or cottage cheese)
1 tablespoon anchovy paste
1 tablespoon capers
   (for garnish)
4 anchovies (for garnish)

Bring cream cheese and butter to room temperature; put in bowl along with remaining ingredients; blend well. Transfer mixture to a serving plate and shape into a smooth mound. Garnish with anchovies and capers. Makes approximately 1½ cups. Serve as a dip with chips or with slices of rye bread as a spread.

Randy Rassmussen arrived in Shenandoah to take the position as KMA farm director on November 5, 1990. He brought with him a broad background of experience in radio, producing, and preparing agricultural products. He was raised on a dairy farm near Morgan, Minnesota, the youngest of four children. He attended technical school in agribusiness and worked in that field for five years before going to Brown Institute in Minneapolis to study broadcasting. After graduation he worked four years at WNAX, Yankton, South Dakota, and three years at KMNS in Sioux City, Iowa, before coming to KMA.

Randy quickly picked up the routine set by previous KMA farm directors, traveling to various conventions, agricultural shows, and fairs. He shares what he learned with the farmers of the Midwest. When appropriate, Randy sprinkles his programs with suggestions based on his experiences in his family's farming operation. He also includes ideas for food raising, preparing, and preserving.

RANDY RASSMUSSEN'S GRILLED PORK CHOPS

American-cut pork chops

Honey barbecue sauce

Randy Rassmussen, KMA farm director, looks the part of an expert chef. Barbecueing, especially with pork, is one of his favorite pastimes.

Slow cook the chops on low heat on a smokeless grill until pork has a grayish center. Baste the cuts with a honey barbecue sauce. Commercial honey sauce is available, like the Sioux Bee Barbecue Sauce, but any will do if it has a high honey content; the honey seals in the juices. Remove from grill after sauce has a chance to warm on the meat. You can make your own honey barbecue sauce as well. American chops are the thick pork chops with the bone removed.

Tom Beavers has had two hitches with KMA. Soon after he graduated from college in 1960, he became KMA's associate farm director. In 1965 he left to pursue an insurance and banking career in Shenandoah. In 1984 he rejoined KMA, first as a salesman and then, in 1989, as associate farm director. Besides carrying out his regular duties, he assists with sales and with special events, such as the station's annual Fall Festival.

KMA staff members take turns hosting visitors on tours through the radio station. Tom Beavers enjoyed guiding this family, who stopped in on a vacation trip to southwest Iowa.

"I like cooking on our gas grill with the usual steaks, hamburgers, and the like, but my wife, Pat, is really the cook in our family," Tom insists. "However, I am happy to share the recipes which have been favorites of mine for years."

TOM BEAVERS' MISSISSIPPI MUD CAKE

1 cup margarine or butter	1½ cups flour
2 cups sugar	1 teaspoon vanilla
4 eggs	1 cup coconut
½ cup cocoa	1½ cups nuts (optional)
¾ teaspoon salt	

Cream together the margarine or butter and sugar. Mix in the eggs. Sift dry ingredients together and add. Stir flavoring and nuts in last. Bake in a greased 9 × 13 × 2 pan for 30 to 35 minutes. Remove from the oven and spread with a 7-ounce jar of marshmallow creme. Then frost with cocoa frosting.

Cocoa Frosting

½ cup cocoa
½ cup margarine or butter
½ teaspoon vanilla

⅛ teaspoon salt
⅓ cup cream or milk
1 pound powdered sugar

Combine ingredients. Spread over top of cooled cake.

Tom reports this is very rich, full of calories, and a little goes a long way.

BEAVERS FAMILY HAMBURGER STROGANOFF

½ cup minced onion
¼ cup butter or margarine
1 pound ground beef
1 clove garlic, minced
2 tablespoons flour
1 teaspoon salt
⅛ teaspoon msg.
¼ teaspoon pepper

¼ teaspoon paprika
½ pound sliced fresh
    mushrooms (or 1 small can)
1 can cream of chicken soup
1 cup sour cream
½ package noodles
½ teaspoon caraway seed
Parsley for garnish

Sauté onion in butter. Add hamburger and garlic and cook, stirring often. Combine flour, salt, pepper, msg., and paprika and add to meat mixture. Simmer on low for 10 minutes; then add soup and sour cream and continue to simmer mixture while noodles are prepared. Cover noodles with boiling, salted water and add caraway seed. When tender, drain and rinse with cold water. Add noodles to meat mixture OR serve meat mixture over noodles. Top with parsley.

This is an old family favorite that started with an aunt of Tom's and has continued to be passed from relative to relative in the manner close families have of keeping recipes alive.

Not many radio stations have a full-time promotion and special events director who is a jack-of-all trades, but KMA has one. Chuck Morris came to KMA in 1980 to head the sports department. He served for a time as KMA's program director before heading up the

Promotion director Chuck Morris, 1990.

promotion department. Chuck announces, does engineering, "runs the board," gives the weather, and has, on occasion, given recipes when the need arose.

Chuck's wife, Monica, who is presently a schoolteacher, has also worked at KMA as a newscaster, broadcaster, and editor for the *KMA Open Line* publication.

CHUCK MORRIS'S PRIME RIB

Select a standing rib roast at your grocer's and have him cut it, allowing ¾ of a pound for each person to be served. Preheat your oven to 325 degrees. Place the beef in your roaster with the fat side up. Incidentally, I put a rack in the bottom of our roaster. By putting the beef fat side up, the meat will baste itself while cooking. Before placing this in the oven, I sprinkle a salt-and-pepper mixture on top of the meat, using approximately ¾ tablespoon of salt and ¾ tablespoon of pepper.

For the proper cooking time in our oven, I use the following chart:
Rare—25–27 minutes per pound
Medium—28–30 minutes per pound
Well done—32–36 minutes per pound
In the latter stages of cooking, I periodically check the meat for proper doneness by removing it from the oven and slicing through the fat. I've found the above chart to be quite accurate.

When the meat is done and removed from the oven, I prepare the Au Jus. The water is already boiling when I dissolve beef bouillon cubes into it at the rate of 4 cubes for every 1 cup of water. The Au Jus is then placed in a gravy boat on the table so everybody can use the amount they want to taste.

This is simple and that's why I like it—not to mention the great taste when served with a baked potato and vegetable of your choice.

Ned Dermody was a newscaster with KMA from 1971 to 1990. He began his career at KXEO in Mexico, Missouri, and worked in a number of other stations before coming to Shenandoah. He joined veteran newscaster Ralph Childs in the KMA news department in 1971.

Newscaster Ned Dermody in 1990.

After Ralph's death, Ned was chosen to head the news department. He was recognized through the years for his devotion to broadcast journalism. He held offices on various boards of directors, including the Missouri Radio and Television News Association, Iowa UPI Broadcasters, Iowa AP Broadcasters, the Northwest Broadcast News Association in Minneapolis, and the Radio and Television Directors Association. The KMA news department won more than fifty awards in regional and national competitions during Ned's years with the station.

NED DERMODY'S ICEBOX CAKE

Melt 2 squares of German sweet chocolate in 2 tablespoons of hot water. Remove from heat. Add 2 tablespoons of sugar, 4 egg yolks, and ¾ cup nuts (walnuts are best). Fold in ½ pint whipping cream (unwhipped) and 4 stiffly beaten egg whites. In a 9 × 13 pan, alternate this mixture with a small box of vanilla wafers or chunks of angel food cake (I prefer the angel food). Leave in refrigerator overnight. Top with whipped cream, Cool Whip, or nothing at all. Eat the first piece yourself or you may not get any—it goes that fast.

Bill Bone, raised in Prairie City, Iowa, arrived at KMA following his college studies at Northwest Missouri State University. He majored in speech and broadcasting and joined the KMA news department in 1973. When Ned Dermody left the news staff in 1990, Bill became head of the news department.

Bill is an excellent newsman and a world traveler of renown. In 1988 he went on a KMA Trade Mission information-gathering trip to Taiwan, South Korea, Japan, and Hong Kong. In 1989 he was chosen to spend one month in Seoul with the Rotary International Group Study Exchange Program. Bill finds news reporting interesting, for each day is different. He classifies as most exciting the weather emergencies that KMA newspeople handle so well. With assistance from other departments, they fan out around the territory to report heavy thunderstorms, warn of tornado sightings, alert listeners to potential flooding, and suggest safety measures.

Director of the KMA news department, Bill Bone.

During emergencies, Bill's post is in the studio coordinating the efforts. "One of the reasons I stay put is my awful sense of direction," Bill explains. "If I am in the station, everyone else knows where I am, and they don't have to go out hunting for me when I get lost."

BILL BONE'S GREEK GRILLED CHICKEN

6 *whole chicken breasts*	2 *teaspoons dried thyme leaves*
½ *cup olive oil*	1 *teaspoon salt*
½ *cup lemon juice*	½ *teaspoon freshly ground*
¼ *cup dried oregano leaves*	*pepper*

Combine ingredients (with exception of chicken) in a glass jar. Shake well. Pour over chicken and marinate, covered, for 4 hours at room temperature or overnight in the refrigerator. Grill chicken, basting frequently with mixture.

BILL BONE'S CHOCOLATE SHEET CAKE

2 sticks margarine
4 tablespoons cocoa
1 cup water
2 cups sugar
2 cups flour

1 teaspoon soda
1 teaspoon salt
½ cup buttermilk
2 eggs
2 teaspoons vanilla

Bring margarine, cocoa, and water to a boil. Combine dry ingredients and pour melted mixture over. Stir well. Add buttermilk, eggs, and vanilla last. Beat well. Bake in a greased jelly roll pan for 30 minutes at 350 degrees.

Frosting

1 stick margarine
4 tablespoons cocoa
6 tablespoons buttermilk

1 pound powdered sugar
1 teaspoon vanilla

Combine margarine, cocoa, and buttermilk in a pan and bring to boil. Remove from fire and stir in powdered sugar and vanilla. Beat well. Frost cake while it is hot.

BILL OVERBEY'S PORK CHOPS MEXICALI

6 Iowa chops
1 teaspoon salt and pepper to taste
¾ cup uncooked regular rice
1½ to 2½ tablespoons taco seasoning mix

1 8-ounce can tomato sauce
1½ cups water
½ cup shredded cheddar cheese
1 medium green pepper, cut in rings

Brown chops. Arrange in baking pan. Sprinkle rice around chops. Combine seasoning, tomato sauce, and water. Pour over chops and rice. Cover tightly with foil. Bake 1¼ hours at 350 degrees. Remove from oven 10 minutes before done. Sprinkle green pepper rings and cheese over surface. Cover again and continue baking until completely cooked. Serves 6.

Bill Overbey, 1990.

BILL OVERBEY'S SPANISH SALAD

¼ cup oil
2 tablespoons wine vinegar
¾ teaspoon salt
½ teaspoon coriander
⅛ teaspoon pepper

3 oranges, sliced thin
½ cup red onions, sliced thin
8 cups greens
½ cup ripe olives

Toss all ingredients together and serve chilled.

Bill Overbey is an enthusiastic culinary expert who gladly shares his recipes. His career with the May Seed & Nursery Company started in 1947 in the advertising office. In 1949 he was promoted to advertising manager. He came to the radio studios with increasing frequency to assist with Ed May's noon weather and gardening program when Ed was out of town. He soon became a favorite guest on the homemaker programs, especially with Colleen Ketcham on "Saturday with Colleen." He is an excellent cook and has shared many of his recipes over the air.

Bill retired in 1985, but as is true of many active persons, he is a "working" retiree. He is busy with volunteer activities, especially in the Shenandoah public library and the local little theater group. He continues to drop by the radio station to do special broadcasts about the library.

DEAN ADKINS'S POTATO SUPREME

12 large potatoes, cooked and
  mashed
1 8-ounce package cream
  cheese
1 pint sour cream

1½ teaspoons garlic salt
Pepper to taste
1½ cups grated cheese
  (optional)

Combine mashed potatoes, cream cheese, sour cream, garlic salt, and pepper to taste. Put in a baking dish and bake in a slow oven (250 degrees) for 1 hour. Sprinkle grated cheese over the top for the last 10 minutes of cooking.

Dean says, "This can also be cooked on low in the crockpot for a couple of hours or so. It is a good recipe for Sunday go-to-meetin' dinners. It's delicious."

Dean Adkins, the youngest of the on-air full-time staff at KMA, was born and raised on a farm near Council Bluffs, Iowa, the sixth of seven children. He graduated from Iowa State University in 1986 with a degree in speech communications and broadcast journalism. He worked in radio in Indiana and then joined the KMA staff in September 1987. Dean hosts the popular "Elephant Shop," a morning program started by Dave White and originally called "The White Elephant Shop." It is a program for people who have items to sell or give away. Dean also has a three-hour afternoon variety program, and he fills in on board shifts and with sports announcing. He is an entertainer, singer, actor, and general all-around good guy.

Dean Adkins, host of the "Elephant Shop" and KMA's afternoon variety program.

In the spring of 1990, Dean announced over the air that he was newly engaged to Kris McClintock of Essex, saying "the wedding will be in a year or so." The "Elephant Shop" phone rang off the wall that day as the listeners congratulated the young man. Dean told his listeners that his interest in recipes and cooking has increased tremendously since this momentous event.

Andy Andersen has held many positions at KMA and KFNF in Shenandoah and at KWWL in Waterloo, Iowa. He came to KMA in 1961 to work in the sales department and as a part-time sportscaster. He advanced to head the sales department in 1969 and in 1971 became general manager for KMA. He retired from that position in 1987. He continues to do public relations work for the station and serves as guide for several of the "See the USA with KMA" tours each year.

Several KMA staff members traveled to Florida to visit the Kansas City Royals spring training camp. Andy Andersen, reverting to his first love— sports—accompanied newscaster Susan Cochran to interview the professional ball players as they began their 1988 season.

Known for his fertile imagination, Andy conceived the idea of a book department for KMA and brought me in as its director in 1983. He has an abiding interest in preserving and handing down from one generation to the next the stories, recipes, and cooking techniques of the people who have been part of the KMA scene through the years. He encouraged me in my efforts to preserve the history of the radio homemakers.

Andy's insistence that he wanted his mother's bean soup recipe included in this book inspired me to develop this "Men in the Kitchen" chapter.

"When I was first married, my wife made bean soup and it didn't taste at all like my mother's," Andy laughs. "Finally, I convinced my wife to put in some potatoes. She tried it, she liked it, and I've been happy ever since."

ANDY'S MOTHER'S BEAN SOUP

1 pound navy beans (Great
  Northern)
Generous ham bone (preferred)
  or smoked hocks

2 medium onions
2 medium potatoes (red)

Sort and wash beans. Put in a 4-quart pan along with bone or hocks. Cover with water and include diced onions. Cook till nearly done, approximately 2 hours. Add diced potatoes. Cook till done. Salt and pepper to taste.

ANDY ANDERSEN'S "LIKE IT THIS WAY" SAUERBRATEN

1½ pounds round steak
1 envelope brown gravy mix
1 tablespoon instant onion
1 tablespoon brown sugar
1 teaspoon Worcestershire sauce

2 tablespoons red wine vinegar
¼ teaspoon ground ginger
½ teaspoon salt
Hot buttered noodles

Cut meat in 1-inch squares and brown in hot shortening. Remove meat from skillet. Add gravy mix and 2 cups water. Bring to a boil. Stir in next 6 ingredients. Add meat. Turn into 1½-quart casserole. Cover. Bake at 350 degrees for 1½ hours. Serve on noodles.

This picture was taken in the fall of 1952 at Cottonwood Farm. Bob and I were going down the lane with the dog, Sparkle, to watch for the school bus that would bring Dulcie Jean from her kindergarten class.

Evelyn Birkby

No matter what you do in life you'll need to know how to talk, so talk. Go do it." My parents repeated this phrase so often I knew it by heart. Their encouragement and support didn't help the situation; following each time I spoke in public I would go home and be sick at my stomach—literally.

My father, Carl Corrie, was a Methodist minister, my mother, Mae, was a musician, so they were accustomed to speaking and performing. They took no pity on me. "Talk until it becomes easy," they insisted. "Don't stop because it makes you sick."

Speaking in public did not get easier for me until after I had attended Simpson College in Indianola, Iowa, and then taught school. After four years of teaching third-graders, I finally conquered my stage fright.

Later, when I was studying at the University of Chicago, I took many courses related to public speaking. By then I was director of youth activities at the First Methodist Church of Chicago (the Chicago Temple). My work required many public appearances, and each one gave me more self-confidence.

I returned to Iowa in 1946 to marry my Sidney high school classmate Robert Birkby. Soon I was speaking to club and church groups in the area.

In the fall of 1949, the publisher of the *Shenandoah Evening Sentinel* advertised for a farm woman to write a weekly newspaper column. By then we lived on the Green Farm south and west of Shenandoah, so I qualified as a farm wife. Robert insisted that I apply. "Writing is just putting the same words you speak down on paper," he encouraged. "Go do it." Shades of my parents! I applied, I was accepted, and I began a weekly column called "Up a Country Lane."

Like a snowball rolling down a hill, writing for a newspaper brought me other opportunities. My column was read by Doris Murphy, women's director for KMA. Ever alert for women she felt had something of value to offer radio listeners, Doris asked me to try broadcasting.

KMA decided that "Down a Country Lane" sounded more poetic than "Up," so they gave my program that title. The lilting tune "Swingin' down the Lane" was my theme music.

With a smile of friendly encouragement, announcer Warren Nielson put me on the air on May 15, 1950. When the program was finished, Warren congratulated me and pronounced the job well done. I, in turn, was happy it was over and that I had not, as I feared, ended up by being sick at my stomach.

SPECTACULAR FROZEN CORN

35 large ears sweet corn   1 pint half-and-half
½ pound butter or good-quality
   margarine

Cut corn from cob and put into 2 large roasting pans (should have 18 to 20 cups cut corn). Add butter or margarine and half-and-half. Place uncovered in 300-degree oven. Bake for 1 hour, stirring well every 15 minutes. Remove from oven and set pans in cold water to chill. (Be careful not to get water into corn.) Package and freeze. When ready to use, heat and add salt and a little sugar to taste.

In August 1950 KMA celebrated its twenty-fifth anniversary. A special broadcast was presented by the radio homemakers from the stage of the Mayfair Auditorium. As the program went on the air, I was not in Shenandoah but at Cottonwood Farm sitting in our pickup truck, which was stuck in the middle of a very muddy lane. It was not the happiest moment of my life!

That evening KMA hosted a banquet at the Delmonico Hotel for staff and special guests. The skies had cleared and Robert had pulled our pickup out of the mud, so I arrived at the dinner on time. I was

KMA homemakers who greeted guests at the Mayfair Auditorium for a
special program in September 1950 are, from left, Bernice Currier, Doris
Murphy, Evelyn Birkby, Ann Mason (visiting specialist from New York),
Adella Shoemaker, and Edith Hansen.

still not reconciled to the circumstances that made me miss my
broadcast; however, it was pleasant to be able to attend the dinner
and know I was part of KMA at this momentous time.

After our marriage, Robert and I made our first home in Shenandoah. Our apartment was just a block from KMA, and I often walked
down the alley to the Mayfair Auditorium to watch the homemakers
as they broadcast from the stage. They became my teachers, and their
special programs were like classes in helping me become a better
wife and housekeeper.

Little did I dream that by 1950 I would be one of the radio homemakers, too. Soon after I began my radio work, KMA sponsored a

I served as specialist Ann Mason's assistant as she presented her decorating ideas for the Homemaker Day in the Mayfair Auditorium in the fall of 1950.

program on home decoration, featuring Ann Mason of New York City. I was thrilled to stand with the other radio homemakers in the lobby of Mayfair to greet more than a thousand visitors. "We hope you enjoyed meeting us as much as we enjoyed saying 'hello' to you," Doris Murphy wrote in the *KMA Guide* following the event. "Next time you hear us on the air you'll know just how we look!"

When I first started broadcasting, Bernice Currier cautioned me about the problems with recipes. "They are booby traps," she warned. "No matter how careful you are in giving a recipe—or writing it down or having it printed—it can trip you up. Numbers get transposed and quantities suddenly grow or shrink. Ingredients can disappear altogether.

"Think about the recipes," she continued. "Be conscious of what they should include. Test them so you are familiar with the way they go together and with the results. Never relax—recipes will clobber you if you do." Another time Bernice told me, "Being a radio homemaker is one of the greatest opportunities a person can have. You'll learn something new every day. What you don't already know, your listeners will teach you. It is like a classroom in living."

GOURMET CHICKEN

1 can crescent rolls
1 5-ounce can boned chicken
1 8-ounce package cream
  cheese

2 ounces water chestnuts,
  chopped
Salt and pepper to taste

Roll out dough very thin and cut into squares. (Can make your own yeast dough, if desired.) Combine remaining ingredients. Spoon a portion of this chicken mixture onto each section of thin dough. Pull dough up around filling like little pillows. Place on baking sheet and bake at 375 degrees for 30 minutes. For an extra touch for company, roll each packet in melted butter and then in fine bread crumbs before baking. These can be made a day or two ahead of time. Then, just before baking, roll in melted butter and bread crumbs and bake as directed. For hors d'oeuvres, make them very small and dainty. These are delicious!

In the summer of 1950, we moved to a farm we had rented seventeen miles southwest of Shenandoah. I told my listeners about the lovely row of tall cottonwood trees lining the creek at the end of our long country lane. When I asked my audience to suggest a name for the farm, Cottonwood Farm was the result.

I commuted from Cottonwood Farm until the needs of my family and the farm made it difficult to prepare a program every day and make the trip back and forth to the studio. For a time I continued broadcasting on Saturdays, and then I gave that up as well. KMA staff discussed the possibility of running a telephone line to our farmhouse but decided the cost was too great. They regretfully gave up their effort to air the first homemaker visit from a farm.

KFNF also tried to put in equipment to lift my voice over the hills between Cottonwood Farm and Shenandoah, but due to iron deposits in a nearby hill the shortwave signals were grounded, and the venture was abandoned.

One of my prized possessions is a *Shenandoah Evening Sentinel* clipping announcing that I would be on KFNF on Monday, November 1st, 1952, at 2 P.M. An enterprising promotional person had gotten ahead of the station's engineering capabilities. The program was never aired.

I was not off the air for long. In the summer of 1955, Leanna Driftmier called me into the bright, cheerful sunroom of her home for a visit. She asked me if I would consider writing a monthly article for the *Kitchen-Klatter Magazine.* "People enjoy reading your newspaper columns, and they miss hearing you on the radio. This will give them another contact with you and your down-to-earth, happy approach to life." In September 1955 my first article appeared in the *Kitchen-Klatter Magazine.*

NEIGHBOR DOROTHY'S TURKEY SOUP

4 quarts water	¼ cup uncooked rice
¼ turkey	½ cup margarine or butter
2 onions, chopped	½ cup flour
3 celery stalks, chopped	2 cups milk
2 to 3 carrots, sliced	

Stew turkey in water until meat is tender (a pressure pan will hurry the process). Remove meat from bone. Cube. Put 4 cups of the broth in a kettle and add vegetables and uncooked rice. Cook about 20 minutes over moderate heat or until tender. Combine the margarine and flour and stir into broth. Cook, stirring, until mixture thickens. Add milk, about 3 cups of cubed turkey meat, and as much of the remaining broth as desired. This is a large recipe but well worth making as the soup freezes well.

Dorothy Stewart has lived near us in Sidney for more than thirty-five years. She has become familiar to my listeners as Neighbor Dorothy.

*Bob and Dulcie Jean with their family of kittens
at Cottonwood Farm, 1952.*

1,2,3,4 ICE CREAM
(From Cottonwood Farm)

1 cup sugar	4 eggs
2 cups cream	1 teaspoon vanilla
3 cups milk	Dash salt

Beat eggs; add sugar and continue beating until thick and lemon colored. Add cream and milk and stir well. Freeze until mushy. Beat until smooth with the vanilla and salt. Return to trays and freeze till firm. This tastes nearly like homemade freezer ice cream.

In February 1957 Leanna and her husband, Martin, traveled to California for a vacation. Daughters Margery and Lucile carried on the broadcast duties. For eleven years the program had been a two-person visit, so when Lucile was suddenly hospitalized, I was asked to fill in for her on the air. I helped with the broadcasts for the next twenty-six years, which meant that when "Kitchen-Klatter" returned to the KMA airwaves in 1972, I was back where I had started.

VIRGINIA'S ELEGANT PORK CHOPS

Marinate 6 pork chops several hours or overnight in the following marinade:

2 cups soy sauce	1 tablespoon molasses
1 cup water	¾ teaspoon salt
½ cup brown sugar	

Lift chops out of marinade and place in a 9 × 13 pan. Put in a 350-degree oven, uncovered, while you prepare the following topping:

⅓ cup water	½ cup brown sugar
1 14-ounce bottle ketchup	1 tablespoon dry mustard
1 12-ounce bottle chili sauce	2 tablespoons French dressing

Bring mixture to a boil and pour over chops. Cover and bake at 350 degrees until done. Turn several times. Any leftover marinade and/or topping can be brought to a boil, cooled, poured individually into fruit jars, covered, and stored in the refrigerator or freezer until time to use again.

This recipe came from my good friend Virginia Miller. She is a gourmet cook who lives in a hundred-year-old farmhouse in southwest Iowa. She has entertained the members of my family at many elegant meals. She also shared numbers of excellent recipes with me, which I have given over the air and printed in my newspaper column. This recipe for Elegant Pork Chops is one of my favorites.

The Birkby family in December 1960: Robert and I, Bob in the center, and Craig and Jeff in front.

HAY-HAND ROLLS

1 package dry yeast
1 cup lukewarm water
1 teaspoon salt
1 tablespoon sugar
3 cups water
4 cups flour

3 eggs, beaten (optional)
1 cup melted shortening or
  cooking oil
1 cup sugar or honey
10 cups flour of your choice
  (approximately)

Combine the yeast and the 1 cup of lukewarm water. When this is dissolved, stir in the salt, 1 tablespoon sugar, the water, and the 4 cups of flour. Beat this well until it is bubbly.

Cover and set aside at room temperature for several hours or overnight. This mixture becomes very spongy and is actually called a sponge by bread-making folks.

After the sponge has set for 2 or 3 hours (or overnight), add the beaten eggs, if desired, the melted and cooled shortening or oil, the sugar or honey, and enough flour to make a soft dough. Turn out on a floured breadboard and knead until smooth and elastic. Place in a greased bowl and let rise until double in bulk. Knead down, cover, and place in the refrigerator. Punch down each day.

When ready to use, remove portion of dough desired from bowl in refrigerator and let stand for 1 hour at room temperature. Knead until elastic, form into rolls, and place on greased cookie sheet. Let rise until double in bulk. Bake at 400 degrees for 20 minutes.

This recipe can be used as a basic recipe for cinnamon or other rolls. It also makes excellent loaves of bread. Shape into loaves after first rising, pat into greased loaf pans, and let rise until double in bulk. Bake at 375 to 400 degrees until the tops are golden and the loaves make a hollow sound when thumped. Turn out immediately on a rack to cool. Coat top with butter or margarine if a soft crust is desired.

For white bread use all white flour. For wheat bread, half whole-wheat flour can be used. For a great multigrained bread, cook 1 cup total of 7-grain cereal, bulgur wheat, steel-cut oats, or a combination of them in 1½ cups water until tender (just like you cook oatmeal). Add a little more water if needed to keep moist. Cool. Stir into sponge along with the flour.

This recipe came originally from a farm wife who really was making them for the men who were putting up hay. The rolls have been used in fairs and won a first-place ribbon at the Oklahoma State Fair in Tulsa. It was featured in the book *Blue Ribbon Recipes* published by Favorite Recipes Press, Louisville, Kentucky. Since I gave it the title of Hay-Hand Rolls, I know the fair participants and cookbook publishers used my recipe.

CRAIG'S FAVORITE PANCAKES

1⅓ cups flour, sifted
¼ teaspoon salt
¾ teaspoon soda

1⅓ cups buttermilk
1 egg, beaten
3 tablespoons butter or
     margarine, melted

Sift the flour and salt together. Combine the soda and buttermilk. Add to the dry ingredients and mix well. Stir in the egg and butter or margarine. Bake the cakes on a hot griddle. Serve with maple syrup.

JEFF'S FAVORITE CUTOUT COOKIES

1 cup butter or margarine	2½ cups flour
1½ cups powdered sugar	1 teaspoon soda
¼ teaspoon almond flavoring	1 teaspoon cream of tartar
1 teaspoon vanilla flavoring	¼ teaspoon salt
1 egg	

Cream butter or margarine, powdered sugar, and flavorings together. Beat in egg. Sift dry ingredients together and gradually beat in. Chill well. Roll out on floured breadboard and cut into shapes as desired. Bake on ungreased cookie sheet for 8 to 10 minutes at 375 degrees or until lightly browned.

I first met Billie Oakley in 1965 at a Shenandoah Farm and Home festival. We were judges for the parade and queen contest, and then we sat beside one another at the evening dinner. It was the beginning of a great friendship.

In 1980 Billie asked me to substitute for her on the air while she was leading a tour group to Switzerland. This led to my broadcasting over KMA whenever Billie had to be gone from her morning program.

In 1983 I resigned from the Driftmier Company and my editing and broadcasting work with Kitchen-Klatter to return to KMA to create and direct a book department and to fill in when needed as a standby broadcaster. My initial project was the *Festival Cookie Book*. In 1985 I wrote and promoted *Cooking with KMA: Featuring Sixty Years of Radio Homemakers*. My third book was *The Come Again Cookie Book*, which came off the press in 1987. During that time, I squeezed in a trip to Britain and wrote a book about my experiences, *Adventure after Sixty: Alone through England and Scotland*.

Speaking to club and church organizations is one of the joys of my continuing contact with the public. Another is the fun of being a judge in the cookie and candy divisions at the Iowa State Fair, a fattening project I have enjoyed since 1983.

Early in 1990, Billie Oakley asked me to write a regular column for her *Home Talk* magazine, so I started "The View from Honey Hill." In addition to my continuing weekly newspaper column for the *Shenandoah Evening Sentinel*, my major writing project is an autobiography based on the early years of my marriage, when I lived with my growing family on the Green Farm and Cottonwood Farm. It is entitled, appropriately, *Up a Country Lane.*

PEPPER JELLY

1 cup chopped green pepper	6 cups sugar
¼ cup canned jalapeño pepper	1 bottle liquid fruit pectin
½ cup sweet red pepper	Green food coloring, if desired
1¼ cups apple cider vinegar	

Remove and discard seeds from green pepper, chop coarsely, and measure. Rinse liquid and seeds from jalapeño pepper and discard. Place the two peppers in blender or food processor with ½ cup of the vinegar. Blend until smooth. Pour into 4-quart saucepan. Rinse the blender with remaining vinegar and add to the pepper mixture. Add sugar and the red pepper, which has been seeded and finely chopped. Bring to a hard boil that cannot be stirred down. Remove from heat and let stand a few minutes to bring foam to top. Skim off foam, being careful to leave red pepper pieces in the mixture. Stir in liquid fruit pectin and green coloring if desired. Stir until well blended. Pour into jelly glasses or small canning jars; seal with paraffin or lids.

Some liquid fruit pectin now comes in little foil-like bags. I used two in the package for this recipe, as the bags indicated they were measured out to equal half of the old bottle measure. It was exactly right for the jelly consistency desired.

This is excellent served with meat dishes. It is also good as a snack when served with crackers and cream cheese.

As is true for all radio homemakers, my listeners followed the experiences of my family. Dulcie Jean died suddenly on April 14, 1953, at the age of five and one-half years. Even though a pathologist performed an autopsy, the infection that took her life was never identified. The year after Dulcie Jean's death Jeff was born, and twenty-two months later, Craig.

FROZEN COLESLAW

1 medium head of cabbage   1 teaspoon salt

Shred cabbage and add the salt. Let set for 1 hour. Make dressing by bringing to a boil and boiling for 1 minute:

1 cup vinegar   1 teaspoon mustard seed
¼ cup water   1 teaspoon celery seed
2 cups sugar

Let cool. Shred 1 carrot and chop 1 green pepper. Drain cabbage thoroughly. Combine cabbage, carrot, green pepper, and dressing. Pack in cartons and freeze.

Craig had a battle with testicular cancer in 1986 just as he was concluding his medical residency. In 1987 I had three serious surgeries, including one for colon cancer. Early diagnosis and excellent medical care brought both of us through these troublesome times. As they had from the beginning of my radio career, listeners expressed loving concern through their letters, phone calls, and prayers and helped our entire family as we coped with the difficulties involved. Their messages indicated also that since I had shared my problems with them, they were helped to adjust to their own life experiences. Radio continues to offer a channel for neighboring.

My son Bob is a writer as well as a wilderness instructor and guide who claims the Pacific Northwest as his home. Under the name of Robert Birkby he writes for a number of outdoor and Scouting magazines. He edited the new *Boy Scout Field Book* in 1984 and wrote *KMA Radio: The First Sixty Years*, published in 1985 for the station's sixtieth anniversary. His book *How to Canoe in One Day* was published in 1989, and in 1990 he authored the tenth edition of the *Boy Scout Handbook*. Middle son Jeff is project manager of the National Center of Appropriate Technology based in Butte, Montana. His work involves conservation, renewable energy, and recycling. Craig, a dermatology surgeon, was married in July 1989 to fellow dermatologist Sharon Nicolazzi. They live in the Seattle area and practice their specialties in Edmonds and Ballard.

Robert and I live in Sidney in the house we built in 1963 on six acres we christened Honey Hill. The long drive in front of the house is covered with asphalt, a great improvement over the muddy country lane at Cottonwood Farm.

BOB'S SOPAIPILLAS

1 package dry yeast
½ cup lukewarm water
1 teaspoon sugar
1 egg, lightly beaten

2 teaspoons salt
1 tablespoon melted shortening
 or oil
½ cup water
3 cups flour (about)

Combine yeast, water, and sugar. Let dissolve about 4 or 5 minutes. Stir in egg. Add salt, shortening, and water. Add flour, stirring, until dough is thick and still sticky. Put about ¼ cup flour on breadboard. Roll and knead dough until springy and not sticky. Take 8 or 10 minutes to knead well. Place in greased bowl, turning once to grease all sides of dough. Let rise, covered, for 1 hour or until double in bulk.

Punch down. Place on lightly floured board. Knead a few times and then roll out with rolling pin until about ¾ inch thick. Cut into oblong pieces about 2 by 3 inches in size (2-inch square pieces work nicely, also). Let rise right on the board about 15 minutes. Drop, top side first, into hot shortening (365 degrees on deep fat thermometer). When brown on one side, turn and brown on the other. Drain on paper towels. Serve hot with honey.

My anniversary broadcast, 1990.

May 15, 1990, found me sitting in the KMA broadcast room ready to go on the air for the fortieth anniversary of my first radio broadcast. The theme song, "Swingin' down the Lane," and the same words the announcer used when he put me on the air on May 15, 1950, were used again. The program featured Edward May, Sr., from Tucson and Ed May, Jr., from Omaha, as well as my sons Bob, who flew in from Seattle, and Jeff, who came from Butte. Susan Christensen, KMA's general manager, shared the microphone, and the rest of my family lent their moral support. Next, Billie Oakley had me on the air for her "Home Talk" broadcast. Then Verlene Looker hosted her "Lifestyles" program, with former station manager Andy Andersen and Billie reminiscing about my years in radio. I joined them for the final moments of the program. By the end of that hour and a half, my professional life had been thoroughly perused.

When we left the broadcast room, a party had begun. Rain was pouring down outside the studio to remind me of that earlier KMA anniversary in 1950 when a torrential rain fell and I was stuck in the muddy lane at Cottonwood Farm. But nothing could dampen my enthusiasm; I felt surrounded by the love of every colleague and listener I had known on radio since that first program forty years before.

PELLA APPLE BREAD

1 cup sugar
½ cup vegetable shortening or
   margarine
¼ cup sour milk or buttermilk
1 teaspoon soda
2 eggs

1 teaspoon vanilla flavoring
2 cups flour
½ teaspoon salt
2 cups raw apples, peeled and
   finely diced
½ cup chopped nuts

Cream sugar and shortening. Combine sour milk or buttermilk and soda. Stir into creamed mixture. Add eggs, vanilla, flour, and salt. Beat well. Lastly, fold in apples and nuts. Put in greased and floured bread pan.

Topping

2 tablespoons butter or
   margarine
2 tablespoons sugar

2 tablespoons flour
1 teaspoon cinnamon

Mix all ingredients together. Drop by bits on top of apple batter in the pan. Press in lightly with a fork. Bake at 350 degrees for 45 to 50 minutes, until done. Turn out on cooling rack. Excellent eaten warm. Very good cold. Freezes well.

During 1975 and 1976 I was on the Iowa Bicentennial Commission. The commissioners were in Pella during the city's tulip festival and we were served this elegant apple bread. It has become one of my favorite quick breads.

On May 15, 1990, KMA hosted a reception honoring me on the fortieth
anniversary of my original broadcast of my morning homemaker show
"Down a Country Lane." Shown with me in the memorabilia room at
station KMA are, from left, my sons Jeff and Bob, Edward May Senior, Ed
May Junior, and my husband, Robert.

SIDNEY RODEO BARBECUE

10 pounds ground beef	1 cup brown sugar
3 cups grated or chopped onion	¼ cup prepared mustard
3 tablespoons salt	¼ cup vinegar
¾ teaspoon pepper	1½ tablespoons Worcestershire
3 cups tomato juice	sauce
3 cups catsup	3 to 4 cups rolled oats
	(uncooked)

Brown meat and onion. Drain off excess fat. Add remaining ingredients except for oats. Simmer, stirring frequently, 30 minutes. Add
oats; cook 10 minutes longer. Serve hot on buns; makes 60.

Florence beside the Falk mailbox that holds an outline of the Old Red Rooster.

Florence Falk

A tornado and a creek propelled Florence Falk into her professional career, and her life as a radio homemaker was similar to both. She worked with the intensity of a whirlwind, and her homey, rural ways were like the flow of the stream through the back pasture.

Broadcasting was a godsend for Florence. The year 1949 had brought a devastating tornado to the Falk farm near Essex, Iowa. After the disaster, Florence appeared on both Adella Shoemaker's and Bernice Currier's broadcasts; listeners responded favorably. In August 1952 when Adella began her syndicated broadcasts, Florence was asked to audition for the position of resident KMA homemaker.

And here is where the creek came into importance. Florence had always pronounced it "crick," with a short *i* rather than a long *e* sound. Owen Saddler, then station manager, liked the natural, country pronunciation and felt that this farm woman conveyed a down-home approach that would appeal to listeners.

Florence started on the air in August after doing a number of introductory broadcasts with Adella. By September she was actually broadcasting from the dining room of her farm home, some eight miles north and east of Shenandoah. Her program was called "The Farmer's Wife." As far as anyone can discover, she became the first radio homemaker to actually send out her programs live from a farm.

On "The Farmer's Wife," Florence talked about such things as the mailman driving by, someone's having a flat tire, her most recent activity or trip, and the time when "the Farmer" fell into the stock tank. Life was never dull for Florence, and she made life exciting for all with whom she came in contact.

SOUR CREAM APPLE PIE

2 tablespoons flour
⅛ teaspoon salt
¾ cup sugar
1 egg

1 cup sour cream
½ teaspoon vanilla
2 cups chopped apples

Sift flour, salt, and sugar. Add beaten egg, cream, and vanilla, and beat. Add apples. Put in pie shell (no top crust). Bake 15 minutes in a 400-degree oven. Reduce heat to 350 degrees and bake 30 minutes more.

Crumb Topping

⅓ cup sugar
⅓ cup flour

1 teaspoon cinnamon
¼ cup butter

Blend together and sprinkle over top of pie. Sprinkle with nutmeg. Return to 350-degree oven and bake 10 minutes more.

CINNAMON APPLESAUCE TOAST

This toast is good as "snackers" or "go-betweens." Butter each toast slice, sprinkle with cinnamon-sugar mixture, and toast sugar-side-up in a moderate oven (350 degrees) for 5 minutes. To serve, spoon hot applesauce on each slice of cinnamon toast and top with two half-slice toast triangles.

Karenann Falk Manley vividly remembers the tornado that affected the lives of the members of the Falk family so dramatically:

"It happened on June 6, 1949, at 6:05. The day had been hot and humid. Mother made strawberry jam; Dad worked in the field. Bruce, who was seven years old, and I (I was nine) had attended Bible school in the morning.

"As the day went on, it got hotter and the wind picked up. Modern weather forecasts were not as yet developed and no warning was

Byron surveys the tornado damage done to the Falk farm in 1949.

given. Just as we sat down for our evening meal, everything became dark and the wind increased in intensity. Hail began to fall, and Bruce and I went out on the front porch and picked up some. We put them in the refrigerator in the basement. They were cold, sharp, pointed things that looked like hedge balls.

"About that time, Dad looked out the window and saw the tornado moving across the fields. It was huge, black, and about a block wide, moving like a giant roller along the ground. We rushed out to the car, which Mother had uncharacteristically parked facing out of the driveway, and drove as fast as we could toward Essex. We were going at right angles to the storm, which undoubtedly saved our lives.

"After the storm was over we returned to the farm. Everything was gone except for a few dead animals. EVERYTHING! No buildings, no trees, no garden, no house. All that was left in the basement were the cream separator, the refrigerator that held the hailstones, and the foundation bricks piled on top of the ruined furnace. If we had gone to the basement for protection we would never have survived.

"Neighbors were searching through the rubble looking for us— they did not know we had gotten away. As midwesterners do in time of trouble, more friends came and helped with the cleanup. They brought us clothes, household items, canned goods—all the things needed to start life again.

"Mother grieved over the loss of little things, our baby pictures, for example. Mother had lost all the treasured family recipes and the cookie sheet that was the only item she had owned which had been her mother's. Although in many ways she never got over the effects of that terrible day, she felt the experience deepened her faith in God and gave her added courage she might not have had otherwise."

COTTAGE CHEESE SOUFFLE

Melt 2 tablespoons butter in saucepan; add 2 tablespoons chopped onion and cook until light brown. Stir in 2 tablespoons flour and 1 teaspoon dry mustard. Add 1 cup milk and cook over low heat until slightly thickened, stirring constantly. Add:

1 cup creamed cottage cheese	⅛ teaspoon paprika
1 teaspoon salt	1 teaspoon Worcestershire sauce
Dash pepper	

Continue cooking over low heat until all ingredients are thoroughly mixed. Remove from heat and add 3 beaten egg yolks. Beat 3 egg whites until stiff and fold into the above mixture. Turn into buttered baking dish. Set in pan of hot water and bake 35 minutes or until firm in 350-degree oven.

The tornado was not the first catastrophe to affect the Falk family. In 1942 a fire destroyed all the outbuildings on the farm. These were rebuilt, only to be annihilated along with the house in the 1949 tornado.

The family carried no insurance, and after the tornado they moved

The Old Red Rooster became the symbol for Florence's programs. She did her broadcasts live from her farm home, usually from the table in the dining room. Obviously, the rooster was sometimes part of the program.

in with cousins in Essex for a short time. Then Byron and Florence decided that the only permanent place they could afford was Byron's old family home.

The farmhouse had been empty and untended for a number of years. Moths were in the carpet, wallpaper was hanging in strips, plaster was crumbling down, and mold and an accumulation of years of dirt were layered over everything. The house had no electricity or water. It was all they had, so Florence and her family turned to the difficult task of making the place livable.

It was in the dining room of this now pleasant home, on a small table given to Florence by a neighbor after the tornado, that "The Farmer's Wife" program originated over KMA for eleven years.

Florence and her younger sister, LaVerne, were born to Charles and Lydia Karlsson. Mr. Karlsson had emigrated from Sweden to southwest Iowa, where he obtained employment. When he had enough money, he sent for his wife, Lydia, to join him. Their two children were born north of Shenandoah near the town of Essex.

When Florence was three years old, her mother experienced the loss of a leg and soon died. Mr. Karlsson worked as a thresher, taking his two tiny girls with him to play along the fencerows while he worked. It soon became evident that this was not a safe environment. An adoptive home with the Lundeens was found for LaVerne, and the Charles Englund family of Essex took Florence to raise as their own. Charles Karlsson then disappeared from the lives of his two little girls.

The Englunds were excellent parents to raise the rambunctious red-haired Florence. She was taught the arts of homemaking and later helped her foster mother with catering, sometimes in the nearby hotel in Essex.

Florence attended country school, Essex High School, the Iowa State Teachers College in Cedar Falls, and the University of Colorado in Boulder. She taught in the historic Page County Goldenrod country school (where Leanna Driftmier's sister, Jessie Field Shambaugh, was teaching when she originated the 4-H club movement). She also taught in town schools in Yorktown and Essex.

Florence married Byron Falk on Sweden's Midsummer's Day, June 24, 1939. They had two children. Bruce Falk now lives and teaches in Joliet, Illinois. Karenann Falk Manley lives in Essex and is a teacher in the local school system. Florence's youngest grandson, Scott, is a student in the Essex high school. Her two older grandsons are Eric Manley, who lives in Bloomington, Illinois, and Wayne Manley, who resides in Oakland, Iowa.

Florence was a down-to-earth person whose early struggles made her practical, efficient, and almost unflappable. She shared every detail of her family life on the farm with the listeners: her husband, Byron, whom she always called "the Farmer" on her broadcasts, their two children Karenann and Bruce, five border collies who, in sequence, were named Tippy, and the Old Red Rooster, whose shape and sounds became the trademark of her programs.

HAM LOAVES

2 pounds ground beef   3 eggs
2 pounds ground ham   1½ cups milk
2 cups graham cracker crumbs

Mix together and shape into one large loaf or individual loaves.

Sauce

1 can tomato soup   1½ cups brown sugar
1 tablespoon prepared mustard   ½ cup vinegar

Combine ingredients in a saucepan and heat. Pour over ham loaves
and bake at 350 degrees until meat loaves are done.

Florence left KMA in 1963. She continued broadcasting from her farm home over Shenandoah station KFNF, and for a time KOAK in Red Oak, until her retirement. Her final program on KFNF was broadcast September 6, 1975. In August of that same year, Florence appeared on the air during the homemaker program celebrating KMA's fiftieth anniversary.

After a series of strokes, "the Farmer's wife" died on May 12, 1983. "The Farmer" continues to live on the family's century farm two miles east of Essex (a century farm is so designated when the members of one family have lived on the same farm for more than one hundred years). He enjoys a daily visit from his daughter, Karenann.

The mailbox that once held the outline of the Old Red Rooster still stands at the end of the driveway.

CORNMEAL MUSH

Put 3½ cups water and 1 teaspoon salt in top section of double boiler; set directly on high heat and bring to boiling point; pour 1 cup cornmeal slowly into water while constantly stirring, and cook 3 minutes. Put over lower section of boiler, which contains hot water, and cook the mush 30 minutes longer. Stir occasionally. Serve warm or cold with milk or cream, or put in molds for slicing and frying.

Mush may be cooked in this manner for 2 to 3 hours and is improved with each minute of cooking.

BUTTER MINT SALAD

1 package lime jello	½ pound marshmallows,
1 can crushed pineapple	quartered
1 package butter mints, crushed	2 cups whipping cream,
	whipped

Drain pineapple. Add water to juice to make 2 cups. Heat and dissolve jello in it. Stir in butter mints until they are dissolved. Chill until thick. Whip. Fold in pineapple, marshmallows, and whipped cream. Pour in 9 × 13 pan. Chill until set.

RICE GRIDDLE CAKES

1 cup cooked rice	1 cup flour
1 cup milk	2 teaspoons baking powder
1 tablespoon butter	1 egg, beaten
1 teaspoon salt	

Mix rice, milk, butter, well-beaten egg, and salt; gradually add and stir in flour and baking powder, sifted well together; mix well; bake on hot, slightly greased griddle, turning but once.

SNICKERDOODLES

Mix together thoroughly:	Sift together and stir in:
1 cup soft shortening	2¾ cups flour
1½ cups sugar	2 teaspoons cream of tartar
2 eggs	1 teaspoon baking soda
	½ teaspoon salt

Chill dough for 1 hour (this is important because the dough then handles much better). Roll into balls the size of a walnut. Do not flatten. Roll in a mixture of 2 tablespoons sugar and 2 teaspoons cinnamon. Place on a cookie sheet about 2 inches apart. Bake at 400 degrees about 12 to 15 minutes or until nicely browned. These may be made into smaller balls and rolled in finely chopped pecans to use for a fancy cookie. They may also be topped with a large pecan half before baking.

ROSETTES

1 cup flour	1 cup milk
½ teaspoon salt	1 tablespoon oil
2 eggs, slightly beaten	1 tablespoon sugar

Mix and strain into a deep bowl. Let stand for 1 hour before using. Heat oil ¾ inch deep to deep fat fry. Dip rosette iron into batter so ½ of iron is covered. Dip iron into fat and hold until batter is a light golden brown. Drain on paper towel. Sprinkle with powdered sugar. Eat plain, or pour creamed peas or chicken over rosette.

For a cookie, frost each rosette lightly with a colored powdered-sugar icing.

PEANUT BUTTER FUDGE

2 cups white sugar   ½ stick of butter
⅔ cup milk

Boil to soft ball stage. Remove from fire and add: 1 cup marshmallow creme and 1 cup peanut butter. Mix well and fast. Pour into buttered pan.

PECAN TASSIES

Shells

2 sticks margarine   2 cups sifted flour
2 3-ounce packages cream
   cheese

Blend well.

Roll in small balls and chill. Line tassie or very small muffin pans with dough, pressing to fit.

Filling

2 eggs   ⅛ teaspoon salt
1½ cups brown sugar   ¼ teaspoon vanilla
2 tablespoons melted butter

Combine ingredients. Beat thoroughly.

Fill each shell with 1 teaspoon chopped pecans. Then add filling to ¾ full. Bake at 350 degrees for 15 minutes, then 250 degrees for 10 minutes. Cool and carefully lift out of tins.

Florence Falk at the table display she created for one of the KMA cookie teas.

The famous early KMA cookie teas provided a showplace for the radio homemakers. Each homemaker had a table and baked her fanciest cookies. Florence always included sugar cookies, staying up for hours before the festival to put little decorations onto each cookie. She rarely used frosting but put raisins, cherries, and candy decorations on with egg white for "glue." The results were such elaborate works of art that no one wanted to eat the cookies. One year she even fashioned a complete manger scene. Her rosettes, pecan tassies, and snickerdoodles became traditions at the teas.

Along with making cookies, Florence liked to collect cookie cutters. She had a collection that numbered in the hundreds.

The Falk family's Swedish background was never more evident than when the holidays were near. Karenann and Bruce enjoyed helping their mother make cut-out cookies and rosettes just as much as Florence enjoyed having them.

SWEDISH SPRITZBAKELSER

Cream together 1 cup butter and ⅔ cup sugar. Add 3 egg yolks and mix well. Blend in 2½ cups sifted all-purpose flour. Add ½ teaspoon each almond and vanilla flavoring. Use in cookie press with the star cutter. Shape into circles or s. Bake in moderate oven (350 degrees) until delicately browned.

OSTKAKA
(From Cottage Cheese)

3 cups creamed cottage cheese   *¾ cup all-purpose flour*
¾ cup sugar   *2 cups milk*
5 eggs, beaten   *½ teaspoon almond flavoring*

Combine the cottage cheese (if necessary, drain excess liquid) with sugar and well-beaten eggs. Mix flour and milk until free from lumps. Add to cheese mixture. Fold in flavoring. Pour into greased 9-inch square pan or baking casserole. Place in water as for custards. Bake in 370-degree oven for 50 minutes. Serve with strawberry juice thickened with cornstarch for topping. Garnish with spoon of whipped cream.

SWEDISH PASTRY

1 cup all-purpose flour	1 tablespoon water
½ cup butter	

Combine the butter and flour and mix as for pie crust, adding the water to bind together. Spread on ungreased cookie sheet into two long strips about 4 inches wide and 13 inches long. Let stand while mixing the following:

In saucepan bring to a full rolling boil:

1 cup water	½ cup butter

When the mixture boils hard, add ½ cup all-purpose flour and beat very hard until all lumps disappear. Remove from heat and beat in 3 eggs, one at a time. Beat hard after each addition. Add 1 teaspoon almond flavoring and mix. Spread the mixture evenly over the two strips of unbaked pastry. Bring the batter well to the edges. Bake in a moderate 350-degree oven for 50 to 60 minutes. The mixture will puff up much as cream puffs. Remove when baked and cool. Frost with a powdered sugar frosting flavored with almond flavoring. Delicious! Cut in squares to serve.

Through the years, each of the radio homemakers took her turn at public appearances at the Iowa and Nebraska state fairs as well as many county fairs. Many times Florence had the pleasure of judging such events. In 1962 she was one of the judges for the "Best of Iowa Baking Contest" at the Iowa State Fair in Des Moines. The winner won a $500 check, a double-oven electric range, and the chance to go on to a national bake-off contest. The recipe for date nut–filled banana cake was the prizewinner.

DATE NUT–FILLED BANANA CAKE

½ cup shortening	2 cups sifted flour
1½ cups sugar	½ teaspoon baking soda
2 teaspoons vanilla	2 teaspoons baking powder
2 large eggs	½ teaspoon salt
1 cup mashed bananas	½ cup buttermilk

Cream shortening well and add sugar gradually; beat until fluffy. Add vanilla and then the eggs one at a time, beating thoroughly after each addition. Add mashed banana. Sift the dry ingredients in alternately with the buttermilk. Mix until smooth. Pour into 2 square 9-inch pans that have been oiled and floured. Bake at 350 degrees for 30 minutes. Remove from oven and let stand for 3 to 5 minutes; then turn out on wire racks until cool. Spread with filling between layers, frost with frosting and sprinkle nuts over the top.

Filling

Combine:	1 cup chopped nuts
1 8-ounce package pitted	1 cup mashed bananas
dates, finely cut	1 teaspoon lemon juice

Let stand at least 10 minutes before using.

Frosting

Combine:	¼ teaspoon salt
1 cup sugar	⅓ cup strong coffee
¼ teaspoon cream of tartar	

Cook to 240 degrees or until a small amount in cold water forms a soft ball. Beat three egg whites until stiff but not dry. Add syrup grad-

Florence had a number of opportunities to appear on television. She is shown here with Bettie Tolson, Omaha KMTV television homemaker. Florence was demonstrating some of her Swedish holiday foods.

ually, beating constantly. Add 1 teaspoon vanilla. Beat thoroughly and cool. Cream ½ cup butter, well. Add the egg white mixture 2 or 3 tablespoons at a time, beating thoroughly after each addition. Spread on top and sides of cake. Sprinkle ½ cup finely chopped English walnuts or pecans on top.

FISH CROQUETTES

To 1½ cups cold cooked flaked halibut or salmon, add 1 cup thick white sauce. If salmon is used, add lemon juice and finely chopped parsley. Season with salt and pepper and spread on a plate to cool. Make into balls or oval shapes. Roll in cracker crumbs. Combine an egg with 2 tablespoons water, beating to blend. Dip croquettes into this "egg wash" and roll in crumbs again. Fry in deep hot lard (or shortening of your choice); drain. Arrange in hot dish for serving; garnish with parsley.

Florence, Karenann, Bruce, and "the Farmer," Byron Falk, measure a
shock of grain sorghum, one of the crops raised on their farm near Essex.

The fact that Florence lived out in the country did not deter the
radio listeners who wanted to come see the farm, the family, and "the
Farmer's wife." Visitors came as early as 6:00 A.M. and they arrived
as late as 10:30 P.M. The Falks always greeted them graciously. On
regular tour days when cookies were offered to the guests, Florence
would have at least twenty-five dozen cookies baked and ready.
Homemade cookies were a treat in those days; stores did carry
cookies, but they were commercially made and packaged and did not
taste homemade.

None of the radio homemakers received any extra funds for the purchase of ingredients for all these cookies or for their time and fuel to prepare them. Even though it was exceptional public relations for the station, it was simply considered part of their job.

PRUNE KUCHEN

Cover the bottom of a baking dish with cooked and stoned prunes. Make a soft rich biscuit mixture (but do not have it stiff enough to knead) and spread this over the prunes. Let bake until done in 400- to 425-degree (hot) oven. Bake about 20 minutes. Cut in squares and serve with cream and sugar. Sliced apples or peaches or canned apricots may be used in place of the prunes.

During the eleven years she was on KMA, Florence sent out thousands of recipe sheets, contributed letters and recipes to the *KMA Guide*, assisted with the KMA cookbooks, and published her own Swedish *Smorgasbord Cookbook*. She attended every convention, fair, contest, club meeting, and church activity that time and distance permitted. She belonged to a number of professional organizations— American Women in Radio and Television, National Press Women, and Farm Women of the World, to name a few.

Coworker Bernice Currier said of Florence, "She is an indefatigable worker in civic affairs: church, school, and projects to benefit the community. She is broad-minded, well read, and welcomes people of all races and cultures into her home and onto her radio program. She has an amazing personality. Her strength and cheerfulness will be remembered by her listeners just as they will remember how she ends each of her programs with 'Keep Smiling.'"

Mary Williams

ndependent Mary Romdall had five brothers and one sister. "I came from a stretched-out family," Mary says. "Two of my brothers and my sister were a generation older than I. My sister died during the flu epidemic near the close of World War I, so by the time I was born I really was the only girl."

During World War II, death touched the Romdall family again. Mary's brother was killed while flying for the Army Air Corps in the China-Burma-India theater of war.

"I was surrounded by fliers," Mary remembers. "Most of my brothers flew, and their enthusiasm led me to grow to love flying. I decided I wanted the independence of being able to control a plane, so I took lessons and earned my pilot's license in 1948."

Flying was only a hobby for Mary. Her talent, interest, education, and profession all centered on journalism and print media.

Mary enjoys making casseroles. The one her family calls Mary's Surprise Casserole originated when a close friend of Mary's son arrived unexpectedly for a meal. "I threw everything I could find into a casserole to try and fill up those bottomless pits," Mary laughs. "Through the years I've served it many times and no one ever knows what may be in Mary's Surprise Casserole."

Mary was raised in Mexico, Missouri, where she graduated from high school. She attended Hannibal-LaGrange College in Hannibal, Missouri, and graduated from the University of Missouri School of Journalism.

For a time Mary worked on newspapers in her hometown and in Norfolk, Nebraska. In Norfolk she met Charles Williams, a radio announcer for WJAG. They were married, and their daughter, Lory, was born while they were living in Norfolk. They moved to Red Oak,

Mary interviewed Polly Stoehr, a seventy-three-year-old pilot who had flown her own plane from California to Shenandoah to participate in an International Flying Farmers' Convention. She had learned to fly at the age of sixty-four and encouraged Mary to continue flying as much as possible.

Iowa, where Charlie worked at a studio that Shenandoah station KFNF maintained. Their son, Loche, was born in Red Oak.

The family came to Shenandoah in 1955. Charlie continued with KFNF until 1957, when he began working for Central Surveys Inc. Mary worked for the *Iowan* magazine and then part-time for the *Kitchen-Klatter Magazine*. In 1963 she had her own women's program on KMA.

In 1966 Mary became editor of the *KMA Guide*. She served in that position until the magazine ceased publication in 1977. She had the longest tenure of any editor in the history of the *Guide*.

Mary retired from KMA in 1986 and is doing many activities she did not have time to do while she was employed. Her genealogy research led her to make a trip to England, Cotland Island, and Sweden. Her love of travel has led to additional trips to Portugal, Spain, China, and Canada. When she is home in Shenandoah, she volunteers her time in her church, club, community, and historical society projects.

BLUEBERRY BARS

1¾ cups sugar
1 cup butter or margarine
4 eggs
1 teaspoon vanilla
3 cups flour

1½ teaspoons baking powder
½ teaspoon salt
1 21-ounce can blueberry pie
   filling
Little ground nutmeg

Cream sugar and butter till fluffy. Add eggs and vanilla and beat well. Sift dry ingredients together. Add to creamed mixture. Stir till blended, using spoon. Spread half of dough on ungreased 15 × 10 jelly roll pan. Spread with blueberry pie filling, using spoon. Sprinkle with nutmeg. Drop remaining dough evenly over top. Bake in 350-degree oven for 45 minutes. Frost while warm with Lemon Frosting. Variation: Omit frosting and make a sugar, water, cornstarch mixture to spoon over individual servings as a dessert.

Lemon Frosting

1½ cups powdered sugar
2 tablespoons lemon juice

1 tablespoon butter, softened

Stir ingredients together and add milk to make a spreading consistency.

When Florence Falk left KMA, station manager Tony Koelker asked Mary to try broadcasting a women's program. Mary based her subject choices upon a wide range of interests. She talked about books, design, fashions, world affairs, art, and music. In many ways, Mary was ahead of her time.

"Just giving recipes and household hints was not my cup of tea,"

Mary smiles. "Broadcasting was a new medium for me, and it really put me on the spot. I feel more comfortable with print journalism, and after six months as 'Woman's Show' hostess, KMA decided they needed someone more old-fashioned who would center the programs on a food-hint-chat format."

DIXIE PORK CHOPS

8 pork chops	¼ cup brown sugar
2 to 3 tablespoons shortening	2 tablespoons flour
½ teaspoon salt	1 cup hot water
½ teaspoon sage	1 tablespoon vinegar
4 tart apples, sliced	½ cup seedless raisins

Brown chops in shortening; sprinkle with salt and sage. Remove chops and put in baking dish; top with apples and sprinkle with sugar. Add flour to drippings in skillet and blend. Add water and vinegar; cook until thick, stirring. Add raisins. Pour over chops. Bake uncovered at 350 degrees 1 hour. (Just guess on smaller amounts for fewer chops.)

LAYERED SALAD

1 head lettuce, torn in bite-size pieces	⅓ cup carrots, grated
½ cup celery, finely diced	1 cucumber, chopped
½ cup green pepper, thinly sliced	1½ cups mayonnaise
1 10-ounce package frozen peas, run under cold water and drained	2 tablespoons sugar
	5 slices bacon, crisp-cooked and crumbled, or 1 3¼-ounce jar Bacos

Spread lettuce on bottom of salad bowl. Add in layers: celery, green pepper, peas, carrots, and cucumber. In separate bowl mix mayonnaise and sugar; spread over top of bowl to seal. Cover and refrigerate at least 8 hours. When ready to serve, toss and sprinkle with

Mary is shown at left with her daughter, Lory, and two grandchildren, Samantha and Jeanette, in front of the mural in Cherry Hills Park, one of the community projects which Mary helped develop.

crumbled bacon or Bacos. Makes 8 servings. Note: ½ cup red onion, thinly sliced, and 4 ounces shredded cheddar cheese may also be layered in salad.

In 1989 one of Mary's dreams came true when, along with other sponsors, the Chamber of Commerce of Shenandoah approved and financed five art murals located in Shenandoah's Cherry Hills Park. The theme for the art work, an environmental walk-through created by artist Christ Lanille of Malvern, is "Bridging the Past and the Future." Mary hopes this is just the first of many such projects she and others in Shenandoah will develop to enhance the city.

Mary's daughter, Lory, is married to Jack Moorehead, Jr., and with their two daughters, Jeanette and Samantha, they live in Des Moines.

Mary's son, Loche, his wife, Laurie, and their son, Charlie, reside in Richmond, British Columbia, where Loche works with the Canadian Mental Health Association.

KENTUCKY PLANTATION DINNER

In a greased casserole put a slice of bread or toast per person. Soak with milk and butter. Put a slice of cooked turkey and a slice of cooked ham on top of each slice of bread. Top with a slice of Swiss or cheddar cheese. Bake at 375 degrees until bubbly. Serve hot with Sauce Poulette.

SAUCE POULETTE

Melt 2 tablespoons butter. Stir in 1 tablespoon flour. Cook, stirring, until smooth and bubbly and lightly browned. Stir in 2 cups chicken broth and 2 sprigs parsley. Bring to a boil; then turn heat low and simmer 30 minutes. Discard parsley. Remove from heat and blend in 2 egg yolks, juice of 1 lemon, 1 teaspoon chopped parsley, and 1 4½-ounce can mushrooms, drained. Pour over baked Kentucky Plantation Dinner or serve over meat.

MARY WILLIAMS'S MICROWAVE SQUASH

2 acorn squash (¾ pound each)   4 teaspoons butter or margarine
4 tablespoons honey   ⅛ teaspoon grated lemon peel

Pierce skin of squash several times. Place on paper towel in microwave oven. Cook on high 5 to 7 minutes. Remove and let stand 3 minutes. Cut each squash in half; scoop out seeds. Arrange in 8-inch square dish, cut sides up. Top with remaining ingredients. Cover with plastic wrap. Cook on high 5 to 6 minutes or until tender. Let stand 2 minutes. Serves 4.

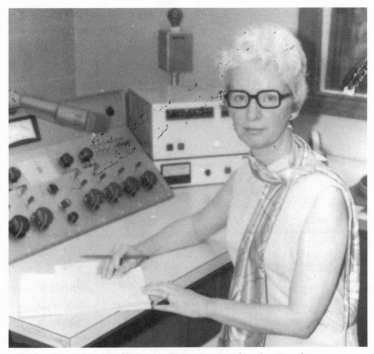

For a time Mary Williams was a reporter for the Sunday
program "You and the UN." Her homemaker program, the
"Woman's Show," was aired for only six months, but Mary
continued working for the station as editor of the KMA Guide
and as head of the promotion department.

After her work as editor of the Guide was no longer needed, Mary
became head of the promotion department for KMA. In addition to
doing the publicity and news releases for the station, she also assisted with special events. One of her favorites was the Brain Bowl.

Started in 1978, KMA's Brain Bowl is patterned after an academic
contest developed by Professor Emeritus George Gayler of Northwest
Missouri State University in Maryville, Missouri. Program director
Del Epperson had attended college in Maryville, and he suggested
that such a program on KMA would be a community service to
young people.

Each year students from sixteen high schools in the KMA region
match wits with each other to answer the questions of veteran
quizmaster Gayler. Mary is proud of the fact that the Brain Bowl, as

of 1986 when she retired, had awarded sixty-seven scholarships to-
taling nearly $13,000. The project had obtained the cooperation of
ten area colleges, all of which offered to match all scholarships.

In 1973 Mary Williams and women's director Brenda Kay Mc-
Conahay compiled *Christmas Treats,* a booklet of recipes gleaned
from a contest. First prize was awarded to Frankly Fancy Cookies.

FRANKLY FANCY COOKIES

Mix together: *½ cup melted butter or*
  2 cups finely crushed graham   *margarine*
  cracker crumbs   *½ cup sugar*

Spread in 9 × 13 pan. Bake 10 minutes at 350 degrees.

Mix together: *2 cups flaked coconut*
  1 can sweetened condensed   *½ cup nuts*
  milk

Spread on cracker crust. Bake 15 minutes at 350 degrees.

Top with: *2 teaspoons peanut butter,*
  1 12-ounce package chocolate   *melted together*
  chips

By 1977 the *KMA Guide* was in trouble. "The loss of live entertainers had something to do with its demise," Mary explains. "The
staff decreased in size as automation arrived, so fewer people re-
mained to draw on for stories. By this time the audiences were no
longer clamoring for information about the radio personalities. The
Guide had served its purpose."

Mary and Brenda Kay McConahay did everything they could to
make the *Guide* survive, but it finally became financially impossible
to keep the magazine going. After more than three decades of sharing
news, columns, pictures, stories, schedules, recipes, and household
hints with the KMA listeners, the final issue was mailed in November 1977.

Mary concluded her editorial farewell with these words: "And so, we bring to an end a communicative effort that brought a radio station and its listeners into a closer, perhaps more personal relationship. For 33 years this unique publication existed on the loyalty of its subscribers and KMA listeners and to them we give a fond farewell and thank you."

OVEN-FRIED CHICKEN WITH HONEY BUTTER SAUCE

1 frying chicken, cut up
1 cup flour
2 teaspoons salt

¼ teaspoon pepper
2 teaspoons paprika
½ cup butter or margarine

Honey Butter Sauce

¼ cup butter, melted
¼ cup lemon juice

¼ cup honey

Melt butter in a shallow baking pan. Combine flour, salt, pepper, and paprika; dip chicken into flour mix and then in the butter, turning each piece. Arrange, skin side down, in a single layer; bake at 400 degrees for 30 minutes. Turn and pour honey butter sauce over all; bake another 30 minutes at 350 degrees until chicken is tender. To make sauce, melt butter in a saucepan; blend in honey and lemon juice. Do not boil.

DRIED BEEF CHEESE ROLL

1 8-ounce package cream
  cheese, softened
2 teaspoons Worcestershire
  sauce
2 tablespoons black olives,
  chopped

1 tablespoon parsley
1 teaspoon minced onion
1 teaspoon milk or mayonnaise
1 3-ounce package dried beef,
  chopped fine

Combine all ingredients except dried beef and make into a ball. Coat the cheese ball with the chopped dried beef. Refrigerate till served.

Billie enjoys a relaxed moment before going on the air with the Martha Gooch Kitchen television program. Billie is giving a taste of the day's special demonstration food to director Mark Silberstein.

Billie Oakley

Wilma Maurine Cisney's father wanted to name her after the famous actress Billie Burke, but Wilma Maurine's mother thought actresses were hussies and such a name was inappropriate for her little baby. However, Mama's name for her firstborn failed to be used. From the very beginning Daddy nicknamed her Billie, and Billie she became.

In spite of any disappointment she might have felt over the naming situation, Mama won her share of altercations. She was an accomplished pianist and saw to it that Billie gained a background in classical music. Billie's father, a frustrated musician at heart, bought her a mail-order guitar and encouraged her to learn to play and sing popular music.

Billie's main entertainment during her high school years was listening to the radio musicians, especially those broadcasting from the stations in nearby Shenandoah.

Both KMA and KFNF were holding big, annual jubilees that included contests for musicians. In the summer of 1932, just before her junior year in high school, Billie traveled to Shenandoah, entered a singing contest at station KFNF, and *won*. She stayed in Shenandoah the rest of the summer and sang at the station for fifteen dollars a week.

The following summer Billie went to Shenandoah whenever she could and sang on both KFNF and KMA. She enjoyed performing, and thus began a lifelong love affair with broadcasting. It is a profession she has never, ever, completely left.

The Indian Cake has, in a way, become Billie's good-luck charm. The original recipe came from a 4-H girl to whom Billie had given a home permanent. The girl decided to bake her favorite cake and give it to Billie as a thank-you gift.

229

This became the cake Billie made through the years to take as a gift to welcome a new baby, to say her own thank-you to a friend, to comfort a family that has had sorrow, or to take to a covered-dish dinner. "I have many memories tied up in that small cake," Billie says.

When Billie began her homemaker broadcasts on KMA in 1963, the first recipe she gave was the Indian Cake. When she started writing a column and providing recipes for the *KMA Guide*, it was her first recipe. So it is appropriate that the first recipe in this chapter be for Billie's special Indian Cake.

INDIAN CAKE

2 cups sugar
½ cup shortening (1 stick
　margarine)
2 eggs
½ cup cocoa
½ cup cold, strong coffee
2 cups flour

1 teaspoon soda
1 teaspoon salt
1 teaspoon vanilla
½ teaspoon burnt sugar
　flavoring
1 cup boiling hot water

Mix in order given until smoothly blended except for the boiling hot water. Carefully blend in the hot water. Pour into greased and floured 9 × 13 baking pan. Bake in 350-degree oven for approximately 30 minutes. Cool and top with following frosting.

Frosting

1 cup sugar
⅓ cup water

⅓ teaspoon cream of tartar
2 egg whites

Mix together in heavy pan the sugar, cream of tartar, and water. Bring to boil. Cook until syrup forms a hard ball in cold water. Stiffly beat the egg whites. Drizzle boiling hot syrup while you continue to beat at a medium-high speed. Flavor with vanilla or your favorite flavoring. I prefer vanilla and almond. For a different flavor and beautiful pink color, substitute maraschino cherry juice for water. Lovely.

Wilma Maurine Cisney at the age of four.

To augment their incomes, many of the radio performers also played and sang in nightclubs and supper clubs. Billie did her share of this type of entertaining as well as playing with dance bands.

It was a time when the staff did many other jobs around the stations. Billie sorted music, wrote continuity, announced, and read news. On station WNAX in Yankton, South Dakota, where she worked in 1937, she also substituted for radio homemaker Susan Taylor.

While she was at WNAX, Billie realized she was not really a singer. It was time she developed the kind of program that would utilize talking, her primary talent. Radio homemaking, she decided, was what she wanted to do.

Billie left one of her jobs because her supervisor asked her to dust the office. Billie had been hired as an entertainer and radio broad-

Billie was twenty years old when she sang and played her guitar at the WLS National Barn Dance programs.

caster, and she believed the woman was trying to embarrass her by making her do the janitor's tasks. Billie maneuvered her boss near some of the other workers, and the boss again insisted that Billie do the cleaning or she would be fired.

"No!" Billie replied in a loud voice.

"Then you are fired," her employer said just as loudly. With witnesses to verify her story, Billie was able to collect unemployment compensation until she found another position. Even in the early days of her career, Billie had a lot of gumption.

Keeping sponsors happy is very important to commercial radio, yet Billie would not agree to advertise a product unless she honestly believed in it.

"One of my first sponsors was a mattress company," she said. "Talking about mattresses made me very uncomfortable. It was a time when broadcasters were extremely careful about what they said, and I simply did not like talking about anybody's mattress. I asked to be taken off that commercial."

PALM SPRINGS POT ROAST

Tear off a strip of foil large enough to completely wrap and seal a 2-to-4-pound pot roast. Place roast in middle of foil; then empty 1 10½-ounce can condensed cream of mushroom soup on top of roast. Sprinkle with 1 envelope Lipton onion soup mix. Bring foil up around roast and do the "drugstore fold" (which seals in all juices). Place foil-wrapped roast on rack in shallow pan and roast 2½ to 3 hours in 320-degree oven. When you open foil, you'll find a delightfully tender roast in its own brown gravy sauce with a delightful aroma!

DRUNKEN CHICKEN

6 large (double) breasts of
   chicken
Olive oil
Cider vinegar
Salt
Coarsely cracked pepper
1 clove garlic, crushed

1 2-ounce can mushrooms and
   liquid
¾ teaspoon sweet basil
1 teaspoon rosemary, crushed
1 stick butter (½ cup)
½ cup dry sherry

Marinate chicken breasts overnight in two parts vinegar to one part oil, crushed garlic, salt, and pepper. Turn once or twice for even marinating. Drain. Arrange breasts upright in shallow baking pan. Brown on both sides in very hot oven (450 degrees). Reduce heat to 350 degrees; pour over mushrooms and liquid. Sprinkle with herbs; dot both sides with butter and add sherry. Cover pan with foil. Continue baking 45 minutes longer or until done (soft to the touch). Serves 12.

RATATOUILLE
(All-Vegetable Stew)

1¾ cups coarsely chopped
  onion
1 clove garlic, minced
2 tablespoons cooking oil
½ pound zucchini, cut in strips
½ pound eggplant, cut in
  ½-inch strips
2 green peppers, cut in strips
4 medium tomatoes, coarsely
  chopped
1 teaspoon salt

Dash freshly ground pepper
2 or 3 fresh basil leaves,
  snipped (or 1 teaspoon dried
  basil leaves, crushed)
2 sprigs fresh thyme, snipped
  (or ½ teaspoon dried thyme
  leaves, crushed)
Other vegetables, like carrots,
  kohlrabi, turnips, etc., may be
  added to suit your taste

In large skillet, cook onion and garlic in oil until tender but not brown (electric skillet set at 300 degrees). Add remaining ingredients. Cover; bring to a boil. Reduce heat to 220 degrees. Simmer 40 minutes, stirring occasionally. Take care not to break up vegetable pieces. Serve hot as a vegetable side dish or cold, if you prefer.

YOUNKERS' DRESSING

½ cup tarragon or wine vinegar
1 cup sugar
2 rounded teaspoons dry
  mustard
2 rounded teaspoons paprika

2 rounded teaspoons celery
  seed
2 rounded teaspoons salt
2 cups corn oil
Grated onion

Mix all ingredients except oil and onion in large bowl or electric mixer. Gradually add oil. Beat all the time you're drizzling in the oil. Add grated onion if you wish. Beat 5 minutes. Then let stand 1 hour. Beat another 5 minutes at moderate speed. Put into jars and store in refrigerator.

When Billie returned to Shenandoah in 1941, she was Billie McNeilly and the mother of three children. She did some continuity writing for KMA and a bit of singing on the air, but she soon decided her family and her home needed her more. Except for some substituting, she stopped radio work for a time.

In 1949 when the children were older, Billie resumed her career in her usual energetic and "whippy" manner. KMA already had several radio homemakers, so Billie went to KFNF and offered to broadcast for two weeks without pay. The management liked what it heard and hired her. The result was Billie's own homemaker program, "It's a Woman's World."

In 1963 Billie McNeilly returned to KMA with her "It's a Woman's World" program. By 1966, her children grown and her name changed to Oakley, Billie moved to Lincoln, Nebraska, to become consumer director for the Gooch Food Products Company.

At the Gooch company Billie tested recipes and Gooch Food Products, presented live cooking programs, assisted with various publications, and managed the Gooch kitchen. Her radio program was syndicated over forty stations, including KMA. She also had a television cooking show on KOLN-KGIN TV in Lincoln and Grand Island, Nebraska, in Sioux Falls, South Dakota, and on Kansas and Iowa stations.

When she reached the age of sixty, Billie realized she was working too hard. She decided to simplify her life and eliminate some of the work her career in Lincoln required. She left the Gooch company and returned to Shenandoah just as KMA was looking for a homemaker to replace Brenda Kay McConahay. "It's a Woman's World" became "The Billie Oakley Show." The roaming days were over. Billie had come home.

After Billie's return to KMA, she began moderating "Party Line," a program commonly known as the talk-back-to-Billie show. The program followed the same format as that started by Warren Nielson and Doris Murphy.

While such a program has a value in providing a forum for opinions to be freely expressed, the moderator must be knowledgeable about both sides of the issues, must know what to do when one person or one subject monopolizes the program, and sometimes must serve as peacemaker.

The
HOTTEST
SPOT IN
MORNING RADIO

now
listeners
can

talk back to Billie
11:00 to 11:30 A.M. - Monday thru Friday

| Availabilities are limited --!! |

So see Andy Andersen
or Pat Patterson
call 246-1020

Ⓚ Ⓜ Ⓐ DIAL
960

Unfortunately, the subjects on "Party Line" became overly controversial. "Running the show as a peacemaker was giving me ulcers and the station fits," Billie remembers. So it was taken off the air.

The "Billie Oakley Show" concluded with its own half-hour segment for listeners to call in. They were welcome to express their opinions, but most callers preferred to discuss recipes rather than attempt to solve the problems of the world.

"It was a lot easier on my stomach and KMA had fewer fits," Billie concluded.

Billie believes that once you open your mouth, nothing is sacred.

"My divorce was very difficult for me. I really didn't want to share that with the listeners, but the only way to cope was to lay the whole thing on the line. I simply told the truth.

"Unfortunately, I remarried. I think I was afraid of growing old alone. But then my husband decided he didn't need to work anymore, and I decided I didn't want to spend the rest of my life supporting a freeloader. The marriage had gone sour and I couldn't live like that. There again, I told my radio listeners what was going on. I don't think any of them held it against me."

RICE AND CHERRIES IN THE SNOW

3 cups water
Dash of salt
1½ cups raw rice
3 cups milk
½ cup sugar
1 tablespoon butter

1 tablespoon Knox gelatin
⅓ cup warm milk
1 teaspoon almond flavoring
1 small tub Cool Whip or 1 cup
    whipping cream, whipped
2 cans cherry pie filling

Boil rice, salt, and water for 15 minutes in covered pan. Add milk, sugar, and butter and cook over low heat until thick. Stir in gelatin that has been softened in warm milk. Let cool slightly. Fold in flavoring and Cool Whip and put in large cake dish. Let set in refrigerator. Spread pie filling on top. Keep cool.

This can be cooked in a microwave. Cook rice 5 minutes on high and then 15 minutes on simmer. Add the milk, sugar, and butter. Cook again on simmer 10 minutes. (Don't have to watch it this way, as it won't stick or burn.)

COOKED POTATO SALAD DRESSING

2 eggs, beaten
⅓ cup sugar
1 tablespoon enriched flour

¼ teaspoon salt
½ cup vinegar
⅓ cup water

Combine egg, sugar, flour, and salt. Beat thoroughly. Add vinegar and water. Cook over medium heat until thick, stirring constantly. Makes about 1 pint.

Billie brought many interesting people to her programs. One week she included a talk from a specialist on cooking eggs, a report on a display in a nearby art gallery, a discussion on how to curb crime in the Midwest, a visit with the head chef of the Broadmoor Hotel in Colorado Springs, Colorado, and a scientist recently returned from an expedition to the Antarctic.

GREEN BEANS FOR THE FREEZER

4 quarts green beans   8 bouillon cubes
8 cups water   1 teaspoon onion powder

Note: Beans should be stemmed, washed, and ready for the freezer container. Also, do not substitute onion salt. It is not strong enough.

Combine water, bouillon cubes, and onion powder in large (8 quarts at least) kettle. Bring to a rolling boil and add the beans. Cover and bring back to a boil. Adjust heat so it won't boil over and continue boiling for 12 minutes. Remove cover and cool well. Pack beans in freezer containers and cover with cooled cooking liquid. Seal and freeze. When ready to use, simply set block into a pan and set heat low to melt liquid. Bring to a boil and serve.

In 1978 Billie decided to reconstruct the famous cookie teas started by Doris Murphy in something like their original form. She planned programs around demonstrations by guest chefs, displays of crafts by specialists, musical entertainment, door prizes, and the introduction of KMA personalities.

The teas grew in popularity. Six hundred persons attended in 1978 and more than fifteen hundred in 1984. After the crowd left the Shenandoah high school gymnasium, Billie observed, "We may have to move the cookie festival to the football field next year to get all the people in."

Each person who attends a cookie festival brings a paper plate containing a dozen cookies and a copy of the recipe. After the program is completed, the guests look at the cookies and sample one or two. The remaining cookies are taken to senior citizen centers and children's homes.

BENNE COOKIES

Cream together in a bowl:
  ¾ cup shortening
  1½ cups brown sugar

Add:
  2 eggs
  1¼ cups sifted, enriched flour
  ¼ teaspoon baking powder
  ½ cup sesame seeds
  1 teaspoon vanilla

Mix well. Drop by spoonfuls about ½ inch apart on a cookie sheet covered with waxed paper. This allows room for the cookies to spread. They're almost flat when baked. Bake in moderate oven (350 degrees) for 12 to 15 minutes. Makes 4 dozen.

SAUERBRATEN WITH GINGERSNAP GRAVY

4 pounds round or rump roast　　2 medium onions, thinly sliced
2 teaspoons salt　　　　　　　　1 stalk celery, chopped
½ teaspoon pepper　　　　　　　1 carrot, minced
8 whole cloves　　　　　　　　　2½ cups water
8 whole peppercorns　　　　　　1½ cups red wine vinegar
4 bay leaves　　　　　　　　　　¼ cup butter

Rub meat with salt and pepper. Place in deep ovenware bowl. Add spices and vegetables. Heat water and vinegar to boiling. Pour over meat immediately. Cool. Cover and marinate in refrigerator 48 hours, turning meat twice a day. Remove meat from marinade. Dry with clean cloth or paper toweling. In heavy kettle, brown meat on both sides in butter. Strain marinade and pour over meat. Cover and simmer 3 hours or until meat is tender. Place meat on heated platter. Serve warm.

Gingersnap Gravy

2 tablespoons sugar　　　　　　½ cup water
1½ cups hot sauerbraten　　　　⅔ cup crushed gingersnap
　　marinade　　　　　　　　　　　crumbs
　　　　　　　　　　　　　　　　Salt

Melt sugar in skillet until golden brown, stirring constantly. Gradually stir in hot marinade and water. Add gingersnap crumbs and cook, stirring constantly, until thickened. Salt to taste. Spoon part of gravy over meat. Serve remaining gravy in separate dish.

Long-distance trips started for Billie in 1970 when she went with an AWRT group to London and Paris. In 1971 she had the Swiss Air chef as her guest on her Lincoln television show. Swiss Air wanted to do something nice for her in return, so they sent her to Switzerland. The trip went so well the airline arranged for her to accompany a study group and tour their country again.

Since that time Billie has hopped a plane whenever possible to fly off to distant places. Often she has been the tour guide who shepherded a group to some of the most fascinating places in the world.

JEWISH CHALLAH
(Traditional Jewish Festive Bread)

3 packages dry or compressed
   yeast
1 teaspoon sugar
½ cup lukewarm water
2 teaspoons salt

1 tablespoon sugar
5 to 6 cups sifted enriched flour
½ cup lukewarm water
3 eggs
¼ cup shortening, melted

In mixing bowl combine yeast, 1 teaspoon sugar, and ½ cup warm water. Let stand a few minutes; stir to dissolve. Set in warm place until mixture is doubled (about 5 minutes). In large mixing bowl combine salt, 1 tablespoon sugar, and 4 cups flour. Make a well in center. Pour in yeast mixture, ½ cup warm water, 3 eggs, and shortening. Stir center ingredients gently; beat until smooth. Slowly blend in remaining flour until dough leaves sides of bowl. Turn dough onto floured surface. Knead about 15 minutes or until it is smooth, elastic, and does not stick when pinched with fingers. Place in greased bowl, turning once to grease all sides. Cover with waxed paper, then a towel. Let rise until double in bulk (about 45 minutes). Punch down and divide into 3 or 4 equal portions. Roll each portion into long rope about 2 inches in diameter at the center and taper to ½ inch at ends. Braid on greased baking sheet. Cover and let rise until double in bulk (about 30 minutes). Brush with solution of 1 egg yolk and 2 tablespoons water. Bake in 400-degee oven 15 minutes. Reduce heat to 375 degrees and bake 45 minutes longer or until golden brown. Place on wire rack. Makes 1 loaf.

Always a strong booster for women in communications, Billie has been a member of the Heart of America chapter of American Women in Radio and Television almost since its inception. KMA encouraged its homemakers to be part of this organization and through the years sent them to various national and regional meetings. This provided Billie with opportunities to meet well-known people, tour interesting areas, and gather material to use on her radio programs.

In April 1965, American Women in Radio and Television cited Billie for excellence in thirty years of broadcasting.

SPEEDY SPUMONI

1 quart vanilla ice cream, slightly softened
½ cup toasted, crushed, slivered, or shaved almonds
1 1¾-ounce milk chocolate bar, chopped

¼ cup drained chopped maraschino cherries
¼ teaspoon grated orange peel
¼ teaspoon grated lemon peel
4 drops anise flavoring

Combine all ingredients. Line muffin pan with 10 paper baking cups. Fill. Freeze until firm. Serves 10.

Some of the radio homemakers who came before Billie opened their homes to the listeners and invited them to stop by for a visit and refreshments whenever they were in Shenandoah.

"I was fortunate to come onto the KMA scene after the great influx of visitors that had almost demanded those visits," Billie remembers. "But everyone has a part of her life which she wants to keep private, and my home has always been the place where I do not welcome intrusion. I'll share everything else, but I did try to protect my children from too much publicity, and I kept my home for myself and my family. It is still special to me and I feel it was the right decision for me."

Through the years, Billie has produced a prodigious number of publications. When she was with the Gooch company in Lincoln, she published the monthly newsletter *Martha Gooch Monthly Memo*. Her *Everybody's an Expert Cookbook* came off the press in 1981. She started a bimonthly publication for KMA in 1984 called *Billie Oakley's Open Line*, which contained the recipes called in by her radio listeners.

Radio homemakers are not only colleagues but also close friends. Billie Oakley and I enjoyed testing cookies in Billie's bright kitchen in preparation for choosing recipes for the Festival Cookie Book.

After "retiring" from KMA in March 1987, Billie found that a life of ease was not for her. Before long she was broadcasting a syndicated radio program carried over more than twenty-four radio stations sponsored by the Shenandoah-based X-TRA-TOUCH Company. That same spring, she began the bimonthly homemaker magazine *Home Talk.* Soon after, she published two *Min Sez* booklets based on the clever sayings of her friend from Gooch days, Min Carver. In 1989 her book of favorite recipes and "remember whens," the *Golden*

Billie is justifiably proud of the Marconi Award presented
to her in 1989 by the National Association of Broadcasters.

Memories Cookbook, came off the press. According to Billie, it is a
project she worked on all her life.

Billie lightened her work load once more in 1990 when she resigned from her syndicated program, but as long as her voice holds
out, Billie will be on the air. She presently has a three-times-a-
week feature program on KMA, and she continues to make public
appearances.

Billie has three children, seven grandchildren, and two great-
grandchildren. Her daughter Marcia Anderson, office controller for
her mother's office operation, lives in Shenandoah with her husband,

Ed. Billie's son, John, and his wife and two daughters live in Nebraska City, where he is a schoolteacher. Daughter Donna coordinates programs for latchkey children in Milwaukee.

Billie has received many awards through the years, including the KMMJ (Clay Center, Nebraska) Hall of Fame award. In 1989 her peers presented her with the prestigious Marconi Award for excellence in radio at the National Association of Broadcasters convention in New Orleans.

PORK CHOPS ROBERT

4 6-ounce center cut pork chops (½ inch thick). Dust chops with flour and sauté in oil and butter (¾ oil and ¼ butter) until chops are completely done. Remove chops to a heated platter. Pour excess fat from skillet. Add 1 tablespoon butter, and 1 tablespoon minced shallots (or green onion), 1 tablespoon dry mustard, and blend in 1 cup Chablis wine (white). Let simmer about 5 minutes to reduce the liquid; then stir in 1 cup brown gravy from a can. Season to taste (I like a little garlic powder added). Pour sauce over hot chops and serve.

POACHED RUSSIAN EGGS

1 can beer
1 8-ounce can tomato sauce
2 tablespoons lemon juice
1 teaspoon Worcestershire sauce
8 drops Tabasco sauce
½ teaspoon horseradish

½ teaspoon sugar
Salt to taste
10 eggs
5 English muffins, split,
    buttered, and toasted

Pour beer into 12-inch skillet. Let stand for at least 30 minutes. Blend in tomato sauce, lemon juice, Worcestershire, Tabasco, horseradish, sugar, and salt. Heat to boiling. Break eggs into sauce. Simmer until whites of eggs are firm, basting with sauce. Remove eggs with slotted spatula, placing each on half of a hot, toasted English muffin. Serve sauce in separate dish to spoon over eggs.

Joni Baillon

Young, vivacious, attractive Joni Baillon arrived in Shenandoah in the midst of a raging thunderstorm. The apartment into which she intended to move had been rented to someone else. Because the nearby Sidney rodeo was being held, all motel rooms were filled. The apartment that KMA station manager Norm Williams finally located for Joni was empty and available, but when Joni moved in she discovered the place had no electricity. That problem was rectified with a few phone calls the following morning.

Despite this rather inauspicious beginning, Joni has only praise and happy memories from her two and one-half years with KMA.

Joni did not plan to become a radio homemaker, but she did have a professional goal of working in radio and becoming a broadcaster. At the time she graduated from Our Lady of Peace High School in St. Paul, Minnesota, she discovered that broadcasting schools were almost nonexistent. Journalism courses were available, but not radio or television training. For two years Joni attended the College of St. Catherine in St. Paul, where she majored in speech and drama. Then she transferred to the Brown Institute of Broadcasting in Minneapolis to become the only woman student among 400 men. (By 1985 there were equal numbers of men and women.)

A fellow student in the Brown Institute became the chief engineer at KJAM in Madison, South Dakota. When the station was looking for someone to do on-air work, the friend suggested to Joni that she apply. When she completed her studies at Brown, she was hired, and she spent four and one-half profitable years in Madison.

"I did everything at KJAM there was to do in a small station. It was a marvelous education. I did continuity writing, log preparation, my own news, markets, interviews, ordered music, the engineering—

247

everything. Eventually I became program manager. A small station where one person can experience all these areas of the work is the best background anyone can possibly have for radio."

When she decided it was time to leave Madison, Joni advertised for a broadcasting position through a national radio magazine. She received offers from fifteen stations; among them was KMA. The air-check tape she sent impressed the station personnel enough for them to fly up to Madison for a personal interview. They liked Joni, and she was pleased with what they told her about their strong mid-western station and life in Shenandoah. Besides, they had flown up in the company plane and Joni liked the idea of working for a business important enough to have its own airplane. It was a happy decision.

CHICKEN ON A CLOUD

1 cup flour	1½ cups milk
1 teaspoon baking powder	¼ cup butter, melted
1 teaspoon salt	¼ cup parsley, chopped
3 eggs, well beaten	1 2½- to 3-pound fryer, cut up

Sift flour, baking powder, and salt. Combine remaining ingredients except chicken; add to dry ingredients. Stir until smooth. Pour mixture over chicken that has been placed in a baking dish. Bake at 350 degrees for 1 hour. Makes 4 to 6 servings.

Joni suggests that this be made with skim milk, egg whites or egg substitutes, and low-cholesterol margarine. Skinning the chicken before preparing will lower both the cholesterol and calorie count for this dish.

Chicken on a Cloud was featured in the April 1989 issue of *Redbook*. The article, "Favorite Chicken Dinners," prefaced the recipe with the following statement: "Dispensers of homey advice since 1925, the 'radio homemakers' on station KMA in Shenandoah, Iowa, are best known for their hearty country recipes, like Joni Baillon's rich Chicken on a Cloud. This . . . fowl comes cushioned on a big butter-topped biscuit that's light-as-air. Is it tough to make? Hardly. Just pour the simple 'cloud' batter over . . . chicken and bake until it puffs up good and golden."

The *Redbook* version of the recipe includes rubbing crushed garlic and butter over the chicken pieces and browning them before putting them in the baking dish. The remainder of the recipe is exactly as Joni gave it to her listeners.

Joni swung into the mode of radio homemaker with great enthusiasm. Never one to work by the clock, she spent long hours gathering and preparing material, testing recipes, presenting programs, and doing public appearances.

A few days after her arrival in Shenandoah, Joni was sent to Des Moines to represent KMA at the Iowa State Fair. She conducted interviews, visited with people who stopped by the KMA booth, and sent her programs back through the Shenandoah station by remote control. In the months to come, she did her share of judging contests, narrating fashion shows, and writing for the *KMA Guide*. Joni's "tasting teas" were a simpler form of the cookie festivals. She prepared and sent out recipes and a casserole booklet. Her training and experience in other areas of radio were utilized as she wrote commercials, produced spot announcements, and ran the engineering board from 1 to 2 P.M. each day during the "Swap Shop."

PEANUT QUICKIES

1 package *fluffy white frosting*   ½ cup *crunchy peanut butter*
    mix
½ cup *all-purpose flour*

Grease and flour cookie sheets. Prepare frosting mix as directed on package. Fold in flour, then peanut butter. Drop dough by rounded teaspoonfuls onto cookie sheets. Bake at 375 degrees for 10 to 12 minutes until golden. Remove from cookie sheets immediately. Yield: about 50 cookies. Tip: If desired, ½ cup salted peanuts may be added to dough.

BROWNIE MIX

4½ cups sifted flour   1¼ teaspoons salt
1½ cups nonfat dry milk   2½ teaspoons baking powder
5 cups sugar   1¼ cups cocoa

Measure all ingredients into a large bowl and mix thoroughly, or use
an electric mixer at low speed for 10 minutes. Makes 10 cups.

BROWNIES

2 cups brownie mix   ½ cup nuts
2 eggs   1 teaspoon vanilla
1 tablespoon water   ½ teaspoon black walnut
⅓ cup shortening or vegetable   flavoring
   oil

Blend ingredients, using mixer at medium speed for 2 minutes. Turn
into greased 8 × 8 cake pan and bake at 350 degrees for 25 minutes.
Cool in pan before cutting. To fill a 9 × 13 pan, double the recipe.

Joni says: "In the late sixties we were beginning to look for more
shortcuts in preparing food. Women were going into the labor force.
Time was becoming more difficult to ration out and do everything
you wanted in your spare time. Homemade mixes were popular."

MIXED VEGETABLES WITH ALMONDS

1 package frozen or fresh   1 can cream of chicken soup
   cauliflower   1 6-ounce package cheddar
1 package frozen or fresh green   cheese, shredded
   beans   1 small jar pimiento, chopped
1 package frozen or fresh peas   1 can small round onions
½ cup milk   ½ cup slivered almonds

Cook cauliflower, beans, and peas until half done. Add milk to soup and heat with cheese. Combine all ingredients except almonds. Place in greased dish and cover with slivered almonds. Bake 30 minutes at 350 degrees. Note: This recipe may be prepared in advance. Yield: 10 servings.

"It was not easy to be a radio homemaker," Joni remembers. "Many times people would bluntly ask me how I knew enough to tell them how to run their homes, prepare food, and care for their families. What they didn't seem to understand was that my life wasn't much different from that of other housewives.

"I did cook more simply than many of the women who stayed home much of the time, and that certainly was reflected in my program. I gave simple, easy-to-prepare recipes most of the time. Weight consciousness really surfaced during the years I was with KMA. Blenders and fondue pots were the big new kitchen items, and everyone was trying out combinations using mixes."

CREAMED ONIONS

18 to 20 medium onions
⅓ cup salad oil
3 tablespoons all-purpose flour
1½ cups milk

1 cup shredded processed
American cheese
Peanuts, chopped

Peel onions and cook in a large amount of boiling salted water until tender; drain. In a large saucepan, blend salad oil and flour; stir in milk and cook slowly until mixture thickens, stirring constantly. Add the shredded cheese and stir until melted. Add drained onions and heat through. Place in bowl and sprinkle with peanuts. Makes 6 to 8 servings.

Joni loves working with people, and radio provided the opportunity to meet folks from a variety of backgrounds. "I interviewed
many people on my daily half-hour 'Joni's Journal' and we talked
about all kinds of subjects. It was a period of time when people were
finally coming to realize that women have many interests and concerns far beyond just cooking and cleaning and family care. I tried to
reflect that change.

"Then, the second half-hour was the 'Party Line' call-in show. It
was a chance for people to air their opinions and they wanted me to
give mine. Sometimes the discussions got very heated. I remember it
was the period when day-care centers were just developing and many
of the listeners were horrified—callers said it was 'a Communist plot
to take the children away from their mothers.' That may seem funny
now, but it was a dead serious idea in the 1960s.

"One horrible day I did the call-in portion of the show and not ONE
person called in. I talked for a solid half-hour!

"Another time we had a particularly hot discussion going and both
sides of the problem insisted on equal airtime. I finally got two
phone lines into the station, put one party on each line, and we had
an excellent three-way discussion of the situation."

Having been in both media, Joni can compare radio and television:
"On radio you are a real person. A friendly neighbor. I even had
mothers sending me pictures of their single sons. I received hundreds of letters a month. I was a friend. In television, somehow, you
are not made a part of the family.

"The radio homemaker fills a particular place in the lives of listeners—friend, advisor, educator—this goes for men, too, not just

women. During my stay in Shenandoah, I saw a move away from stereotypes. Men are as interested in cooking and nurturing children as women are, and they were beginning to feel free to express those feelings. Women are interested in all kinds of things: politics, sports, books, films, civic affairs, and business, the same topics which men find interesting.

"Women are trusted on the air," Joni concludes. "Listeners feel that what they say is true; they know and trust them. Women are trained from childhood to develop varied talents and skills more than men are. We are expected all through life to be able to play many roles. We continue wanting to grow and learn—perhaps that is another reason homemaker broadcasts are so popular.

"I'm glad I'm a woman!"

MEAL ON A MUFFIN

1 teaspoon butter	4 slices pineapple
8 thin slices ham or cooked Canadian bacon	1 cup Nippy Cheese Sauce
	2 English muffins, split and toasted

Melt butter in frying pan. Sauté meat and pineapple until lightly browned. Heat cheese sauce. Arrange muffin halves on four serving plates. Top each with two slices of meat and a slice of pineapple. Pour on cheese sauce just before serving, or serve cheese sauce at the table. Makes 4 servings.

Nippy Cheese Sauce

½ pound Old English cheese	Dash of yellow food coloring
1 quart thick white sauce	1 teaspoon dry mustard
Dash of Tabasco	¼ teaspoon salt
1 teaspoon Worcestershire sauce	

Melt cheese in thick white sauce and add seasonings. Cool and store in refrigerator.

QUICK PUMPKIN CAKE

Use one package of spice cake mix, and add one 1-pound can of pumpkin, 2 eggs, and 2 teaspoons soda. Mix as usual, but DO NOT add any other liquid. Bake according to directions on the cake-mix box. It makes a moist cake, similar to a pound cake, and is delicious with caramel frosting.

TURKEY CASHEW HOT DISH

1 cup diced celery
¼ cup minced onion
¼ cup green pepper
3 ounces Chinese noodles
2 cups cubed cooked turkey

1 small jar pimiento, diced
1 can cream of mushroom soup
¼ cup water
1 chicken bouillon cube
1 cup cashew nuts

Sauté celery, onion, and green pepper in butter. Add noodles, cooked turkey, pimiento, soup, water, and bouillon cube. Mix gently. Spoon into casserole. On top, pour the cashew nuts. Bake at 325 degrees for 40 minutes.

DANCING SNOWBALLS

Here's a clever idea to use as a centerpiece for the holidays. You need:

1 quart water   1 heaping tablespoon soda
1 cup vinegar   Mothballs

Put the water and vinegar together in a large glass bowl or rose bowl. Put in mothballs and add the soda. The mothballs, combined with the other ingredients, will dance up and down within the bowl. To reactivate, add more soda.

CHERRY HOT CROSS BUNS

1 12¾-ounce package hot roll   1¼ cups sifted confectioners'
  mix   sugar
¼ cup chopped green glacé   5 teaspoons milk
  cherries   1 8-ounce jar red, stemmed
¼ cup chopped red glacé   maraschino cherries
  cherries

Prepare the hot roll mix according to package directions, adding chopped glacé cherries. After dough rises, shape into 1½-inch balls and place on greased baking sheets. Let rise in a warm place until double in size. Cut deep cross in each bun with scissors. Bake in a 400-degree oven for 10 to 15 minutes or until golden brown. Cool slightly. Combine sugar and milk, mixing until smooth. Pour into crosses. Top with whole maraschino cherries. Makes about 18 buns.

MINTED PEAS WITH LEMON

1 10-ounce package frozen peas   ½ teaspoon dried mint
2 tablespoons butter or   1 teaspoon grated lemon peel
  margarine

Cook peas according to package directions; drain. Add butter, mint, and lemon peel; toss to coat peas. Heat through. Serves 4.

Joni left KMA in 1969 to go to its sister station—KMTV in Omaha—where she became the host of the program "Conversations." She was named producer in 1974. In 1981 "Conversations" was named Best Local TV Show by the *Omaha Magazine*. In April 1982 Joni became cohost on the "Good Day" hour-long weekday show, a position she held until the show's cancellation in the fall of 1983.

In December 1983 Joni joined the city of Omaha as public events marketing coordinator. From her office in the Civic Auditorium, she promotes events, conducts advertising campaigns, helps with scheduling, and works with local and national news media.

Joni particularly enjoys doing advertising and promotion, including television guest appearances, because they keep her in touch with friends in the media. She is concentrating her volunteer efforts on downtown Omaha development projects. She also is working with her husband, Vern, on the 1998 TransMississippi Exposition's one-hundred-year celebration.

She fondly remembers her years as a radio homemaker. "I liked the close relationship to the listeners radio gave me. In television I discovered that the camera gets in the way and seems to make a person more of a performer who is unapproachable. In radio, people feel as if they can reach out and touch you. I always knew when I was communicating with people. They let me know, like the father who called to thank me for a program I did on treatment of birthmarks. He did not know such help was possible, and through my program he found help for his son.

"I liked the sense of value and heritage which are so evident at KMA. I hope they are never lost."

SEASONED SALT

6 tablespoons salt	½ teaspoon curry powder
½ teaspoon dried thyme leaves	1 teaspoon dry mustard
½ teaspoon marjoram	¼ teaspoon onion powder
½ teaspoon garlic salt	⅛ teaspoon dill seed
2¼ teaspoons paprika	½ teaspoon celery salt

Combine. Mix well. Store in covered jars.

Johnny Carson, who grew up in southwest Iowa and eastern Nebraska, returned to Omaha in 1969 and was interviewed by Joni on her "Conversations" program on KMTV, KMA's sister station.

SPINACH LASAGNE

1 pound Monterey Jack cheese, grated
8 ounces lasagne noodles, cooked
2 packages frozen chopped spinach, cooked and drained
1 cup grated Parmesan cheese

2 pounds cottage cheese (may substitute part sour cream)
2 raw eggs
1 tablespoon parsley
Salt, pepper, and garlic powder to taste
2 tablespoons melted butter

Mix cottage cheese, seasonings, and raw eggs. Grease a lasagne pan. Place a layer of noodles in pan followed by a layer of cottage cheese, Monterey Jack cheese, spinach, and Parmesan. Repeat layers. Drizzle with melted butter. Bake at 350 degrees for 30 minutes, uncovered.

During her days with KMA, Joni shared many of the events in the lives of her family. She was raised in St. Paul, Minnesota. Her father was an evaluation engineer for the Northern Pacific/Burlington Northern Railroads. After his retirement, he became an active volunteer with the Minnesota State Historical Society, Meals on Wheels, and his local church. Joni's mother achieved the goal of her lifetime when, after ten years of study, she graduated with a four-year degree in counseling. Joni's brothers—Jim, John, and Jeff—were always special to her, and they became special to her KMA listeners as well.

When Joni moved from KMA in Shenandoah to KMTV in Omaha, she naturally made many new friends. Among them was Vern Wood, a history teacher who worked during the summer and weekends at the KMTV station as a camera operator and audio engineer. Joni and Vern married in 1971 and live on ten acres in northwest Omaha. Vern teaches American history at North High School in Omaha and is active with the Nebraska State Council of Social Studies.

"Our companions," Joni relates, "are cats in the house, two dogs, several barn cats (who wandered by, stopped in, and stayed), and Vern's horse. I've started to pay more attention to the wildlife near our acreage—all types of birds, deer, rabbits, squirrels, possum, raccoons, and anything else which wanders through. My garden consists of flowers, mostly begonias and impatiens in planters and clay pots."

If only the people who thought Joni could not be a radio homemaker because she was single could see her now!

CHEESE BALL

1 glass Roko cheese (Kraft)	½ cup chopped pecans
1 glass Old English cheese	2 teaspoons Worcestershire
1 large package cream cheese	sauce
	1 very small onion, minced

Let cheese soften at room temperature. Then add sauce and onion and mix well. Shape into a ball and roll in chopped pecans. Wrap in foil and chill in refrigerator overnight. Bring out before serving to soften for spreading.

Vern and Joni.

CHEWY CHOCOLATE COOKIES

2 cups sugar
1¼ cups margarine, softened
2 eggs (or egg substitute like Egg
  Scramblers)
2 teaspoons vanilla

¾ cup cocoa
2 cups flour
1 teaspoon baking soda
½ teaspoon salt

Cream together the sugar and margarine. Stir in remaining ingredients in order given. Drop by teaspoonfuls onto ungreased cookie sheet. Bake at 350 degrees for 8 or 9 minutes. *Do not overbake.* Let set for 1 minute on cookie sheet after removing from oven. Cookies will flatten during this time. Remove to cool. Store in tightly covered container. Excellent! Yield: 4 dozen.

Jo Freed

I t is amazing that the small town of Essex, Iowa, population 1,001, could produce a number of dynamic, energetic, personable women who became KMA homemakers: Jessie Young, Florence Falk, and Jo Freed.

Jo even followed in Florence's footsteps by being nicknamed (by then-salesman Andy Andersen) the Essex Whirlwind. Florence had a hand in Jo's first appearance as a radio homemaker as well.

Jo was working for radio station KFNF as a secretary. She also wrote commercials, did book work, compiled the log, taped spot announcements, and did a few on-air interviews. Florence Falk was broadcasting her homemaker program over KFNF when her daughter Karenann, who lived in Colorado, gave birth to her first baby. Florence went to be with Karenann and the baby while Jo filled in on the "Farmer's Wife" program until Florence could arrange to make and mail back tapes.

When Joni Baillon left KMA in January 1969, Jack Katz, sales department manager, suggested that Jo come in for an interview. Jo's "Today's Woman" program was the result.

Jo was born and raised in Council Bluffs, Iowa. Her father worked for the Pacific Freight Express. There were six children in the family, and the years were difficult. Economizing was the order of the day, so Jo learned much about managing a home with very little.

One of Jo's earliest memories is of her mother telling the family good-bye each time she left for the hospital to have a baby. Each birth was a stress-filled situation because every one of the six babies was born by cesarean section. To have six by this method and live was almost unheard of in the 1930s. Jo's mother tried to prepare her children for the possibility of a tragedy. "I was the third from the oldest in the family," Jo relates. "The last three children born were younger by six years, nine years, and twelve years, so I vividly remember Mother trying to prepare us each time she left, saying a sad farewell in case she did not return."

AU GRATIN SHOESTRING POTATOES

Peel 10 medium-size potatoes. Cut them in shoestring style until you have filled a 9 × 12 oblong dish ½ inch from the top. Melt 6 table-spoons butter and combine with 1½ cups half-and-half. Pour over potatoes. Shred over the potatoes 1½ cups cheese. Cover dish with aluminum foil or other cover and bake in oven 30 to 45 minutes at 375 degrees. Serves 15 people.

CARROT CASSEROLE

¼ cup butter
2 cups grated carrots
1 cup grated American cheese
½ teaspoon salt
1 cup celery, cut fine

1 small onion, chopped
1 cup soft bread crumbs
2 eggs, beaten
¼ cup coffee cream

Mix all ingredients together and pour into a greased casserole. Cover and bake for 40 minutes in a preheated oven at 350 degrees.

BEEF STROGANOFF

2 pounds round steak, cut into
  strips or cubes
½ teaspoon salt
½ teaspoon pepper
½ cup butter
4 green onions or 1 tablespoon
  minced onion
5 tablespoons flour

1 can beef broth
1 teaspoon prepared mustard
1 6-ounce can mushrooms,
  drained
⅓ cup sour cream
⅓ cup cooking sherry

Brown seasoned meat in butter; add onions and brown slowly. Stir flour into meat and onions. Add beef broth and bring to boil, stirring constantly. Turn heat to low; stir in mustard. Cover and simmer for 1 hour or until meat is tender. Add mushrooms, sour cream, and sherry. (Heat just to boiling point.) Salt to taste; serve with hot rice or noodles. Serves 6.

DARK BLUE PUNCH

1 gallon water

½ cup sugar

11 cans frozen lemonade

1 tablespoon blue coloring

¼ tablespoon green coloring

Combine ingredients and pour in punch bowl over ice rings. Add 11 12-ounce bottles of 7-Up, chilled. Makes enough to fill 100 punch cups.

LIGHT BLUE PUNCH

Make above recipe, except for the coloring. Add just a little of the colors at a time, starting with ½ teaspoon of the blue and a few drops of green coloring until desired blue is achieved.

"As the name of the show, 'Today's Woman,' suggested, I gave many shortcuts for cooking contemporary foods," Jo says. "The sixties and seventies were a time when lifestyles began to get busier." Jo emphasized cooking with electric skillets and the use of mixes. Commercial mixes were in popular use by the late 1960s, and many more varieties were available than when they were first introduced about 1955. Energy-efficient oven meals were another special interest Jo shared with her listeners.

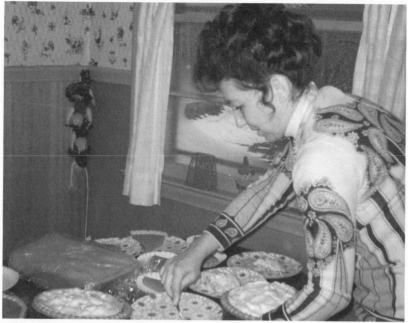

Jo has long been a prodigious baker. She is pictured cutting pies she has prepared for her family's Thanksgiving dinner.

FRESH STRAWBERRY PIE

Place 1 quart cleaned strawberries, cut in large pieces, in a baked 9-inch pie shell; set aside.

Combine in saucepan 1 cup sugar, 2 tablespoons cornstarch, and 1 cup water.

Cook together until thick and clear. Then add 2 tablespoons strawberry gelatin, mixing well. Cool slightly and pour over the strawberries. Chill and top with sweetened whipped topping. This recipe is also good with fresh peaches mixed with peach gelatin.

Jo says this of her family history: "My mother was a plain, basic cook who put out delicious meals. She had a week's plan for her menus and they seldom varied. Sunday we had a roast beef dinner, Monday was bean soup, and, I remember, Saturday we had pork chops with gravy and biscuits. I think one reason I enjoy experimenting with food is because my mother had a routine which did not allow for such maneuvering.

"My father's work on the railroad also had to do with food. He put ice into boxcars which carried fruits and vegetables. He was only sixteen years old when he married, and since it was during the Depression he worked for the WPA. Evenings in the late thirties and early forties, he wallpapered and painted homes and commercial buildings. When I was old enough, I would go along and help paste and paint. From this experience I learned to enjoy redecorating older homes—something I still like to do."

STUFFED ROUND STEAK

4 slices bacon, diced
1 onion, chopped
1½ cups toasted bread cubes
2 tablespoons minced parsley
½ teaspoon celery salt
¼ teaspoon sage
2 to 2½ pounds thin round
    steak, cut into 5 portions,
    tenderized

½ teaspoon salt
⅛ teaspoon pepper
1 cup bouillon
1 8-ounce can tomato sauce
Minced parsley for garnish

To make stuffing, sauté bacon with onion. Mix in bread cubes, parsley, celery salt, and sage. Sprinkle steak with salt and pepper. Spread each portion of steak with stuffing and roll up. Hold together with toothpicks. Place in large skillet. Pour bouillon over; cover and simmer for 1 hour. Pour on tomato sauce. Replace cover and simmer another 45 minutes or until done. If gravy is too thin, cook uncovered until of desired consistency. Garnish with minced parsley.

    5 servings.

Even in 1969, trade names and certain subjects were still taboo. Jo remembers that comments on religion and race were "tiptoed around." Brand name products were carefully eliminated from food chat. "I had to say 'prepared whipped topping.' Now radio home-makers can talk about Cool Whip and Dream Whip without any problems. Even if only one brand was available—Eagle Brand sweet-ened condensed milk, for example—using a trade name was frowned upon."

ICE CREAM DELIGHT

2 cups crushed Rice Chex   ⅔ cup brown sugar
1 cup shredded coconut   ⅓ cup melted butter
½ cup chopped nuts

Mix together and put ⅔ mixture on bottom of 8 × 12 oblong cake pan. Spread ½ gallon softened vanilla ice cream or ½ gallon flavored sherbet on the mixture in the pan. Top with the remaining mixture. Put back into the freezer until serving time.

DICED APPLE COOKIES

½ cup shortening   ½ teaspoon cinnamon
½ cup white sugar   1 teaspoon baking powder
½ cup brown sugar   ½ teaspoon soda
1 egg   ¼ teaspoon salt
1 teaspoon vanilla   ½ cup nutmeats
2 cups sifted flour, plus a little 1 cup diced raw apples
   more if needed   ⅛ teaspoon nutmeg

Mix. Drop by spoonfuls on ungreased cookie sheet. Bake at 375 de-grees 10 to 12 minutes.

Style shows were part of the programming at many of southwest Iowa's festivals and craft sales. At the Clarinda Carnival in 1961, Jo Freed (center) and two other women modeled the latest fashions from local stores.

Jo's busy days at KMA included working closely with the editor of the *KMA Guide*, Mary Williams. Jo helped choose a theme for each issue. She also took pictures, wrote the "Party Line" column, and contributed recipes. Jo sent out a monthly "Today's Woman" mailer and put together the cookbook *Recipes for Today's Woman*. She enjoyed meeting people, judging at fairs, doing public appearances, and guiding visitors through the KMA radio station. "It was a time of great fun and lots of joy," Jo says fondly.

Funny mistakes on the air happen to every broadcaster. "Recipes," as Bernice Currier had said, "are booby traps." One day Jo Freed gave a recipe for cranberry relish. Instead of saying "1 orange" when she listed the ingredients, she said "1 onion." She did not realize the error until a friend called to say she didn't think she'd make up the cranberry relish, "It doesn't sound appetizing with that onion included." Jo went on the air the next day and made the correction. "I just hope the mistake was outlandish enough to keep cooks from try-ing," Jo says ruefully.

Jo graduated from Thomas Jefferson High School in Council Bluffs, Iowa. She attended an Omaha business school and did secretarial work. Then she married Wilbur Freed and moved to Essex.

"Willy" Freed enjoyed restoring and redecorating older houses along with Jo. They lived in a number of homes that they remodeled and then sold, moving on to repeat the process. Jo became interested in the real estate business after leaving KMA. She became a licensed real estate broker with her own business, a profession she continued to enjoy until Willy retired in 1987.

JO'S CARROT CAKE

Sift together and set aside:
   3 cups flour
   2 cups sugar
   2 teaspoons soda
   2 teaspoons baking powder
   2 teaspoons cinnamon
   ½ teaspoon salt

Mix:
   1 teaspoon vanilla
   4 eggs, slightly beaten
   1¼ cups oil
   2 or 3 cups shredded cooked carrots
   ½ cup nuts (black walnuts chopped a little)

Cook carrots in small amount of water; then mash. Combine all ingredients.

Bake in 13 × 9 × 3 greased pan for 55 to 60 minutes in a 350-degree oven.

Frosting

1 teaspoon vanilla
½ cup butter or margarine
1 4-ounce package cream
   cheese

3 cups sifted powdered sugar
½ cup nuts

Cream cheese, butter, and vanilla. Add powdered sugar a little at a time. Then add the nuts.

The Freeds now live in Mesa, Arizona. Jo and Willy enjoy taking interesting trips around Arizona, like riding the 1906 Steam Train to the Grand Canyon. They like to pick peaches, grapes, and other fruits just for fun. With desert rock landscaping, the two have no grass to mow in their yard, but they grow rosebushes, shrubs, flowers, and many trees to remind them of their midwestern roots.

Jo continues to enjoy entertaining and trying new recipes. She dries her own raisins, cooks up orange marmalade, and experiments with recipes of the Southwest. Sometimes she gives food demonstrations to church groups, trailer court gatherings, and club meetings. Her enthusiasm for a growing number of friends and acquaintances plus the energy she puts into enjoying life and family are in many ways an extension of her work with KMA.

The Freeds' two daughters are now "thirtysomething" young women. Lori and her husband, Glen Waters, and two children live on the family farm near West Branch, Iowa. Lori is an interior designer. Lynn works in the senior division of an insurance group and lives in the Mesa area.

EASY CHERRY CRISP

½ cup melted butter
1 cup flour
1 cup brown sugar
1 cup dry oatmeal

¼ teaspoon baking powder
¼ teaspoon salt
¼ teaspoon soda

Mix all together and pat ½ mixture into bottom of 9 × 9 pan. Add 1 can cherry pie filling spread on top. Top with remaining ½ mixture. Bake 30 minutes in 350-degree oven.

Brenda Kay McConahay

When Brenda Kay was first hired by KMA in January 1972, someone told Billie Oakley that KMA had a new homemaker and she had a degree in home economics from Iowa State University in Ames. "I don't care anything about a degree," Billie shot back. "Is she going to be any good?"

When Brenda heard what Billie had said, she realized that while she did have a wealth of background, resources, and education, she was going to have to use every ounce of her ability to prove that she could, indeed, fill the role now hers. "I decided to show Billie that I could be a good radio homemaker."

Brenda did agree that Billie's statement made sense. The two became good friends as the years went by. Brenda went to Lincoln several times and appeared on Billie's television program. Billie in turn came to Shenandoah to help with homemaker days. When Brenda left KMA on March 1, 1978, it was Billie who moved into the position she vacated.

Brenda Crow was raised in smalltown Iowa. Her father, Nelson Crow, is a teacher who imbued his daughter with a love for music. Her mother, Virginia, is extremely talented in crafts, cooking, and related interests. Both her parents passed their interests along to their daughter. Brenda was born in Des Moines during the time her father was teaching in Madison County. The family lived in Indianola while Mr. Crow completed his education. They moved to Clarinda, Iowa, in 1955.

After graduating from high school, Brenda spent a year at Stevens College in Columbia, Missouri, and then transferred to Iowa State University in Ames to complete her undergraduate studies in home economics. Then she decided she wanted to go east—why she is not

271

Brenda in 1972.

certain, but probably because she had never been there—so off she went to teach in New Jersey.

During a summer back in Clarinda, Brenda met Richard Mc-Conahay, a native of Sidney. He was the catalyst that brought her back to the Midwest. Soon after her return, Brenda learned that KMA was searching for a radio homemaker. She came to Shenandoah and did the traditional air-check. KMA liked what they heard and hired her for what turned into six happy years of broadcasting.

After she left KMA, Brenda lived in Clarinda, where she was the homemaking supervisor for Page County Public Health Nursing Services. She had a daily program over radio station KQIS-FM, and she shared the many interests and activities of her growing family.

Brenda used a great deal of imagination in her programming. "Living Today" was chosen as the title for her main homemaker half-hour. (Naturally, a contest was held and the winner for the title received $100 worth of groceries.) Brenda took over the call-in show for the station and called it "Potpourri" because it encompassed such varied subjects from so many listeners. She developed a Saturday "Feminine Focus" program that featured a "This Is Your Life" type interview with women from the area who had been nominated by listeners as being of worth and accomplishment.

CHERRY MASH CANDY

2 pounds powdered sugar
2 boxes cherry frosting mix
2 tablespoons melted margarine

1 can sweetened condensed
  milk
1 10-ounce jar maraschino
  cherries
1 tablespoon vanilla

Drain and chop cherries. Mix frosting mix and sugar together. Add remaining ingredients and blend thoroughly. You will probably need to use your hands for blending. Chill for 1 to 6 hours. Roll in small balls (½ to 1 inch in diameter) and chill for 2 to 3 hours.

Melt together in double boiler 2 12-ounce packages chocolate chips and ½ bar paraffin. Add 1 pound chopped peanuts, with skins removed.

Dip cherry balls in chocolate mixture in top of double boiler.

Brenda frequently used educational tapes sent out by the Iowa State University Extension Service to broaden the scope of subject matter and to bring valuable information to her listeners. Women, she insisted, are interested in *everything*.

"Everything" included such topics as women's role in society, crisis hot line needs, child study, and venereal diseases. Radio subject matter had come a long way from the days when a broadcaster could not talk about toilet training or sleeping on a mattress!

"One of the most difficult tasks I had on the air," Brenda remembers, "was to learn to cover my emotions. So many things happened to me during the six years I worked for KMA. I was married and had all the excitement of the wedding to tell about. Then I had the trauma of three miscarriages. It was a long time before I could talk publicly about the hurt of those difficult days, but finally, when I had a live child and had shared my pregnancy and Ricky's birth with the listeners, I told them about the unhappy times.

"One of the greatest results of that experience was when a lady wrote to tell me her daughter had had a series of miscarriages and would I please send her the name of the doctor in Omaha who had helped me to finally carry a baby full term. I did so, and the daughter went to see the doctor. In due time she had a fine, sturdy baby."

Sadly, Richard and Brenda's marriage did not survive. In 1985 Brenda and her two children, Ricky and Claire, moved to Des Moines, where she continues to serve others in need. She works for the Polk County Department of Human Services as a specialist in the child abuse division. She teaches classes and assists with support groups in the First United Methodist church in Des Moines, emphasizing ways to help divorced persons and single parents.

Coping with her own painful experiences, Brenda has developed a strong foundation from which to help people who are hurting.

CAULIFLOWER WITH SHRIMP SAUCE

1 medium cauliflower, cut in
  flowerets
Salt to taste
1 can (10 ounces) frozen
  condensed cream of shrimp
  soup (unfrozen soup may be
  substituted, but do not dilute)

½ cup milk
¼ cup shredded cheese
1 tablespoon dry bread crumbs

Cook cauliflower until tender in boiling, salted water. Place in baking dish and cover with soup-milk mixture. Sprinkle with cheese and crumbs. Bake at 350 degrees for 30 minutes.

CHOCOLATE ZUCCHINI BUNDT CAKE

Mix *well*:
  4 eggs
  ¾ cup oil
  2 cups coarsely grated
  zucchini
  1 teaspoon vanilla
  1 box chocolate pudding
  (instant)

Add:
  1 chocolate cake mix, dry

Pour into greased and floured bundt pan. Bake in 350-degree oven for 1 hour and 10 minutes.

Brenda liked to give easy-to-make, simple recipes, the kind she used for her own family. As a busy wife and mother who worked outside the home, she knew how important it is to make meal preparation less complicated. She seldom gave a yeast bread recipe because she felt it is hard to explain over the air; quick breads were more to her liking. She had many requests for the kinds of salads and desserts that listeners could take to luncheons and covered-dish dinners.

The crockpot had become popular, and Brenda experimented with many recipes using this new piece of kitchen equipment. Electric skillets also added interest and ease to cooking.

FROZEN PERFECTION CHOCOLATE DESSERT

Mix: 1½ cups coconut and 2 tablespoons melted margarine. Press in bottom of an 8 × 8 pan, baking in 325-degree oven for 10 minutes.

Mix: 1 teaspoon instant coffee in 2 tablespoons hot water.

Melt: 7-ounce chocolate bar with almonds over low heat or in double boiler. Cool. Fold into large container of refrigerated whipped topping. Fold in coffee liquid. Pour into cooled crust. Sprinkle with small package of slivered almonds. Freeze.

HOMEMADE CORN BREAD MIX

4 cups flour
2 tablespoons baking powder
2 teaspoons salt

½ cup sugar
3 cups cornmeal

Mix ingredients. Cut in ½ cup lard or homogenized shortening. Store in cool place. To use, mix 2 cups mix, 1 cup milk, and 1 egg. Stir until mixed. Bake in 450-degree oven for 10 to 15 minutes for muffins, 20 to 25 for bread.

LARGE CHOCOLATE CHIP COOKIES

Cream together:
  2 cups butter
  3 cups sugar
  1½ cups brown sugar

Add and beat well:
  6 eggs
  1 tablespoon vanilla

Sift together and add:
  2 cups flour
  2 teaspoons soda
  1 teaspoon baking powder
  1 teaspoon salt

Add a little at a time:
  6 cups flour
  Beat hard at end of flour
  addition

Add:
  2 12-ounce package chocolate
  chips
  1 cup chopped nuts

Chill several hours or overnight. Bake on ungreased cookie sheets in 375-degree oven for 10 to 15 minutes, depending on the size of the cookies.

When she started her own family, Brenda also planned a contest for those who wished to submit advice for new parents. The response was tremendous, and a fine collection of suggestions were published in a booklet. The winning entry began:

"Enjoy, take time and enjoy them when they are little. The time is preciously short and goes by so very fast. Laugh, laugh out loud with your kids—at yourself, with them. Make happy sounds, humming, singing. It cheers up Mommie even if she doesn't feel cheery and it always helps a grumpy youngster."

When someone asked Brenda to point out the highlights of her years of broadcasting at KMA, she included her marriage and little Ricky's birth. Her tenure included the bicentennial year 1976, and Brenda participated by bringing guests on her shows, helping with pageants, and speaking at various events. Then, when KMA celebrated its fiftieth anniversary on the air, Brenda was mistress of ceremonies for the Homemakers' Day.

"It was great fun to have those women all together in one place," Brenda remembers. "Some of them I knew personally and very well. I had worked with Billie and Evelyn, and I knew Florence and the members of the Kitchen-Klatter family. Adella was a new friend, as was Jessie Young, who came all the way from her home in Colorado to be with us."

During the fiftieth anniversary broadcast, Billie Oakley was talking about the changes that had taken place through the years she had been on radio: "Today many women use mixes and shortcuts in their food preparation. We need to reflect that in our programming."

Old-timer Jessie Young suddenly sat up very straight and began to pound the table. "No! No! No! If you are really a good cook you make all of your dishes from scratch, even today!"

It took all of Brenda's tact to resolve the difference on the air, but everyone knew that neither homemaker had changed her mind.

SKILLET BISCUITS

Preheat electric skillet to 350 degrees and grease lightly with margarine. Place biscuits in skillet, not letting them touch. Cover and bake 3 to 5 minutes. Turn biscuits; cover and bake about 3 minutes longer.

Vivian Steinbauer is a home economist who lived in Shenandoah. She and Brenda met while they were both judges at a Page County Milk Made Magic contest. With their similar interests—church, sewing, family, and professional goals—the two become fast friends. When Brenda took a leave of absence from the air to have her first baby, it was Vivian who substituted for her.

VIVIAN'S PIZZA-STYLE SPAGHETTI

1 cup milk
2 eggs
1 pound spaghetti, cooked
2 jars (15½ ounces each)
  spaghetti sauce

1½ cups thinly sliced pepperoni
2 cups shredded mozzarella
  cheese

Beat milk and eggs together and toss with spaghetti. Spread spaghetti mixture in a large flat baking dish. Top with spaghetti sauce. Arrange pepperoni over top, as desired. Sprinkle with cheese. Bake for 30 minutes in 350-degree oven. Let stand for 5 minutes before cutting into squares.

VIVIAN'S RICH CHERRY FREEZE

1 can cherry pie filling
1 small can crushed pineapple,
  drained
1 cup small marshmallows

2 cups whipped cream or
  topping
1 can sweetened condensed
  milk

Mix together and freeze. Remove 30 minutes before serving. May be placed in loaf pan and sliced or in a square pan and cut in squares. Serve on lettuce.

Brenda talks to visitors in KMA's "bull pen," a busy area that held many desks.

HAYSTACKS

1 3-ounce package cream
    cheese
2 tablespoons milk
2 cups sifted confectioners'
    sugar
2 1-ounce squares unsweetened
    chocolate, melted

¼ teaspoon vanilla
Dash of salt
3 cups mini marshmallows
Flaked coconut

Combine softened cream cheese and milk, mixing until well blended. Gradually add sugar. Stir in chocolate, vanilla, and salt; fold in marshmallows. Drop rounded teaspoons of mixture in coconut; toss until well covered. Place on baking sheet; chill until firm. 4 dozen.

PURPLE SALAD

1 3-ounce box grape or dark
   raspberry gelatin
1 cup boiling water

1 small can crushed pineapple,
   undrained
1 can blueberry pie filling

Dissolve gelatin in water; stir in pineapple and pie filling. Chill. May be frosted with whipped topping before serving.

PINEAPPLE DREAM CAKE

1 small (Jiffy) yellow cake mix
1 package instant pineapple
   pudding mix
2 cups cold milk

1 8-ounce package cream
   cheese, softened
1 cup crushed pineapple, well
   drained
Small container whipped
   topping

Prepare yellow cake mix according to directions on box, only bake in a 9 × 13 pan for 10 to 15 minutes or until it tests done. Cool. Stir pudding mix and milk together. Blend in softened cream cheese. When thick and smooth, spread over baked cake layer. Spread crushed pineapple over pudding layer. Top with whipped topping. Chill. Makes 16 to 20 servings.

PEPPY BURGERS

1 pound ground beef
½ cup chopped onion
1 10½-ounce can vegetable
   soup

4 tablespoons catsup
1 teaspoon mustard
Dash of pepper

Brown beef and onion, stirring to separate meat. Pour off excess fat. Add soup and seasonings. Simmer 5 to 10 minutes to blend flavors, stirring often. Serve as a casserole, over a slice of toast, or in toasted buns.

One summer KMA covered thirty-one county fairs in Iowa, Missouri, and Nebraska plus the Iowa and Nebraska state fairs, craft fairs, community days, and special homemaker days. Brenda assisted with most of them. In her *KMA Guide* column that fall Brenda spoke from her own experience when she wrote: "Movement is the character of life; immobility is the character of death. If you want to stay alive, keep moving."

FROZEN STRAWBERRY SQUARES

1 cup flour   ¼ cup brown sugar
½ cup chopped nuts   ½ cup melted butter

Bake in oven at 350 degrees, stirring every few minutes until golden brown. Put 1⅓ cups in bottom of 9 × 13 pan and use the rest for top.

2 egg whites, beaten stiff   1 cup sugar
2 10-ounce packages   2 tablespoons lemon juice
   strawberries (or 1 16-ounce
   package) or 2 cups

Beat at high speed till stiff peaks form—10 to 15 minutes. Fold in 1 large package whipped dairy substitute. Spoon over bottom layer. Freeze and cut in squares. This is a good dessert to have in the freezer to use as needed.

Brenda was not raised on a farm. When farmers began telling her they listened and enjoyed her program, she honestly did not believe that these men could be out in the fields and the barnyards and listening at the same time. One year, when she was making a personal appearance at the Iowa State Fair, a farmer commented that he listened to her "every day."

"How is this possible?" Brenda asked him. "You surely don't come into the house each morning just to listen to 'Living Today.'"

The farmer laughed: "Why, Brenda, farmers have radios in their tractors. We can work and listen all at the same time."

In March 1985 Colleen helped provide the commentary for the Business and Professional Women's annual fashion show held in Shenandoah. This photograph was taken just at the conclusion of the evening.

Colleen Ketcham

One of Colleen Ketcham's prize possessions was the wedding photograph of her great-great-grandmother. It showed a Cherokee maiden dressed in Native American regalia standing beside her new husband. Colleen was proud of her heritage, which also included English, French, and Irish ancestry. With her Cherokee and European ancestry, she was truly an all-American woman.

"I was born to Stanley and Lesta Exceen," Colleen said. "We lived on a farm near Coin, Iowa, southeast of Shenandoah. When I was in the fourth grade, my daddy had a farm sale and we got out of farming. It was really traumatic and a great adjustment for all of us.

"We moved to a farm south of Emerson. My mother worked at Union Carbide in Red Oak, and for a time my daddy got on as a hired hand on a farm. Later, he got on at Union Carbide too, and we moved to town."

Colleen attended the Nishna Valley Consolidated School, graduating in 1969. That summer she went to Omaha and began working for the Northwestern Bell Telephone Company. It was on-the-job training for the new graduate, a pattern Colleen continued throughout her professional life.

Late in 1969 Colleen was married. "He was a young man I'd grown up with," Colleen recalled. "We were married in December, and in January he went to Vietnam and we were apart for nearly a year. When he returned, we went to Ft. Leonard Wood for about a year and had our first baby, Shalee Dawn. My husband was from Coin so we moved back there. Then Jake William was born.

"I didn't work when the kids were real little," Colleen continued. "I was lonely with only a three-year-old and a six-month-old to keep

283

me company most of the day. I got a job working part-time writing advertising copy for a Shenandoah store. I worked there about four years. It saved my sanity."

It is not easy to talk about the difficult times in one's life, but Colleen was open about herself. "The radio listeners know that I had a divorce, so I see no reason to try and hide it," Colleen said with a wry smile. "When I was faced with a divorce I needed some way to support the kids, so I applied at KQWI in Clarinda and got a job in sales. I also wrote and taped commercials which were used on the air."

Darrell Murphy, an announcer at KMA, was also from the Coin area and knew Colleen. He liked the way her voice sounded on the radio and suggested that she apply for work at KMA. She was offered a part-time position.

TWO-MINUTE FUDGE

½ cup butter or margarine	¼ cup milk
1 pound powdered sugar	½ cup nuts
5 tablespoons cocoa	1 teaspoon vanilla

Place margarine, powdered sugar, cocoa, and milk in mixing bowl. Microwave on high for 1 minute. Stir to combine all ingredients. Microwave on high for 1 minute. Add nuts and vanilla and beat until smooth. Pour into a greased 8-inch square pan. Refrigerate until set. Yield: 36 pieces.

BANANA SPLIT DESSERT

2 cups finely crushed graham crackers	4 or 5 bananas
1 stick melted butter	1 20-ounce can crushed pineapple, well drained
¼ cup sugar	1 12-ounce container Cool Whip
2 cups powdered sugar	Chopped pecans
2 eggs	Maraschino cherries
1 stick soft margarine	Chocolate or strawberries, if desired

Mix first three ingredients and press into 9 x 13 pan and refrigerate. Combine powdered sugar, eggs, and margarine in blender, mixer, or food processor. Blend well and spread over chilled graham cracker crust. Slice bananas over powdered sugar mixture; spread pineapple over bananas. Top with Cool Whip, and then chopped nuts and maraschino cherries. Drizzle with chocolate, if desired, or use strawberries. Refrigerate several hours (will hold overnight). Serves 12 to 16.

FRENCH ONION SOUP

2 tablespoons butter or
    margarine
4 onions, sliced
4 cups water

2 tablespoons beef bouillon
    granules
⅛ teaspoon pepper

Combine butter and onions in a 3-quart casserole; microwave, covered, on high for 6 to 8 minutes until onions are tender, stirring occasionally. Add remaining ingredients. Microwave, covered, on high for 6 to 8 minutes until soup boils. Let rest 5 minutes before serving. Top each bowl with croutons, Swiss, and Parmesan cheese and microwave until cheese melts. Serve immediately.

Colleen liked what she saw and knew about KMA and decided, with a great deal of courage for a single mother with two children, to leave her full-time position with KQWI.

On August 1, 1979, Colleen became an "apprentice everything" at KMA. She learned to run the control board and she liked it. "I came to the station a lot and watched the others work the board and took notes. People were very encouraging. Mac McDonald was program director and he helped me, and Don Hansen. Once I knew how to do it myself, I'd turn the knobs and put people on the air. It was a great feeling to have that kind of power," she remembered. "I played the records, pushed 'carts' into their proper slots to air the taped commercials, reported time and temperature, did live advertising, and read the markets. They even had me sorting and cataloguing the music records. Eventually, I went on full-time."

*Colleen and her children, Jake and Shalee, at her
wedding to Bruce Ketcham.*

For a number of years, Colleen "ran the board," which meant doing
the engineering work that put the programs out over the air. She became the very popular host for "Elephant Shop," which she headed
for over three years.

Colleen married Bruce Ketcham in August 1982. Two of their at-
tendents were Colleen's children, Shalee and Jake. They moved to
Bruce's farm eight miles east of Shenandoah, where they farmed 450
acres of soybeans and corn and raised Simmental cattle. Colleen was
always interested in school, church, and 4-H activities.

Shalee graduated from high school in Shenandoah in the spring of
1990 and is a student at Northwest Missouri State College in Maryville, Missouri. Jake is a Shenandoah high school student and makes
his home with Bruce.

"In 1983," Colleen related, "I decided I wanted to broadcast in the
women's department. I began by doing some programs on 'The Billie
Oakley Show,' and I liked the work. In September 1984 I started air-

ing 'Saturday with Colleen.' It's a great feeling," she continued, "and most days I feel like I am getting paid just for having fun. I am doing something I'd like to do even if I didn't get any salary."

CROCKPOT CHILI DIP

1 10-ounce can Hormel chili
  with no beans

1 8-ounce package cream
  cheese

Combine and pour into a crockpot. Cook on low for a couple of hours and serve with Doritos or other corn chips.

Colleen's life as a farm wife was far different from the lives of the radio homemakers in the early days of the business. "I enjoy my modern kitchen so much that I wonder how the women ever managed without some of the equipment I take for granted. My favorite kitchen gadget (if you can call it that) is my microwave oven. It helps so much when I work to be able to come home and pop something in that oven and have it done in minutes."

CHIPPED BEEF CHICKEN

10 chicken breasts (deboned
  and skinned, if you like)
1 package chipped beef
10 bacon strips

1 cup sour cream
1 can cream of chicken soup
1 6-ounce package cream
  cheese
Dash of Tabasco sauce

Use a 9 x 13 glass baking dish and line the bottom with the chipped beef. Take a single bacon strip and wrap around each chicken breast. If you like, you may cook the bacon until it's half done before you start wrapping; this makes it crispier. Combine your sour cream, chicken soup, softened cream cheese, and dash of Tabasco. Lay the chicken evenly in your baking dish; then pour over the above mixture. Cover with aluminum foil and bake one hour at 350 degrees. Take off foil and let bake another 10 minutes or so.

"Working people, men in particular, are changing their attitudes about homemaking," Colleen insisted. "Husbands are involved with the family and home as never before. They help raise the kids, do the cooking, take care of the laundry, buy the groceries, and clean the house.

"Types of food are changing, too," she continued. "Health foods are easy to find, even in the frozen food sections of the stores. Less sugar and salt, more low-calorie dishes, and easy-to-prepare mixes are popular. Some of the old-fashioned ideas will always be good, though. There is nothing like Grandma's cooking. It will always be IN."

Colleen was aware of the fact that she had no formal education in radio or broadcasting, but she wanted to keep learning and progressing in the profession. "I don't want to be pulling the ten-to-three board shift when I'm fifty; when I'm sixty I don't want to be spinning records," Colleen explained. "I want to develop in more areas of radio, and the women's department is a good one to work in."

Colleen had part of that desire granted. She will never be working on the board shift or spinning records at the age of fifty or sixty. In July 1987, in the middle of a remote radio broadcast that she was doing live from the Mills County Fair in Malvern, Iowa, Colleen collapsed. Following hospitalization, she returned home, but she was later rushed to an Omaha hospital in a coma. On August 29, 1987, at the age of thirty-six, she died of a brain aneurysm. On September 1, more than seven hundred relatives, friends, colleagues, and radio listeners attended her memorial service.

Colleen had stated on one of her "Elephant Shop" programs: "Our own troubles are worth enduring if they show us how to have sympathy for others. Keep your face into the sun and the shadows will fall behind."

After her death, Andy Andersen, station manager when Colleen started, likened her to an unpolished stone with a flair for the dramatic when she started on KMA. "Now," he insisted, "she is a *polished* stone, one that we cherish."

Mike LePorte, KMA farm director, commented: "Colleen always had the ability to lift you right up. She had a great vitality with which she approached life. She was quick with a smile, quick with humor, and quick with getting down to work when a job needed to get done."

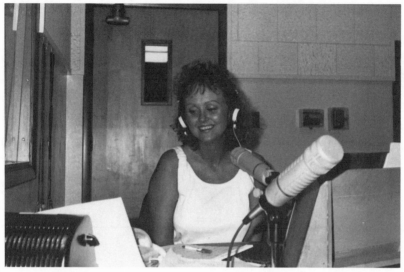

Colleen Ketcham was a popular host for the "Saturday with Colleen" homemaker show.

Fellow broadcaster Verlene Looker remembered: "Colleen would find a saying or a poem to use at the end of each program, and then she would conclude with the words, 'I am not going to say good-bye; I'm just going to say, Until we meet again.'"

COLLEEN'S ROUND STEAK

1 package round steak
Prepared mustard
1 package onion soup mix
1 can mushrooms, drained

6 slices bacon, browned and
    drained
1 can cream of mushroom soup

Cut round steak into serving pieces and spread one side with prepared mustard. Sprinkle on top the onion soup mix and drained mushrooms. Lay strips of bacon on meat and roll up. Put in jelly roll pan with the open edge down; pour soup over. Cover with foil and bake at 250 degrees for 5 hours. (This is also good with chopped green peppers and one onion, sliced.)

Sue Jones (left) and Marilyn Lee.

Marilyn Lee and Sue Jones

After Billie Oakley retired in March 1987, KMA searched for new ideas in programming. The station finally contracted for a national call-in program featuring a psychologist and started the daily half-hour "KMA Today" program, which dedicated one or two mornings a week to subjects related to homemaking. Listeners who for more than sixty years had enjoyed radio homemakers with whom they could identify did not relate as well to questions and answers on problems unrelated to their own and did not bond as well with broadcasters who came into their homes once or twice a week instead of every day.

Listeners began to complain. They wrote letters. They called the management at KMA. They talked to their neighbors about their frustration. The ultimate criticism was made by one listener of many years who stated loudly that she hated having people's sex problems in the middle of her dinner preparations. When the contract expired for the psychologist's program, it was not renewed.

What to do next? The management at KMA wanted to appeal to modern women and attract them to the listening audience, but they decided that completely abandoning the format of earlier women's programs was premature. The station sent out requests to home economists asking if they were interested in doing a homemaker program.

Shenandoah resident Marilyn Lee was one of the women in the area who received such a letter. Marilyn's first response was disbelief. Then she thought the suggestion was funny, for she could not visualize herself as a radio broadcaster. After learning that the station planned for a second woman to share the responsibilities, Marilyn said she'd try, wondering what she was agreeing to and why!

Assuming that two people on the microphone would have broader appeal and more diversity than just one, those in charge of broadcasting decisions began to look for another person with a background different from Marilyn's—someone who could bring a dimension beyond home economics to the program. The choice for the second member of the broadcast team was music teacher Sue Jones.

Even though being a radio homemaker was far removed from her professional training, Sue's experiences with community projects, entertaining, and teaching gave her confidence. Speaking to radio listeners was surprisingly similar to performing in front of an audience. Sue discovered that broadcasting was an exciting challenge and that working as a partner with Marilyn was pleasant.

"Family Living" went on the air August 31, 1987. In some ways the program was unique; in others it was a descendant of earlier homemaker shows. "Family Living" was not the first to have two women together in front of the microphone to visit with each other and the audience. Gertrude May and LeOna Teget did some dual programming in 1925, the first year of KMA's life. However, it was the Kitchen-Klatter family whose members gradually developed the two-person homemaker program into a consistent pattern that became almost an art form.

The format of "Family Living" included a wide variety of topics and issues designed to meet the interests of the homemaker–career woman. Marilyn and Sue told stories of their families and their experiences and gave household hints and recipes, just as the radio homemakers had done before them. They added new material, such as area school reports and medical information, and conducted telephone interviews with guests from all over the country on many subjects. The station's telephone lines were opened for part of the hour-long program. Listeners called in to speak with the guests, to ask questions, or to give their favorite recipes. It was much like the "Open Line" program that Doris Murphy had started, and the same technique was used through the years by Billie Oakley, Joni Baillon, and others.

The two "Family Living" broadcasters went singly or together to cover fairs, seminars, expositions, and places of interest. They went to the World Agricultural Exposition in the Amana Colonies in Iowa and to the Botanical Garden in Milwaukee, Wisconsin. They also enjoyed a visit to Reiman Publications in Milwaukee, where they originated two live broadcasts to beam back to KMA listeners. Chris Branstad, Iowa's first lady, helped them judge pies at a Corning, Iowa, annual pie contest and then agreed to do a half-hour radio interview with them. Some of the other special guests on the "Family Living" program were the dean of the Nebraska Methodist College of Nursing, Ann Keiser, editor of the *Country Women Magazine*, and Peggy Fleming, the national spokesperson for the pork industry.

MARILYN'S HERBED TOMATO CHEESE BREAD

Bottom layer:
  ⅔ cup milk
  2 cups biscuit mix

Middle layer:
  3 medium tomatoes, peeled
  and sliced ¼ inch thick

Sour Cream Topping:
  1 medium onion, minced
  2 tablespoons butter
  ¾ cup dairy sour cream
  ⅓ cup mayonnaise
  4 ounces grated cheddar
  cheese (about 1 cup)
  ¾ teaspoon salt
  ¼ teaspoon pepper
  ¼ teaspoon leaf oregano
  Pinch sage
  Paprika (for top)

Preheat oven to 400 degrees. Butter a 13 x 9 x 2 pan. Stir milk into biscuit mix to make a soft dough. Turn dough onto a well-floured board and knead lightly 10 to 12 strokes. Pat dough over bottom of buttered baking dish, pushing dough up sides of dish, to form a shallow rim. Arrange tomato slices over dough. Prepare sour cream topping: sauté onion in butter until tender and blend in remaining topping ingredients with the exception of paprika. Spoon sour cream topping over tomatoes and sprinkle with paprika. Bake 35 minutes. Let stand 10 minutes before cutting.

When Sue and Marilyn were visiting Reiman Publications in Milwaukee, they made this recipe for the judges in the tomato recipe contest. It was one of the winners.

Marilyn and Sue enthusiastically entered into the activities surrounding KMA's annual fall festivals, helping demonstrate crafts, presenting cooking ideas, and staging musical interludes.

"For us the highlights of our radio experiences were the listeners and the special guests we met, all of whom made the programs interesting," Sue commented. "It was hard work. No one realizes how difficult it is to keep a half-hour or an hour program fresh and interesting. It is an extremely time-consuming job to research and prepare the material, find and test recipes, and decide how all the pieces should go together. But it was a fun, learning experience."

SUE'S SIMPLE CHICKEN CHOW MEIN

2 tablespoons oil
4 tablespoons minced onion
1 cup sliced button mushrooms
1½ cups shredded cooked
   chicken
1 cup diced celery

1½ cups chicken stock (skim off
   fat)
2 tablespoons light soy sauce
1 tablespoon sugar
1½ teaspoons cornstarch
3 tablespoons cold water

Brown onion and mushrooms in oil. Add chicken, celery, chicken stock, soy sauce, and sugar and simmer for 15 minutes. Blend together cornstarch and water and add to meat mixture. Cook until mixture thickens and is heated throughout. Serve over rice or noodles.

MARILYN'S APPLE DIP

1 8-ounce package cream
   cheese
¾ cup brown sugar

¼ cup white sugar
1 teaspoon vanilla flavoring

Soften cream cheese to room temperature; add remaining ingredients and blend until smooth. A great dip for sliced apples.

Sue Jones and Dean Adkins enjoyed singing a duet as part of the entertainment at KMA's 1988 Fall Festival.

Sue Jones was raised in Lake City in northwest Iowa. Her father was a lawyer whose three sons followed in his footsteps. Both Sue and her sister chose music education as a profession.

Sue attended Simpson College in Indianola, where she met her husband, Floyd Jones. They were married and moved to Des Moines, where Floyd attended medical school and Sue became the breadwinner for the two as a teacher. When Sue discovered she was pregnant, she was desperately afraid she would lose her job. Her school board was more lenient than many during the sixties and seventies in permitting a pregnant teacher to remain in the classroom. With a sigh of relief, Sue continued teaching, Floyd continued medical school, and the Joneses continued eating.

In 1972 Sue and her family, now including sons Bryan and Eric, moved to Shenandoah, where Floyd started his medical career in family practice. He and Sue added Justin and Jessica to bring the number of their children to four.

Like Sue, Marilyn experienced a precedent-setting pregnancy. She was the first teacher in the school system in Tipton, Iowa, to be allowed to teach while pregnant. "After that year was over, I stayed home to care for the baby," Marilyn explained. "It is strange how times have changed. In the 1940s married women were not allowed to teach. That rule was relaxed, but then if a teacher became pregnant she was required to give up her position. Now married is okay, pregnant is okay, and a mother returns to teaching soon after the birth of a child.

"One reason I kept my pregnancy a secret as long as I could was that we had lost our first child. I kept thinking how awful it would be if I was forced to give up teaching, and then, if I didn't carry this baby full term, losing my job would have been for nothing."

Marilyn grew up in Cedar Rapids, Iowa. She received her degree in home economics education from Iowa State University in Ames, where she met her husband, Ken Lee. After their marriage, Marilyn taught school in Tipton until the happy birth of their son Chad. Subsequently two more sons were born to the couple, Brian and Mark.

The Lees moved to Shenandoah in 1984, but Marilyn did not return to teaching. It was not surprising that the opportunity to do radio educating on "Family Living" presented a challenge for her.

"Times have changed," Marilyn exclaimed one day over the air. "Women today are career-oriented, so the listeners at home are older women or young mothers with their babies." She felt that most women in their thirties, forties, and fifties were working and not able to listen.

MARILYN'S CHOCOLATE CHIP BARS

1 cup margarine	½ teaspoon butter flavoring
¾ cup white sugar	1 teaspoon vanilla flavoring
¾ cup brown sugar, packed	2¼ cups flour
2 tablespoons honey or corn syrup	1 teaspoon soda
2 tablespoons water	¼ teaspoon salt
2 eggs	1 12-ounce package chocolate chips

Cream margarine and sugars. Add honey, water, eggs, and flavorings. Combine dry ingredients and add to creamed mixture. Stir in chips. Bake in a greased jelly roll pan in a 350-degree oven for 18 to 20 minutes. These stay nice and moist.

At the 1988 Iowa State Fair, Marilyn Lee and Don Hansen beam out a live broadcast over the KMA airwaves from the Varied Industries building.

"As long as we were on the air, Sue and I tried to present current issues of interest to both men and women. Men did listen. We had letters from farmers and truck drivers and househusbands. We tried to reflect the changing roles men and women were facing. Food talk is interesting, but many people today, especially younger ones, eat out, like quick stuff, and don't want to spend time in the kitchen. Maybe they don't want to spend time copying down recipes either."

The "Family Living" program ceased production in December 1988. Marilyn returned to college to become recertified as a teacher. She then continued her education in nursing. She continues with her many interests—antiquing, crafts, gardening, and cooking. She collects cookbooks, and in 1990 she assisted the Shenandoah United Methodist Church in publishing a collection of recipes.

Sue also returned to college to renew her teaching certificate. The following fall, she was hired to fill in for a music teacher on maternity leave in the nearby Essex public school. She is involved in a number of community activities, including the Shenandoah Music Association and the American Field Service (the Jones family hosted a Swiss boy in 1984–1985 and a Japanese girl in 1990–1991). She is choir director for the Shenandoah United Methodist Church and also helped with their cookbook project.

SUE'S DELIGHTFUL CHICKEN CASSEROLE

2 cups chopped cooked chicken
1 cup cream of chicken soup
¾ cup mayonnaise
1 cup diced celery
1 cup cooked white rice

1 tablespoon grated onion
½ teaspoon salt
1 cup bread crumbs
¼ cup melted margarine
½ cup slivered almonds

Combine chicken, soup, mayonnaise, celery, rice, onion, and salt. Put mixture in a 1½-quart greased baking dish. Bake for 30 minutes at 350 degrees. Mix together bread crumbs with margarine and almonds; put topping on top of baked mixture. Bake an additional 20 minutes.

MARILYN'S MARINATED HERBED TOMATO SALAD

6 ripe tomatoes, cored and
    sliced
3 sweet peppers, sliced
1 sweet onion, diced
¾ cup sliced black olives
⅔ cup salad oil
¼ cup vinegar
¼ cup cut parsley

¼ cup minced green onion
½ teaspoon salt
Dash pepper
1 teaspoon sugar
½ teaspoon fresh or dried basil
½ teaspoon fresh or dried
    marjoram

Slice vegetables into bowl. Add olives. Combine remaining ingredients in another bowl and mix well. Pour over vegetables and refrigerate for several hours before serving.

MARILYN'S HOT ARTICHOKE DIP

1 14-ounce can artichoke
  hearts, drained
1 cup Parmesan cheese
1 8-ounce package cream
  cheese

½ cup mayonnaise
½ teaspoon dry dill weed
¼ teaspoon minced garlic

Put half the ingredients at a time in food processor; blend well and mix together. Spread in a 10-inch greased pie plate. Bake for 15 to 20 minutes. Serve in fresh mushroom caps or on melba rounds.

Chris Branstad shared this recipe with the "Family Living" broadcasters when she was with them on the air.

SUE'S QUICK AND EASY COBBLER

1 cup flour
1 cup sugar (or less)
½ teaspoon salt
2 teaspoons baking powder

⅔ cup milk
2 cups fresh fruit (cherries,
  raspberries, or a can of
  cherries)
1 teaspoon almond flavoring

Combine flour, sugar, salt, and baking powder. Add milk and stir well. Spoon into 8 x 12 greased Pyrex baking dish. Mix fruit, sugar (less for sweet fruit, the total amount for sour), and flavoring and pour over batter. Bake at 45 minutes in 350-degree oven. Good served hot or cold with vanilla ice cream.

Verlene leading a camel at the Iowa State Fair.

Verlene Looker

KMA continued searching for just the right key to a modern women's program that would appeal to as many listeners as possible. After "Family Living" left the air, the new program "Lifestyles" was created. Finding a host did not take long; Verlene Looker gave up her receptionist-secretary position and her twice-a-week "KMA Today" program to head the new daily hour-long broadcasts.

By that time, members of the Looker family had already been a part of KMA radio and the May Seed & Nursery Company for many years.

Verlene and her brother, Roger, were born on a farm some seven miles from Maryville, Missouri. The family moved to Shenandoah when Verlene was six years old. Her father farmed for a time and then began working for the May Seed & Nursery Company in the grass seed department. He became the overseer of the original public trial gardens on Nishna Road. Mrs. Looker was hired by the May Company to work in the seed mail-order department, a position she continues to enjoy.

Becoming a broadcaster was the furthest thing from Verlene's mind when she finished high school. Business was her major interest. After she graduated from business college in Omaha, her first employment was as a secretary with an Omaha credit union. In 1965 she returned to Shenandoah to work for the Driftmier Company. For twenty years she filled a number of positions for Kitchen-Klatter. She took charge of the magazine files, printed name plates, and assisted with the mail at a time when hundreds of letters were received each day. Eventually she became office supervisor, a role that required overseeing the printing of the *Kitchen-Klatter Magazine* and the publication

Continuing the tradition of hosting interesting guests on her homemaker program, Verlene Looker interviews microwave cooking specialist Karen Kangas Dwyer of Omaha. Don Hansen, "Lifestyles" engineer, can be seen through the glass of KMA's live broadcasting studio.

of their cookbooks. She helped owner Lucile Verness choose the premiums that encouraged listeners to buy the company's products, and she tested some of the recipes that Lucile then sampled and gave over the air. In 1966 Lucile arranged for Verlene to attend Iowa Western Community College to study communications, business management, accounting, and, later, computer studies. In 1971 Verlene began doing backup broadcasting on the "Kitchen-Klatter" radio program, which was heard over KMA. By 1977 she was a frequent member of the broadcasting team.

Verlene continued working for Kitchen-Klatter until the company went out of business the last day of 1985. She immediately began doing a homemaker program for Shenandoah-based KQIS. She also became a tour guide for the Central Travel Agency of Shenandoah.

VERLENE'S NUT GOODIE BARS

1 12-ounce package milk
  chocolate chips
1 12-ounce package
  butterscotch chips
2 cups peanut butter (creamy or
  chunky)
1 cup butter or margarine

½ cup evaporated milk
¼ cup dry vanilla pudding mix
  (NOT instant)
2 pounds powdered sugar
½ teaspoon maple flavoring
2 cups salted peanuts

Melt the chocolate chips, butterscotch chips, and peanut butter in top of double boiler over hot water. Put half in buttered 10 x 15 jelly roll pan. Freeze. Combine butter or margarine and dry pudding mix in saucepan. Boil 1 minute. In a large bowl, place the powdered sugar. Pour butter-pudding mixture over it and beat until smooth. Add maple flavoring. Spread over hardened chocolate layer. Freeze. Reheat remaining chocolate mixture and add the peanuts. Spread over powdered sugar layer. Freeze. Just before serving, remove for 5 minutes. Cut into small squares. Keep refrigerated or frozen until time to eat. This is very rich, so cut into small squares.

In April 1986 she joined the office staff at KMA as receptionist-secretary. In the fall of 1987 she returned to the air as host for two programs a week on "KMA Today." In January 1989 KMA asked Verlene to head the women's department and to develop a program that would include both the traditional and the modern. The result was "Lifestyles."

"I enjoy the work," Verlene insists. "It took me a while to decide to become a full-time radio broadcaster, but the longer I do it, the more I appreciate this profession. Pleasing the listeners is my number 1 priority. When I go to fairs and food contests and conferences, I find I am among caring radio friends.

"Interviews and personal appearances are a challenge. I enjoy meeting and interviewing people like actresses Debbie Reynolds and Shelley Fabares and Chris Branstad, the wife of the governor of Iowa," she continues. "I've done remote broadcasts from such places as the National Beef Conference in Portland, Oregon, a child abuse convention in Washington, D.C., the Donna Reed Festival in Denison, Iowa, and from many county and state fairs.

"The first test of a live remote is to see whether the equipment will work. At one fair, nothing functioned properly, and I had to turn to the telephone lines to get the broadcast on the air. The only telephone available at that moment was in the restroom. There I was, inside that stifling hot place, trying to talk with enthusiasm to the radio audience about the activities going on outside at the fair."

ESCALLOPED CABBAGE

1 small head cabbage, chopped
Salt and pepper to taste
3 tablespoons butter
1 egg

3 cups club crackers, crushed
1 cup half-and-half or cream
1 8-ounce package Velveeta
  cheese

In a saucepan combine chopped cabbage, seasonings, butter, and water just to cover. Cook until tender. Drain. In a buttered 3-quart casserole, place a layer of cabbage, a layer of sliced cheese, and a layer of crackers. Repeat layering until all ingredients are used, ending with a cracker layer. Beat egg and half-and-half together. Pour over cabbage and bake, covered, in a 350-degree oven for 20 minutes. Remove cover and continue baking for 10 more minutes to brown lightly.

RICE–PORK CHOP CASSEROLE

4 thick pork chops
¼ cup diced onion
¼ cup chopped green pepper

½ cup uncooked wild rice
1 quart tomato juice
Salt and pepper to taste

Brown pork chops, onion, and green pepper in a little shortening. Place in a 2-quart casserole dish; place rice on top of chops and pour tomato juice over all. Bake, covered, in a 350-degree oven for 1 to 1½ hours.

CUCUMBER RELISH

10 cups ground cucumber
8 medium onions, ground
4 medium sweet peppers,
    ground
4 teaspoons pickling salt
2 cups vinegar

4 cups sugar
2 teaspoons turmeric
2 teaspoons celery seed
4 teaspoons mustard seed
½ teaspoon black pepper

Combine first four ingredients. Let stand for 30 minutes. Drain well. Combine remaining ingredients, add vegetable mixture, and boil for 5 minutes. Pack into jars; seal and process in hot water bath for 10 minutes.

BUTTERMILK PIE CRUST

6 cups flour
2 to 3 teaspoons salt
2 cups shortening (preferably
    lard)

½ cup margarine
1 cup buttermilk
2 tablespoons oil
1 teaspoon vanilla flavoring

Combine flour and salt. Cut in shortening. Combine buttermilk, oil, and flavoring. Blend well. Refrigerate. Take out enough for a pie as desired. Keeps well. Yields 4 to 6 pie crusts.

Verlene got this recipe during a public appearance she made in Worthington, Minnesota.

Other interesting events happened during fair appearances. One year at the Iowa State Fair, Verlene led a camel around the grounds, not a normal homemaker project. It is an experience she does not care to repeat. In Iowa, fairs can occur during some of the hottest days of the year. Verlene and I were judging a baby contest at the Mills County Fair in Malvern, Iowa, when the temperature zoomed to more than one hundred degrees. Poor kids! Poor parents! Poor judges!

Besides telling of such experiences on her broadcasts, Verlene also shares stories about her family activities. She helps her brother, Roger, with his farming operations near Essex. She helps plant, cultivate, harvest, and walk beans. ("Walking beans" means to walk between the bean rows and pull or cut out weeds and maverick plants.) The work is a relaxing change of pace from broadcasting.

Verlene's father died in November 1987. She and her mother continue to make their home together in Shenandoah. "We still enjoy cooking but we don't do nearly as much as we used to. I do try to make a good share of the recipes I give over the air. Doing them myself makes them easier to talk about," she explains. "When listeners send in recipes, I always assume they have already tried them. I've worked with recipes so much now that I can read a recipe and tell if it is good."

GROUND PORK CASSEROLE

1 pound ground pork	1 can tomato soup
1 medium onion, chopped	1 can creamed corn
Salt and pepper to taste	1 cup grated cheddar cheese
1 small package noodles	

Brown the pork and onion; salt and pepper as desired. Drain off excess fat. Cook noodles according to package directions. Drain well. Combine meat mixture with noodles. Add the tomato soup and creamed corn. Place in a 2-quart casserole. Sprinkle with cheese. Bake at 350 degrees for 30 minutes.

Verlene is editor of the bimonthly *Open Line Memo*, a publication made up primarily of the recipes given over the air. For several years, a cookie contest was held in connection with each Fall Festival. The cookies were terrific, tasty, and a resource for new ideas to use on the broadcasts and in the *Memo*. After the judging was completed, the cookies were taken to care facilities and children's homes in the area.

Verlene tries to bring variety into her "Lifestyles" program by in-

This photograph was taken during an open house at the original Earl May Seed & Nursery Company test and display gardens, where Verlene's father used to tend the acres of flowers and vegetables. The present gardens, south and west of Shenandoah close to Highway 2, are open to the public all summer long.

terviewing guests. For example, there was Jamie White, a fourteen-year-old girl who, with her father, runs camps in the Ozarks for handicapped children. Jamie designs clothes for a large clothing store chain and uses her profits to support the camp.

Occasionally, controversial subjects are aired on Verlene's programs, but she always tries to show both sides. "I often feel that no one changes anyone else's mind, but the listeners deserve to be informed.

"No matter how modern the times, homemakers and the subjects in which they are interested are needed," Verlene states firmly. "People want recipes and helpful hints; they want to hear knowledgeable guests talk, and they want to call in and share their ideas on the radio. I think radio homemakers will always be around."

KMA general manager Susan Christensen at her desk.

Susan Cochran, KMA associate news director.

The Adventure Continues

As we have seen, KMA is a unique radio station in a unique time in the history of the Midwest. It now has two women named Susan on the staff, but each is unique in her own way. In some respects, they are bringing KMA, now more than sixty-five years old, full circle. As with the other women on the staff who hold responsible positions, both have a deep sense of the heritage of the station and a commitment to its listeners.

Susan Christensen, general manager of KMA and KMA-FM, is involved in every aspect of the stations, a position her background, education, and experience have fitted her well to assume. Susan served as sales manager for KFAB-AM and KGOR-FM in Omaha just prior to coming to Shenandoah. However, her learning experiences go back to her earliest days on the farm.

She and her three brothers and one sister were born and raised in a close-knit family in McCook, Nebraska, where her family still farms. Her parents, E. J. and Nadine Friehe, encouraged her to travel, read, and learn about people outside of Red Willow County, Nebraska, and to keep her mind stimulated.

Susan explains: "Children in our family were raised with traditional roles, but their expectations were not treated according to gender. My mother was actively involved in all the farming operations. My grandmother managed my grandfather's implement dealership (Grandfather was the mechanic in the partnership). As a result of this background, I did not know that women were supposed to be gentle, submissive creatures until I left home; by then the damage had been done. I was, and still am, an independent person.

"My family expected me to get an education, to play a role in society, and to choose for myself whatever I wanted to do. I was expected to do well."

SUSAN CHRISTENSEN'S GERMAN PFEFFERNUSS COOKIES

4 cups brown sugar
1 cup molasses
1 cup butter
2 to 3 eggs
7 cups flour
2 teaspoons cinnamon
2 teaspoons cloves

2 teaspoons pepper
2 teaspoons allspice
2 teaspoons nutmeg
2 teaspoons soda
1 teaspoon salt
1 teaspoon grated lemon rind

Mix sugar, molasses, and butter in a saucepan and bring to a boil. Let cool. Then add well-beaten eggs and the flour, which has been sifted with the other dry ingredients. Add lemon rind. Cover dough and let stand at room temperature for several hours, overnight, OR up to 2 weeks (right!). Add more flour if needed to hold shape but no more than needed. Roll into a long 1-inch-thick rope. Cut into 1-inch cubes and roll into balls. Place on greased cookie sheet. Bake at 350 degrees for about 15 minutes. Store in a tight container. The longer they set, the better the flavor.

Susan Christensen's great-grandparents came from Germany and, like many other German natives, settled in Nebraska. No wonder Susan enjoys German cooking. And this little traditional cookie is one of her favorites.

SUSAN CHRISTENSEN'S SOFT GINGERSNAPS

¾ cup shortening
1 cup sugar
1 teaspoon cloves
1 teaspoon cinnamon
1 teaspoon ginger

4 tablespoons molasses
2 teaspoons soda
1 egg
2 cups flour

Combine ingredients and roll in balls the size of a walnut. Roll in granulated sugar. Bake at 350 degrees approximately 8 to 10 minutes.

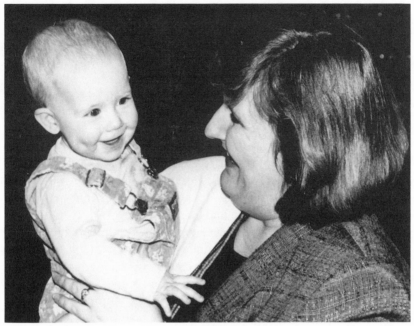

Susan Christensen with her daughter, Megan.

One of Susan's major interests as a child was music, which undoubt-edly is one of the reasons she was so attracted to radio. The sounds, voices, blends, harmonies, and artistry were appealing to young Susan. During her high school days, she worked evenings as a disc jockey at a radio station and days as a guide at a local historical site.

While earning her degree in broadcast journalism at the University of Nebraska in Lincoln, Susan worked for radio station KLIN-FM as a news reporter and also as a television newswriter and photographer. She did some on-air work in both media. After college she started working for May Broadcasting in Omaha as a writer-producer for commercials. These experiences gave Susan a knowledge of every as-pect of broadcasting and prepared her well for her present position.

Susan met her husband, Larry Christensen, while he was an engi-neer at KMTV. He now has his own company based in their Shenan-doah home. An expert in electronics, he designs and installs video production facilities. Susan and Larry are the parents of Megan, who was two years old when her mother became general manager of KMA.

"I enjoy homemaking and find it a creative outlet. I like the basics—sewing, cooking, baking at Christmastime. I do not do anything spectacular but I like it all, except I don't like to garden much. My greatest delight is being a mother. Megan is terrific and is already a great companion for me when I work around the house."

Susan has expressed deep feelings about the station: "KMA was built on listeners' needs, and we are still committed to serving them. Stability and continuing what is proven to be of value are part of the ongoing work of the station, but in new ways. We now live in a thirty-second world. Few people sit by the radio for hours at a time as they did in the early days of radio. Everyone gets impatient no matter what age they are, young and old alike. People have changed through the years, and radio needs to change with them."

As a woman working in a normally male-dominated position, Susan has experienced some prejudice—the odd look, criticism voiced openly, sometimes snide comments. She feels keenly that it is the quality of the person, not the gender, or race, or lifestyle, or age, that is important. "I do respect differences of opinion; that's what keeps the work interesting," Susan hastens to add.

"I do like the way women think. They bring more nurturing skills to their profession, are better listeners, and are more aware of people's feelings. Women try to keep in touch with people as individuals, to think of the entire person rather than just the circumstances at hand.

"If I have my way," Susan concludes emphatically, "KMA will continue with news, weather, sports, agriculture, music, and homemakers' programming as it has in the past, but in fresh, energetic, creative ways. The future is impossible to predict, but we can work toward it with enthusiasm. No matter what is done, our dedication to the listeners won't change."

SUSAN CHRISTENSEN'S GRANDMOTHER'S GOOEY POPCORN

½ cup heavy cream   Popped corn
1 cup sugar

Combine cream and sugar and boil together until a soft ball forms. Pour over popped corn. Mix and enjoy.

SUSAN CHRISTENSEN'S QUICK EASY CHICKEN

4 boneless chicken breasts
1 teaspoon chopped onion
¼ butter or white wine
1 can cream of mushroom soup
1 cup sour cream

1 teaspoon chopped onion
½ teaspooon parsley
Dash celery salt
Salt and pepper to taste

Sauté chicken breasts and onion in butter or white wine for 3 or 4 minutes. Add remaining ingredients. Cover and simmer for about 20 minutes or until chicken is done. Serve over hot cooked rice or noodles.

SUSAN CHRISTENSEN'S COLESLAW

2 cups sugar
3 pounds shredded cabbage
1 small onion, chopped
½ cup chopped green pepper
1 cup vinegar

1 cup Mazola oil
1 teaspoon dry mustard
1 teaspoon celery seed
1 teaspoon salt

Pour the sugar over the shredded cabbage. Add onion and green pepper. Set aside while you prepare the dressing. Heat remaining ingredients to a boil. Pour over cabbage. Refrigerate and let stand overnight.

The other unique Susan at KMA is the station's associate news director. She has been with the station since 1981. Susan Cochran worked in a number of positions—as the weekend announcer, as a seven-to-midnight disc jockey, and as the morning announcer—until she finally moved to her present position as a member of the news department. She received her B.A. degree in education from Graceland College in Lamoni, Iowa, in 1980, and a B.S. degree in broadcasting from Northwest Missouri State University in 1985.

To date Susan has earned nine news and sports awards as a news reporter and an Award of Merit for her interesting and informative

"KMA Today" program dealing with the subject of animal rights. She is committed to international understanding. She was chosen as one of the reporters to travel with Governor Terry Branstad in the summer of 1988 to report on the Sister State Agreement with the Stavrapol region of the Soviet Union. The Iowa contingent also made stops in Hungary, Switzerland, and Germany.

"I enjoy doing all kinds of topics, even sensitive subjects," Susan says. "I got some flak for having a real witch on one program, but she was sincere and it was an interesting discussion on a subject few people know. I like to give people the right to talk, the right to disagree, to give both sides of a problem or situation. Everyone has a right to express his or her opinion." Susan adds, "I am not offended if people disagree, but I am offended if they do not have the opportunity to give an opinion or refuse to listen to what another person has to say. I give information so people can make informed decisions."

Susan's husband, Jeffrey Moores, is an elementary physical education teacher and head high school coach for boys' basketball and girls' cross-country track for the Shenandoah public schools. Susan and Jeffrey are the parents of two children, Dane Cochran Moores and Faith Cochran Moores.

SUSAN COCHRAN'S GRANDMOTHER'S CHOCOLATE PUDDING

⅓ cup cornstarch
3 tablespoons cocoa
¼ teaspoon salt

½ cup sugar
3 cups milk
1 tablespoon butter or
   margarine

Sift dry ingredients together 3 times. Put in top of double boiler over hot water and add the milk. Cook over medium heat until pudding is boiling hot and begins to thicken, stirring all the time. Add butter or margarine and stir well. Remove from heat and add flavoring. Stir well and chill. (I sometimes use powdered chocolate mix instead of cocoa for a milder pudding.)

Susan Cochran with her two children, Faith and Dane.

SUSAN COCHRAN'S PARTY CHICKEN SALAD

4 cups cubed cooked chicken
1 cup grated carrots
1 cup finely chopped celery
1 cup sliced ripe olives
1 cup green seedless grapes
1 tablespoon chopped green
   onion or flaked dried onion
1 7-ounce can pineapple
   chunks

1 cup mayonnaise
½ cup cream cheese, softened
1½ cups frozen whipped
   topping or ¾ cup heavy
   cream, whipped
2 cups canned shoestring
   potatoes

In a large bowl combine all ingredients with exception of last four. In a small bowl, mix mayonnaise, cream cheese, and whipped topping or whipped cream. Stir into ingredients in large bowl to coat. Chill 3 to 5 hours. Mix in the shoestring potatoes just before serving. Serve over lettuce. Serves 8.

SUSAN COCHRAN'S SAUERKRAUT BALLS

1 pound ground beef
½ pound sausage
½ cup flour
½ cup onions
½ cup fresh mushrooms

1 cup sour cream
1 can sauerkraut, drained and
    chopped
2 eggs, beaten
Toasted bread crumbs

Cook and drain the meats. Stir in flour, onions, and mushrooms. Heat thoroughly. Remove from fire and add sour cream and drained, cut-up sauerkraut. Cool and roll into balls. Dip balls into beaten eggs, roll in toasted bread crumbs, and fry in deep fat until golden brown.

SUSAN COCHRAN'S POPPY SEED BREAD

3 cups flour
½ teaspoon salt
1½ teaspoons baking powder
2½ cups sugar
1½ cups milk

1⅓ cups cooking oil
3 eggs
1½ tablespoons poppy seeds
1½ teaspoons vanilla flavoring
1½ teaspoons almond flavoring

Combine ingredients and beat well for 2 minutes. Pour into two lightly greased and floured loaf pans. Bake at 350 degrees for about one hour or until done. Remove from oven and immediately pour over the following glaze.

Glaze

¾ cup sugar
¼ cup lemon juice
2 teaspoons margarine

½ teaspoon almond flavoring
½ teaspoon vanilla flavoring

Combine and bring to a boil. Pour immediately over hot loaves. Let remain in pans for 30 minutes and then turn out on rack.

SUSAN COCHRAN'S RASPBERRY PRETZEL SALAD

3 cups crushed pretzels
1 cup melted margarine
3 tablespoons sugar
1 8-ounce package cream
  cheese
1 cup powdered sugar

1 egg
1 8-ounce container prepared
  whipped topping (like Cool
  Whip)
1 6-ounce box raspberry gelatin
2 cups boiling water
2 small boxes frozen raspberries

Combine pretzels, margarine, and sugar and pat into a 9 x 13 pan. Bake 10 minutes at 350 degrees; cool. Combine cream cheese, powdered sugar, and egg until well blended. Fold in whipped topping. Spread over top of cooled crust. Dissolve gelatin in boiling water and stir in raspberries. The cold raspberries should cause the gelatin to cool and become syrupy. Pour over cream cheese layer. Chill until firm.

Ed junior says, "Today women play a very significant role in all the departments at station KMA and, for the first time in the station's history, the overall operation is managed by a woman, Susan Christensen.

"The talents and skills of women are still needed at KMA, just as they were in 1925. I am glad for all those who have carried on the traditions started by my grandparents, Earl and Gertrude May, efforts which were continued by my father, Edward senior. I will strive to retain the values the radio homemakers helped establish through the years."

The adventure continues.

Edith Hansen.

Postscript

It is impossible to exaggerate the closeness the listeners felt toward the women who were radio homemakers during the early days of broadcasting. When Florence Falk said on the air that "the Farmer" had just fallen into the stock tank, they waited breathlessly for her to tell them what was going to happen next. When Leanna Driftmier had the car accident that eventually put her in a wheel-chair for the remainder of her life, her listeners prayed for her, sent her cards and gifts by the thousands, and gained strength to face their own tragedies through her courage. When Aage Hansen and Don Shoemaker and Dulcie Jean Birkby died, hundreds of women and men all over the Midwest sent messages of condolence as if to close friends.

The listeners became emotionally attached to the broadcasters. Recently a letter arrived in my radio mail from a young woman who lives near the tiny unincorporated town of Brooks, Iowa: "I listened to the radio homemakers while I was growing up. My mother would turn on the radio, take the telephone off the hook, and tell us children to keep quiet. In the process we heard most everything that was said right along with our mother. I grew up hearing the voices of the radio ladies. They made me feel that they were friends who cared about my entire family. They were closer to us than some of our own relatives."

The radio homemakers created a sense of credibility, and because of that trust they were super salespeople. If Jessie Young told folks to buy soap, her listeners bought bar after bar of the brand she recommended. If Bernice Currier said to get a certain kind of vitamin, people bought it in huge quantities. When Lucile Verness broadcast ways to use the company's flavorings, shoppers flocked to the grocery counters to stock up. When Billie Oakley suggested that Bag Balm (a product she knew from her years on the farm where her father used it on cows' udders) was a good skin moisterizer, the sales for Bag Balm in Jay's Drug Store in Shenandoah jumped from six cans per year to more than two thousand cans in a matter of months. The radio homemakers prepared their own commercials, and they made the presentation sound so easy that listeners thought the ads were given extemporaneously.

Although the radio homemakers came from a variety of backgrounds and had disparate personalities, temperaments, and appearances, they also had many qualities in common. Energy is one characteristic that comes to mind, plus the willingness to work long hours. They projected sincerity, enthusiasm, optimism, and compassion. Dedication to the listeners was a quality they shared. Each brought her own philosophy of life to the work. Some were trained as home economists; others relied for inspiration on personal experiences. They shared their lives, tragedies and joys alike. They studied and stayed current in the development and techniques of cooking, housekeeping, and family care, as well as other interests pertaining to midwestern life.

The radio homemakers have been women who were not hampered by the fact that radio was (and still is) predominantly a male profession. Leanna Field, for example, was told by her parents never to use the excuse that she was a woman to keep her from doing what she wanted to do. She, in turn, taught her own children the same thing. Other women in the broadcasting field, like Susan Christensen and Susan Cochran, were raised in the same manner.

The world has changed greatly since 1925, when the rural audience was flung in large numbers across the landscape. As the years went by, the population distribution changed. Traditions changed. Work patterns for both men and women changed. Electricity came into homes, and energy-saving equipment was invented to make the physical tasks of caring for a house easier. More women became part of the work force. Communications technology improved and the world moved into the home via television, with all its challenging, inventive, and sometimes frightening aspects.

Just as the rest of the world is changing, so broadcasters and listeners change every day. Now when you turn on the radio, you are apt to hear a woman's voice giving the news, listing the markets, reporting health updates, and sending back live reports from political meetings and sports events. No longer is the woman's role on the air that of "just" a homemaker. When someone says, "Let's talk homemaker things," they mean a broad range of subjects. As important as cooking and eating are, women are interested in all aspects of living, and radio programming reflects that fact.

No matter how times have changed, in many ways the needs of listeners remain the same. People get lonely. They face worrisome, sometimes seemingly insurmountable problems. This means that neighboring still is the keystone for radio homemaker programs—kindness and compassion are close at hand.

Members of the present generation of broadcasters are not as willing to share as much of their lives as their predecessors were—and perhaps that is proper. Few listeners today go to a broadcaster's home, knock on the door, and expect to be invited in for cookies and tea. Microphones are no longer located in the radio homemakers' kitchens or dining rooms, from which the sense of relaxed friendliness and down-home atmosphere once was carried out across the airwaves.

But just as it was when the majority of women listened from far-flung country farmhouses, so today the broadcasters try to reach women where they live and in whatever situation they find themselves. Programs include information to appeal to all ages, not just older people, not just younger ones. The radio homemakers reach out to women in the work force, to those with latchkey children, and to those who work full-time at home. They give women a sense of worth and identity in a society that frequently gives them neither.

The radio homemakers were unique pioneers who opened up the field of broadcasting for every woman who followed.

Leanna Driftmier.

Index